AI AND THE RULE OF LAW

This book considers the ways in which the concept of the Rule of Law will need to evolve in order to ensure that the exercise of power by Artificial Intelligence (AI) does not become arbitrary and does not proceed unchecked. It presents the Rule of Law and its impact on the past and the present; it considers what AI is, what it does, and what it might become in future; and it looks at how AI will need to be harnessed to allow power to be exercised more effectively in the future.

The book argues that the Rule of Law has for centuries been the concept that protects against the arbitrary exercise of power. However, the exercise of power by AI unchecked by humans strains the concept's ability to provide this protection.

AI and the Rule of Law

The Necessary Evolution of a Concept

Paul Burgess

•HART•
OXFORD • LONDON • NEW YORK • NEW DELHI • SYDNEY

HART PUBLISHING

Bloomsbury Publishing Plc

Kemp House, Chawley Park, Cumnor Hill, Oxford, OX2 9PH, UK

1385 Broadway, New York, NY 10018, USA

29 Earlsfort Terrace, Dublin 2, Ireland

HART PUBLISHING, the Hart/Stag logo, BLOOMSBURY and the Diana logo are trademarks of Bloomsbury Publishing Plc

First published in Great Britain 2024

A catalogue record for this book is available from the British Library.

A catalogue record for this book is available from the Library of Congress.

Library of Congress Control Number: 2023949400

ISBN: HB: 978-1-50996-317-1
ePDF: 978-1-50996-319-5
ePub: 978-1-50996-318-8

Typeset by Compuscript Ltd, Shannon

To my own Past and Present:
To my Mum and Dad, and to Hal, Spike, and Tash

ACKNOWLEDGEMENTS

Everything must start somewhere. My journey to this book has come about through the support, guidance, and assistance of a number of people. Without them, this project would not only have remained incomplete, but also would likely have never started.

I have been fortunate enough to receive academic support and encouragement from a number of the most influential Rule of Law thinkers that are explored within this book. My first postgraduate class with the ever-generous Prof. Jeremy Waldron. My curiosity (and confusion) was piqued from day one, and Jeremy was kind enough to foster and support that interest. During the course of my ongoing interest, Prof. Brian Tamanaha has been an invaluable source of information and encouragement – his passion for exploring the history of the concept was infectious and contributed to my own historically-motivated focus. Whilst this book project looks toward the future, the historical context of the concept plays a fundamental role thanks to Brian's influence.

Two other Rule of Law thinkers that play a prominent role throughout this book have demonstrated the most wonderful collegiality over a number of years: Prof. Jeff King and Prof. Martin Krygier. They have commented, critiqued, and supported many of my projects. Because I approach the concept of the Rule of Law from a very different perspective to both of them, it has been an amazing privilege to be able to learn from (and be swayed by!) their deep and rich ideas. I can only hope that the prominence I afford to their Rule of Law ideas throughout this book does some justice to their work.

As any author will appreciate, the writing endeavour cannot be completed with academic support alone. Enormous thanks must go to my best friend and wife for allowing me to escape on numerous occasions to get this done.

To each of these individuals, I express my sincere and profound thanks. You were there at the beginning of the project, you framed and shaped the project, and you have remained there through to the end. Everything must start somewhere, but you have been there for the whole journey.

CONTENTS

1

Artificial Intelligence and the Rule of Law

Artificial Intelligence (AI) and the Rule of Law are frequently discussed; yet they are infrequently discussed together. They each play vital roles in various societies around the world. The increasing use of AI promises huge speed and efficiency benefits in all forms of decision-making. For this reason, the role AI plays in the exercise of power through its greater involvement in legislative and administrative decision-making seems certain to increase. The Rule of Law has, for centuries, constrained the arbitrary exercise of power. However, it has only ever been deployed in order to constrain *human* decision-making – and it does not necessarily follow that the application of the Rule of Law to a non-human would have the same application.[1] The intersection of the increasing use of AI in the exercise of power and the ability of the Rule of Law to provide a protection from that exercise is, and will increasingly be, crucial. In this book I consider the ways in which the concept of the Rule of Law – and our conceptions of the same – will need to evolve in order to ensure that the exercise of power by AIs does not become arbitrary and does not proceed unchecked. Broadly stated, I will seek to answer the question: how will the concept of the Rule of Law need to evolve in order to account for artificial intelligence being used to exercise public power in the future?

I look to a not-too-distant future in which AI is used in order to make decisions that reflect the exercise of state power. I consider three hypothetical situations where AI could be used in the exercise of power: first, in administrative decision-making; second, in the creation of secondary (delegated) legislation; and third, in the creation of primary legislation. Whilst AI is already used in some states' decision-making situations, the hypotheticals are future-facing (but are not fanciful). By looking forward to a time when AI – inevitably – plays a more active and substantive role in exercising state power, and in considering how its exercise of power may be restricted, I do not propose technical or mechanical solutions; this book is not about code or algorithmic design. Even though it would be possible to limit an AI's exercise of power by *not* giving it access to a particular system or by designing the AI so that it cannot perform a certain action, I do not provide this as a solution. Whilst these are, undoubtedly, valid ways in which the exercise of power

[1] Y Bathaee, 'The Artificial Intelligence Black Box and the Failure of Intent and Causation' (2018) 31(2) *Harvard Journal of Law & Technology* 889.

could ultimately be checked, in circumstances where the benefits of AI make it ever-more-likely that it will be deployed in ever-greater-capacities, I consider the limitation of power in more constitutional theoretical terms. I consider whether the Rule of Law – in the ways that it is currently conceived and has been conceived in the past – can apply to and limit an AI's actions. In other words, I consider whether it is possible to extend conceptions of the Rule of Law – and the forms of protection that they are taken to provide – to the exercise of power by AIs in order to limit their exercise of power. Through the course of this book, I argue that the various ways in which the Rule of Law has been popularly conceived provide inadequate means to limit the exercise of power by AIs and, for this reason, the concept must evolve in order to meet the new challenges that AI presents.

The evolution of the Rule of Law is not unprecedented. In circumstances where it is not unusual to see conceptions that range over more than two millennia being deployed side-by-side to justify the meaning and contents of the concept, it seems that the contemporary meanings attributed to some of the conceptions cannot mean precisely the same *now* as they were intended to at their inception.[2] If the concept of the Rule of Law has been capable of change in the past, there seems to be no reason why it cannot be conceived of in different terms in the future. Where this is the case, the question that must first be addressed is whether the Rule of Law, as it is presently understood, can address the challenge presented by AI's exercise of power. Where it cannot, and if it is intended that the protections previously provided by the Rule of Law should continue, it will be necessary for the concept of the Rule of Law to evolve in order to continue to prevent the arbitrary exercise of power where the power is exercised by an AI. As I argue that the past or present conceptions cannot be applied to the exercise of power by AIs, and that it will be necessary for the concept to evolve, the shape and nature of that evolution is vital. This book does not provide all of the answers in this respect. But it does provide an outline of the problems that are faced and some suggestions as to the ways that the Rule of Law will necessarily need to evolve in the future.

In this brief introductory chapter, I provide an overview of the argument that I will make across the book's chapters. I also provide some context to the terms that will be used through the book in a way that will, hopefully, illustrate why the intersections of the ideas that I discuss in the book more widely are of paramount importance to the future.

I. The Rule of Law and AI

The Rule of Law and AI have captured the attention of academia and the wider public. Their popular appeal is clearly evident both through their frequent mention

[2] P Burgess, 'The Rule of Lore in the Rule of Law: Putting the Problem of the Rule of Law in Context' (2020) 12 *Hague Journal on the Rule of Law* 333 ('Rule of Lore').

in the national media or in relation to the relatively broad – and justifiably unsophisticated – understanding that any member of the public may have of the ideas. Whilst these popular understandings exist, there is a more sophisticated way in which the ideas can be considered. In this respect, there are deep and differing conceptions of what exactly 'the Rule of Law' or 'AI' means. These may, or may not, reflect the more popular understandings or the realities of the ideas. I dedicate a chapter to exploring exactly what is meant by both 'the Rule of Law' and 'AI' in chapters two and three respectively. Here, I provide only the briefest outline of each of the ideas in order to illustrate the broad argument that I make across the book.

Whilst there is frequent media coverage of both the Rule of Law and of AI individually, there is very little popular coverage of the two ideas together.[3] There is, however, clearly the scope for an overlap of the ideas. This is reflected in a slew of recent articles or chapters that consider both ideas.[4] This suggests that the importance of the interaction and the overlap is becoming increasingly apparent. Yet, what has been absent from previous consideration of the two ideas together is how exactly the Rule of Law applies to the exercise of power by an AI. This book remedies that situation and starts what will certainly be a longer conversation about the necessary form that the Rule of Law will need to take if it is to provide the protections that it has done in the past.

Given the focus of the book on AI, and where AI is increasingly used to solve more complex problems, it may be useful to start the whole process by considering the way that AI would answer the question that I seek to answer. I asked ChatGPT to answer the question that frames this book (posed at the end of the book's opening paragraph). The introduction, in part, was:

> The increasing use of AI in public decision-making necessitates a reevaluation of the traditional understanding of the Rule of Law. The existing legal framework, built on human-centric principles, may struggle to effectively regulate and govern AI systems. The Rule of Law principles, such as accountability, transparency, and fairness, must be reexamined in the context of AI to ensure that the exercise of public power remains within acceptable boundaries and upholds democratic values.

[3] The broader proposition – that there is little consideration of whether and how current legal doctrines apply to the use of AI – has also been stated by Allen. JG Allen, 'Agency and Liability' in JG Allen (ed), *Artificial Intelligence: Law and Regulation* (Cheltenham, Edward Elgar, 2022) 146.

[4] For some recent examples, see R Kennedy, 'The Rule of Law and Algorithmic Governance' in W Barfield (ed), *The Cambridge Handbook of the Law of Algorithms* (Cambridge, Cambridge University Press, 2020) 209; M Zalnieriute et al, 'From Rule of Law to Statute Drafting: Legal Issues for Algorithms in Government Decision-Making' in W Barfield (ed), *The Cambridge Handbook of the Law of Algorithms* (Cambridge, Cambridge University Press, 2020) 251; M Zalnieriute, LB Moses and G Williams, 'The Rule of Law and Automation of Government Decision-Making' (2019) 82(3) *The Modern Law Review* 425; P Burgess, 'Algorithmic Augmentation of Democracy: Considering Whether Technology Can Enhance the Concepts of Democracy and the Rule of Law Through Four Hypotheticals' [2021] *AI & Society*; P Gowder, 'Transformative Legal Technology and the Rule of Law' [2018] *University of Toronto Law Journal* www.utpjournals.press/doi/abs/10.3138/utlj.2017-0047.

As part of the conclusion to the answer that was provided to the question, ChatGPT stated:

> Enhancing legal frameworks and reconceptualizing the Rule of Law for AI require proactive measures, international collaboration, and continuous adaptation. This article underscores the need for clear legal standards, the updating of existing laws, the integration of ethical considerations, the establishment of robust oversight mechanisms, and international cooperation to foster a cohesive global approach to AI governance.
>
> In conclusion, by addressing the challenges posed by AI in the Rule of Law and embracing the opportunities it presents, we can shape a future where AI systems operate within legal boundaries, respect fundamental rights, and promote transparency, fairness, and accountability. The reconceptualization of the Rule of Law for AI is essential for navigating the complexities of AI-driven public power and ensuring a just and ethical society. By implementing the recommended strategies and safeguards, we can strike a balance between harnessing the potential benefits of AI and safeguarding the principles that underpin the Rule of Law.[5]

These responses are – somewhat annoyingly for an academic author – relatively reflective of some of the findings in this book. ChatGPT rightly identifies some of the key issues – for example, transparency and accountability – that reflect problems for the use of AI in exercising public power that represent a core aspect of the thesis in this book. What was more comforting for an author was the fact that the AI generated comments – in both the extracts above and in the full series of responses (in which I also requested authorities for the various claims made through the response) – failed to identify the questions as to '*why?*' the problems arise and '*what?*' the future of the Rule of Law may need to look like in order to address the problems that are identified. These sorts of questions are, in an academic thesis, essential.

In order answer the question that I pose, and in order to avoid the oversimplification that ChatGPT provides, I consider the concept of the Rule of Law in a way that takes account of the contested nature of the concept and considers a variety of levels of abstraction. I also use three hypothetical ways in which AI may be used to exercise public power in order to draw out the problems (and some solutions). Whilst this does not fundamentally result in the identification of problems that differ fundamentally to those identified in seconds by ChatGPT, it does allow a deeper and more critical approach to the Rule of Law accounts that have been broadly accepted over time. In turn, this allows me to identify *how* our idea of the Rule of Law will need to change in order to solve these problems.

[5] The full dialogue with ChatGPT can be viewed here: chat.openai.com/share/a0ce3cfe-b88d-45c8-b6c5-1cf616b07c00.

A. The Rule of Law – In this Book

The Rule of Law has long been seen as a vital concept in controlling the exercise of state power.[6] It is in this sense that the term is frequently deployed in common discourse and the media. Whilst the concept's precise terms are contested, it is universally seen as a 'good' thing.[7] The nature of the contest is unpacked further in the chapters that follow; however, as already suggested above, it is frequently taken to be one that operates so as to prevent the arbitrary exercise of power.[8] It is in virtue of the concept's enduring popularity and importance to societies around the world, and in virtue of its apparent ability to evolve over time, that its continued use and deployment in terms of the exercise of power made by AIs is relevant. Given the concept's universal appeal and wide application, it seems unlikely that an *alternative* concept would be created to supplant the Rule of Law in terms of the exercise of power by an AI in the future. As will be explored – particularly in chapter two – the concept of the Rule of Law has been applied to control the exercise of power across a range of different scenarios. There is no reason to expect that a hard line has or will be reached in the concept's utility in this respect. Accordingly, consideration of the *way* in which the concept must evolve in order to ensure that its core anti-arbitrariness function can be retained in the face of AI exercising power is vital.

The Rule of Law is contested concept.[9] In circumstances where its precise conceptual boundaries are not agreed upon, any consideration of the kind proposed in this book is rendered difficult. If a single conception – even a broadly acceptable one – is adopted, questions can be raised as to how generalisable any conclusions reached may be in terms of *other* conceptions of the Rule of Law. Accordingly, in order to get around this problem and to consider whether any broadly accepted or acceptable form of the Rule of Law can apply to a future in which AI makes laws or other administrative decisions, I adopt a methodology that considers (at different levels of abstraction) and aggregates a number of popular forms of conceptions of the Rule of Law into broad Rule of Law categories: the Past Rule of Law; and, the Present Rule of Law.

[6] It has been described as the 'most important political concept': J Waldron, 'The Concept and the Rule of Law' (2008) 43 *Georgia Law Review* 1, 3.

[7] The concept is 'an international hurrah term': M Krygier, 'Four Puzzles About the Rule of Law: Why, What, Where? And Who Cares?' in J Flemming (ed), *Getting to the Rule of Law* (New York, New York University Press, 2011) 64, 64. 'Everyone happens to be in favor of the rule of law at the moment': J Waldron, 'Legislation and the Rule of Law' (2007) 1(1) *Legisprudence* 91, 118.

[8] M Krygier, 'What's the Point of the Rule of Law?' 67 *Buffalow Law Review* 50, 746; JP Reid, *Rule of Law: The Jurisprudence of Liberty in the Seventeenth and Eighteenth Centuries* (Dekalb, IL, Northern Illinois University Press, 2004) ('*Rule of Law*').

[9] There is a detailed literature that explores the contested, or essentially contested, nature of the Rule of Law as a concept. For a summary of the various positions and debates, see J Waldron, 'Is the Rule of Law an Essentially Contested Concept (in Florida)?' (2002) 21(2) *Law and Philosophy* 137; P Burgess, 'The Rule of Law: Beyond Contestedness' (2017) 8(3) *Jurisprudence* 480.

In chapter two I set out in detail the meaning of the Past Rule of Law and the Present Rule of Law. However, it is relevant to note at the outset that the terms I adopt are intended only to represent the *periods* in which the conceptions that make them up were authored. It is not intended as a reflection of whether either category is more – or less – correct than the other. Before considering more detailed ways in which the way in which AI and its decision- or law-making abilities will be considered through this book, it is useful to provide a little more detail about what I mean by the Past and Present conceptions of the Rule of Law and how the categories are formed. I include some of the most popular, and frequently relied upon, statements of the Rule of Law. In this respect, the conceptions that I use cannot be subject to complaints about cherry-picking by me or any specific individual. The selection of conceptions is largely made for me; they represent a broadly aggregated idea of the concept as given in the past or the present.

The Past of the Rule of Law is constituted by the conceptions provided by the 'usual suspects' of the Rule of Law:[10] Aristotle, Locke, Dicey, Hayek, Fuller, and Raz. In terms of their Rule of Law accounts, these thinkers have been described as a 'Who's Who? of Western political thought …'[11] They are frequently deployed to illustrate what the Rule of Law *is*,[12] and can be used to define the meaning, content, and boundaries of the concept of the Rule of Law.[13] As their conceptions range over more than 2,000 years, there is clearly a historical diversity. There is also a philosophical diversity.[14] They provide very different accounts of the Rule of Law. Yet, two broad criteria can be used to unite the usual suspects: their conceptions can all be seen to be thin/formal accounts of the Rule of Law; and, each can be seen to be intended to solve a problem associated with the imposition of *state* arbitrary power. These two criteria provide points of contrast to the Present Rule of Law.

The Present of the Rule of Law is not to be taken as an absolute statement of what the Rule of Law *is* now. It is, instead, reflective of trends that have emerged in relation to the meaning of the concept of the Rule of Law in recent years. Two – different – forms of the Present Rule of Law are suggested here. Each providing a point of contrast to the uniting criteria for the Past Rule of Law outlined immediately above.

[10] P Burgess, 'You Say It Best When You Say Nothing At All: "[The Rule of Law]"' (2021) 25(1) *Edinburgh Law Review* 1.

[11] J Møller and S-Erik Skaaning, *The Rule of Law: Definitions, Measures, Patterns and Causes* (Basingstoke, Palgrave Macmillan, 2014) 2. A similar list is provided by Waldron. J Waldron, 'The Rule of Law' in EN Zalta (ed), *The Stanford Encyclopedia of Philosophy* (Fall 2016, 2016) plato.stanford.edu/entries/rule-of-law/.

[12] Examples of this approach include: Reid (n 8) 5–8; C Sampford et al, *Retrospectivity and the Rule of Law* (Oxford, Oxford University Press, 2006) 14; J Waldron, 'Stare Decisis and the Rule of Law: A Layered Approach' (2011) 111 *Michigan Law Review* 1, 4 ('Stare Decisis and the Rule of Law'); Waldron, 'The Rule of Law' (n 11). For a critique of this approach, see Burgess, 'Rule of Lore' (n 2).

[13] See, eg, the Stanford Encyclopedia entry: Waldron, 'The Rule of Law' (n 11). In terms of their status as usual suspects, see Burgess, 'Rule of Lore' (n 2).

[14] They are, however, largely, white, frequently bearded, mostly dead, men. This, undoubtedly, impacts our conception of what the Rule of Law is.

The first form reflects the Rule of Law as a thick or substantive idea. This goes beyond the Past's idea that the Rule of Law is merely a thin/formal requirement and takes the Rule of Law to be related to substantively good outcomes; the Rule of Law can be achieved if the laws that are made attain a particular end.[15] There are a wide number of thick accounts of the Rule of Law. Two will provide the core basis for the idea in this book: the United Nations' (UN) approach to the Rule of Law and Lord Bingham's approach. Both have proved to be popular in recent years.

Whilst no single definition of the Rule of Law has been adopted by the UN, an illustrative example is that the UN Rule of Law requires 'fairness in the application of the law, separation of powers, participation in decision-making, legal certainty, avoidance of arbitrariness and procedural and legal transparency'.[16] Where the UN's Rule of Law can and should be deployed to accomplish other things (like the achievement of Human Rights),[17] this goes beyond the mere prescription of formal or procedural ideas contained in the Past ideas. Lord Bingham provides a similarly thick idea in his popular text on the Rule of Law. He provides eight subrules of the Rule of Law that include several thick/substantive ideas: that public officials should exercise their powers in good faith (and act within those powers); the law must protect fundamental rights; and, adjudicative procedures must be provided and be fair.[18] Whilst Bingham and the UN provide only two examples of the substantive turn, they are influential and important examples. They illustrate the first form of the Present Rule of Law: the Rule of Law should aim for and achieve substantive ends.

The second form of the Present Rule of Law reflects an alternate point of difference to the Past Rule of Law that relates to the state-based exercise of power. Instead of having its applicability decided by the application of arbitrary *state* power, this form of the Present Rule of Law relates to the application of *arbitrary* power (whether it be by the state or any other entity).[19] Whilst the idea that the focus of the Rule of Law's prevention of arbitrary power should not be confined to the state is not new,[20] it has recently seen a wave of arguments in support of

[15] The classic statement of the thin and thick ideas of the Rule of Law is provided by Craig. P Craig, 'Formal and Substantive Conceptions of the Rule of Raw an Analytical Framework' [1997] (Autumn) *Public Law* 467.

[16] UN Security Council, *The Rule of Law and Transitional Justice in Conflict and Post-Conflict Societies – Report of the Secretary-General* (No UN doc S/2004/616, 23 August 2004) 6: www.un.org/ruleoflaw/files/2004%20report.pdf.

[17] ibid.

[18] T Bingham, *The Rule of Law* (London, Allen Lane, 2010). (This is a somewhat simplified version of the list.).

[19] Krygier (n 7); JA Sempill, 'What Rendered Ancient Tyrants Detestable: The Rule of Law and the Constitution of Corporate Power' [2018] *Hague Journal on the Rule of Law* 1 ('What Rendered Ancient Tyrants Detestable'); JA Sempill, 'The Lions and the Greatest Part: The Rule of Law and the Constitution of Employer Power' (2017) 9(2) *Hague Journal on the Rule of Law* 283; J King, 'The Rule of Law' in R Bellamy and J King (eds), *The Cambridge Handbook of Constitutional Theory* (2024) papers.ssrn.com/abstract=4487306.

[20] See, eg, P Selznick, *Law, Society, and Industrial Justice: 50th Anniversary Edition* (New Orleans, Quid Pro, 2020).

the idea.[21] The shift in this form of the Present of the Rule of Law is both subtle and significant. Whilst the unobjectionable aspect of the Rule of Law as being fundamentally against the application of arbitrary power is retained, the state-only application (in the usual suspects' – Past – accounts) is abandoned; the Rule of Law is directed at the application of *any* arbitrary power.

In this book, the Present Rule of Law will be seen to take the above two forms: the first related to the substantive application of the Rule of Law; and the other related to the wider – non-state-centric – application of arbitrary power. These contrast with the Past idea of the Rule of Law that sees both a thin/formal structure aimed at preventing the arbitrary exercise of state power. Considering the Rule of Law in this way ensures that all popularly accepted ideas associated with the concept of the Rule of Law (in the Anglo-American world) are included. Both the Past and the Present ideas will be used in order to consider whether the Rule of Law can provide an adequate form of protection in the future when AI exercises power.

B. Artificial Intelligence – In this Book

A computer is, fundamentally, a calculation machine. The idea of what a computer *is* was first explained to me (in the 1980s) as being 'a machine that under the control of a stored program automatically accepts and processes data and supplies the results of that processing'.[22] Whilst this may seem relatively simplistic in terms of what we understand AI to be (or be able to do), it is important to remember that AI systems are still – albeit highly sophisticated – calculation machines.

'AI' can cover a vast range of technologies. Whilst it is a very broad term that has no single agreed definition, it is also well-know and would be recognised as something that broadly already plays a significant role in many aspects of our daily lives. It is driving the fourth industrial revolution,[23] and advancements in a range of fields – including in law and the wider exercise of public power – will likely be able to benefit from its application in the future. The use of technology in making decisions within the public sphere offers a number of potential benefits. These include increased efficiency, increased accuracy, improved consistency, and

[21] LM Austin and D Klimchuk (eds), *Private Law and the Rule of Law* (Oxford, Oxford University Press, 2014). For a critique of the extension of the Rule of Law in this way, see P Burgess, 'Googling the Equivalence of Private Arbitrary Power and State Arbitrary Power: Why The Rule of Law Does Not Relate to Private Relationships' [2021] *International Journal of Law in Context*.

[22] Whilst I learned this definition in the 1980s, it is still used. See, eg, O Bevan, TJ Dixon and S Hargitay, *Microcomputers in Property: A Surveyor's Guide to Lotus 1-2-3 and DBASE IV* (Oxford, Taylor & Francis, 2014) 1.

[23] AI is commonly referenced in terms of the fourth industrial revolution. Its impact on the public sector and related industries is clear. G Velarde, 'Artificial Intelligence and Its Impact on the Fourth Industrial Revolution: A Review' [2020] *arXiv:2011.03044 [cs]* arxiv.org/abs/2011.03044; S Makridakis, 'The Forthcoming Artificial Intelligence (AI) Revolution: Its Impact on Society and Firms' (2017) 90 *Futures* 46.

the ability to re-focus staff to 'higher value' activities.[24] The uses of technology are already making the process of legal practice more streamlined in a way that may see tangible benefits to clients. As one simple example, the use of technology exponentially speeds up the process of document review in large litigious matters by reducing the number of documents that require review from tens of millions, to mere thousands. In considering further benefits, these could extend to the increased provision of access to justice together with the potential enhancement of transparency and legitimacy in decision-making and the idea of democracy more generally.[25] Again, as a simple example, the use of technology in the broadest sense is already assisting potential litigants to challenge decisions or administrative rulings or achieve outcomes through 'the world's first robot lawyer'.[26]

AI would likely be recognised as being related to applications like driverless cars as well as in contemporary personal assistant applications like Siri or Alexa and, as illustrated earlier, generative AI like ChatGPT. These broad applications demonstrate AI's ability to assist in decision-making, automate tasks, and improve accuracy across a vast spectrum of processes. Given these benefits, AI can also offer substantial efficiencies in terms of decision-making in the public sphere.

The term 'AI' can be taken to include any machine that acts intelligently – as a machine that can make correct decisions in a given circumstance.[27] (I refine this further in chapter three.) This encompasses both narrow/weak AI processes – like chess-playing AIs that may outperform humans in some limited tasks – and strong AI (artificial general intelligence) – as a form of AI that does not yet exist but would be able to simulate thinking in ways that cannot be distinguished from human intelligence.[28] The application of AI has been increasing over recent years.

[24] NSW Ombudsman, *The New Machinery of Government: Using Machine Technology in Administrative Decision-Making* (NSW Ombudsman, 29 November 2021) 4: www.ombo.nsw.gov.au/news-and-publications/publications/reports/state-and-local-government/the-new-machinery-of-government-using-machine-technology-in-administrative-decision-making.

[25] Burgess, 'Algorithmic Augmentation' (n 4). See also, eg, S Chesterman, *We, the Robots?: Regulating Artificial Intelligence and the Limits of the Law* (Cambridge, Cambridge University Press, 2021); J Boughey and K Miller (eds), *The Automated State: Implications, Challenges and Opportunities for Public Law*, 1st edn (Alexandria, NSW, Federation Press, 2021) federationpress.com.au/product/the-automated-state/.

[26] See DoNotPay, 'Save Time and Money with DoNotPay!' join.donotpay.com.

[27] For weak AI see Y LeCun, Y Bengio and G Hinton, 'Deep Learning' (2015) 521(7553) *Nature* 436. For strong AI see W Naudé and N Dimitri, 'The Race for an Artificial General Intelligence: Implications for Public Policy' (2020) 35(2) *AI & Society* 367, 367–8. Within the broad AI definition included here, other sub-fields – for example, machine learning (as a class of statistical methods aimed at detecting patterns or correlations between dependent and independent variables (classification) or predicting an outcome (prediction)) – are included. Y Hermstrüwer, 'Artificial Intelligence and Administrative Decisions Under Uncertainty' in T Wischmeyer and T Rademacher (eds), *Regulating Artificial Intelligence* (Cham, Springer International Publishing, 2020) 199, 201: doi.org/10.1007/978-3-030-32361-5_9.

[28] In these respects, and as will be apparent from what follows, I bring a more specific – old fashioned – idea of AI, big data, and machine learning together under my single umbrella term. This sort of approach is not unique. For example, big data and AI have been brought together in the past. See, eg, MC Elish and danah boyd, 'Situating Methods in the Magic of Big Data and AI' (2018) 85(1) *Communication Monographs* 57. Whilst not ideal, taking a broad approach adds a level of simplicity to the examination conducted herein.

AI's ability to efficiently process vast volumes of data has already been extended into the public sphere where automated decision-making and the provision of information is necessary to make (data-driven) decisions.[29] Furthermore, it has already been used in circumstances that directly impacts humans where the use and application of AI may be more efficient than the application of human-only operations.[30] In many respects, applications of AI related to popular social media platforms would be familiar.[31] What may be less familiar, however, would be AI's use in predicting recidivism or in making parole decisions.[32] In these respects, the potential benefits that AI can offer have already been applied – and to some degree realised – in the public sphere more broadly.[33]

Given the potential for efficiency gains,[34] the use of AI in the exercise of power being wielded by the state seems to be both evident and likely. Whilst the

[29] Here construed to be a decision that is made by automated means without the involvement of a human actor in the decision. For a similar definitional structure, see *General Data Protection Regulation (GDPR) 2016*. In relation to the use of AI to guide (human) decision-making generally, see S Newell and M Marabelli, 'Strategic Opportunities (and Challenges) of Algorithmic Decision-Making: A Call for Action on the Long-Term Societal Effects of "Datification"' (2015) 24(1) *The Journal of Strategic Information Systems* 3.

[30] A data-driven 'technocracy' may outperform the human-only decision-making processes in a way that avoids opaque motivations. P Khanna, *Technocracy in America: Rise of the Info-State* (CreateSpace Independent Publishing Platform, 2017); B Lepri et al, 'Fair, Transparent, and Accountable Algorithmic Decision-Making Processes' (2018) 31(4) *Philosophy & Technology* 611. In some senses, people may prefer algorithmic judgment: JM Logg, JA Minson and DA Moore, 'Algorithm Appreciation: People Prefer Algorithmic to Human Judgment' (2019) 151 *Organizational Behavior and Human Decision Processes* 90. See also PB de Laat, 'Algorithmic Decision-Making Based on Machine Learning from Big Data: Can Transparency Restore Accountability?' (2018) 31(4) *Philosophy & Technology* 525.

[31] E Ferrara et al, 'The Rise of Social Bots' (2016) 59(7) *Communications of the ACM* 96; Z Chu et al, 'Detecting Automation of Twitter Accounts: Are You a Human, Bot, or Cyborg?' (2012) 9(6) *IEEE Transactions on Dependable and Secure Computing* 811; D Silver et al, 'Mastering the Game of Go Without Human Knowledge' (2017) 550(7676) *Nature* 354.

[32] J Dressel and H Farid, 'The Accuracy, Fairness, and Limits of Predicting Recidivism' (2018) 4(1) *Science Advances* eaao5580; B Shillingford et al, 'Large-Scale Visual Speech Recognition' [2018] *arXiv:1807.05162 [cs]* arxiv.org/abs/1807.05162.

[33] In relation to administrative decision-making: C Coglianese and D Lehr, 'Regulating by Robot: Administrative Decision Making in the Machine-Learning Era' (2017) (105) *Georgetown Law Journal* 1147; D Hogan-Doran, 'Computer Says "No": Automation, Algorithms and Artificial Intelligence in Government Decision-Making' [2017] *Judicial Review: Selected Conference Papers: Journal of the Judicial Commission of New South Wales*: search.informit.org/doi/abs/10.3316/INFORMIT.173260757765464. In relation to public sector decisions: M Oswald, 'Algorithm-Assisted Decision-Making in the Public Sector: Framing the Issues Using Administrative Law Rules Governing Discretionary Power' (2018) 376(2128) *Philosophical Transactions of the Royal Society A: Mathematical, Physical and Engineering Sciences* 20170359; P-Adrien Hanania and A-Laure Thieullent, 'Perform AI for Public Sector: Public Goes AI!', Capgemini Worldwide (4 March 2020) www.capgemini.com/2020/03/perform-ai-for-public-sector-public-goes-ai/. See also, Zalnieriute, Moses and Williams (n 4).

[34] A data-driven government may be more effective and more efficient through being more responsive. S Goldsmith and S Crawford, *The Responsive City: Engaging Communities Through Data-Smart Governance*, 1st edn (San Francisco, CA, Jossey-Bass, 2014). There may be significant efficiency gains – but with existing technology, they may not necessarily result in benefit without human input. H Mehr, *Artificial Intelligence for Citizen Services and Government* (Harvard Kennedy School, 2017) 19. This desire is – generally speaking – one that is applied to the way in which AI is currently being deployed in the public sphere. Hanania and Thieullent 'Perform AI for Public Sector' (n 33).

application of AI and its *actual* ability does lag somewhat behind the popular conceptions,[35] and whilst the form of AI that I will consider below does not yet always exist, the benefits of speed and efficiency that AI can offer make it increasingly likely that it will be used as a tool to assist in decision-making in the exercise of power. In this respect, consideration of the potential impact of decisions made by AIs in the exercise of state power is both timely and necessary.

It is necessary to clarify the way in which AI will be considered in the book more broadly. In the context of considering the trajectory that the use of AI in decision-making in the public sphere seems to suggest, I will consider a hypothetical form of AI that does not yet exist in order to contemplate the role of the Rule of Law in limiting the exercise of (an AI's) power in three situations. There are three general hypothetical situations in which I consider the use of AI: in administrative decision-making; in the creation of secondary (delegated) legislation; and, in the creation of primary legislation. The use of a hypothetical in this way is useful.[36] This approach avoids becoming lost in the technological realities of AI whilst also enabling a consideration of the Rule of Law-related issues that may exist if technology continues to develop in the way and in the direction that is evidenced by AI's current application. Accordingly, the form of AI that I consider below is a form of strong AI that is both able to make decisions in a way that is indistinguishable from a human's thought processes, in a way that is free from any form of bias, and through a decision process that is transparent.[37]

In considering the question of the limitation of AI and the increased role that it will play I take a non-technical approach that falls between utopian and dystopian that could be described as non-dystopian. It is non-technical as I do not propose that algorithmic or mechanical means should be used to provide limitations on the way in which AI may exercise power; whilst this would likely be possible, I am more concerned with the relationships that a power-exercising AI would have to the concept of the Rule of Law that has constrained rulers and governments for centuries. (In this sense, the discussion in the book is squarely grounded in

[35] It has often been suggested as being responsible for various forms of dystopia. Popular examples in film would include: *Avengers: Age of Ultron* (Directed by Joss Whedon, Marvel Studios, 2015); *Terminator* (Directed by James Cameron, Roadshow, 1984). It can also be seen in books – for example AC Clarke, *2001: A Space Odyssey* (Orbit, 2001). Prominent engineers have also expressed their concerns: K Piper, 'Why Elon Musk Fears Artificial Intelligence' (2 November 2018) *Vox* www.vox.com/future-perfect/2018/11/2/18053418/elon-musk-artificial-intelligence-google-deepmind-openai; S Shead, 'Elon Musk Says DeepMind Is His "top Concern" When It Comes to A.I.' (29 July 2020) *CNBC* www.cnbc.com/2020/07/29/elon-musk-deepmind-ai.html.

[36] J Chen and P Burgess, 'The Boundaries of Legal Personhood: How Spontaneous Intelligence Can Problematise Differences between Humans, Artificial Intelligence, Companies and Animals' (2019) 27(1) *Artificial Intelligence and Law* 73; N Bostrom, *Superintelligence: Paths, Dangers, Strategies*, illustrated edn (Oxford, Oxford University Press, 2014).

[37] These are key contemporary difficulties in the development of AI. Furthermore, they are not insignificant hurdles to surmount. I touch on these immediately below but provide more detail in ch 3. The rationale behind the assumptions being made and a discussion of the nature of the contemporary difficulties is also explored in some detail in ch 3.

constitutional theory and not information technology.) It is also non-technical as I do not delve into the core realities of what AI can currently achieve.

The approach I adopt is minimally utopian. It does not imagine a future in which the technology will bring humanity's salvation, nor one in which the technology that is considered within the book is necessarily the thing of science-fiction. Instead, I look toward a not-too-distant future in order to identify the ways in which AI will likely be used in order that I may identify the problems that this may cause in terms of the exercise of states' powers. In circumstances where the current reality of AI is not at the level at which it can exercise state power in the broadest sense (nor is AI at the level at which many members of the public may imagine it to be), this requires that I construct hypotheticals in terms of the likely uses of AI in the future. In doing so, whilst my approach is not utopian, it is also not dystopian. It is non-dystopian in three ways. First, it is non-dystopian as I do not suggest that the advent of general artificial intelligence will necessarily herald an apocalyptic end.[38] I take this approach in order to assess the relationship of the constraints provided by the Rule of Law on a well-constructed 'friendly' AI.[39]

The second reason that my approach is non-dystopian is because the situations that I hypothesise in the chapters that follow imagine that one fundamental problem that has plagued the development of AI can be solved: the operation of bias. Whilst I address this in more detail in chapter three, it is useful to note it here. AI, as it currently exists, may have problems related to in-built biases.[40] In this book, I do not play-down the current problems associated with this aspect of AI and the potential problems that this could have for decision-making and the Rule of Law in general. Instead, in order to get to the content of the broader argument, I imagine a form of AI that has been able to overcome these issues and can make decisions free of these problems.

I do not, however, stipulate that *all* contemporary problems associated with the use of AI can be solved. In addition to bias, AI's use in making decisions has also been hindered by problems associated with the transparency of its decision-making process. In simple applications, the way in which a decision is arrived at can be relatively easily mapped out and a rationale or justification can be provided for the decision. As a very basic example a rule could be put in these terms: if an

[38] There are many suggestions that AIs will not be friendly, even if there is a compelling argument that this is what is needed. RJM Boyles and JJ Joaquin, 'Why Friendly AIs Won't Be That Friendly: A Friendly Reply to Muehlhauser and Bostrom' (2020) 35(2) *AI & Society* 505; L Muehlhauser and N Bostrom, 'Why We Need Friendly AI' (2014) 13(36) *Think* 41.

[39] The technologies I explore will be friendly (and useful). The promotion of friendly or beneficial AI is a vital research goal. SD Baum, 'On the Promotion of Safe and Socially Beneficial Artificial Intelligence' (2017) 32(4) *AI & Society* 543.

[40] C Sandvig et al, 'When the Algorithm Itself Is a Racist: Diagnosing Ethical Harm in the Basic Components of Software' (2016) 10 *International Journal of Communication* 4972; M Spielkamp, 'Inspecting Algorithms for Bias', MIT Technology Review (12 June 2017) www.technologyreview.com/2017/06/12/105804/inspecting-algorithms-for-bias/; E Nissan, 'Digital Technologies and Artificial Intelligence's Present and Foreseeable Impact on Lawyering, Judging, Policing and Law Enforcement' (2017) 32(3) *AI & Society* 441.

application for planning permission is not accompanied by an architectural plan, then the application should be denied. Where an architectural plan is not provided, an AI making a decision in terms of the application for planning permission would be able to relatively easily deny the application. A reason for this decision – that an architectural plan was not provided – could be given. However, as decision-making processes – and hence the algorithms associated with them – become more complicated, transparency can be lost; decisions are made within a black box.[41] Whilst the ideal mode of an AI's decision-making ability would include full transparency – which would generate legitimacy[42] – this is currently unachievable within the confines of current technology – and the absence of transparency can lead to fundamental issues of accountability beyond only the Rule of Law to areas of public decision making more broadly.[43] As a particular example of the problems and ramifications that may follow, the use of an AI system to assist a government official in making a decision may mean the decision making process is opaque (at best), and this may render judicial supervision of that decision-making act more difficult (or impossible).[44] This currently appears to be a problem that is intractable.[45] On this basis, through the vast majority of the book I assume that the use of the sorts of sophisticated AI systems contemplated in this book will also remain relatively un-explainable; however, in the final chapter where I consider the potential Future Rule of Law, I consider what would happen if the explainability problem could be solved. In doing so, whilst explainability represents the most conspicuous problem for the use of AI in the exercise of public power, it is far from the only one that may mean that adherence to the ideas of the Rule of Law may preclude AI's use.

The third reason my approach is non-dystopian is because I take the position that the technical ability of AI will – ultimately – be sufficient to act in the relatively idealised ways that I outline in the hypotheticals. The hypotheticals are structured to imagine differing levels of technological advancement in order to test the way in which the Rule of Law may operate to as to provide levels of protection. As noted above, I take this non-dystopian approach in considering three general hypothetical situations in which I consider the use of AI: first, in administrative decision-making; second, in the creation of secondary (delegated) legislation; and, third, in the creation of primary legislation. Whilst AI is not yet able to achieve all

[41] F Pasquale, *The Black Box Society: The Secret Algorithms That Control Money and Information*, reprint edn (Cambridge, MA, Harvard University Press, 2016); T Wischmeyer, 'Artificial Intelligence and Transparency: Opening the Black Box' in T Wischmeyer and T Rademacher (eds), *Regulating Artificial Intelligence* (Cham, Springer International Publishing, 2020) 75: doi.org/10.1007/978-3-030-32361-5_4.

[42] K de Fine Licht and J de Fine Licht, 'Artificial Intelligence, Transparency, and Public Decision-Making' (2020) 35(4) *AI & Society* 917; T Araujo et al, 'In AI We Trust? Perceptions About Automated Decision-Making by Artificial Intelligence' (2020) 35(3) *AI & Society* 611. Although, *complete* transparency may not be the ideal. de Laat (n 30). See also, Burgess (n 4).

[43] Allen (n 3) 158.

[44] ibid 160.

[45] D Minh et al, 'Explainable Artificial Intelligence: A Comprehensive Review' (2022) 55(5) *Artificial Intelligence Review* 3503.

of these tasks, the non-dystopian approach that I adopt across these three aspects ensures that a 'future-proofed' approach to constitutional theory can be adopted.

In relation to each of these three hypotheticals I consider two functional applications of AI. The first relates to an AI assessing data and providing recommendations to a human 'supervisor'. It is likely apparent that this function is not vastly different to the current exercise of power – and, in fact, reflects what is already happening in some instances.[46] It accordingly is, generally, dealt with relatively quickly. Notwithstanding the familiarity and similarity of this function, it is a useful consideration in order to identify the connections between the human-focused form of the Rule of Law as it has been seen up until now and the necessary future of the concept. This becomes apparent in the more detailed consideration of AI's other functional application as an autonomous entity that operates without the immediate control or supervision of humans.[47]

Despite the importance of both AI and the Rule of Law, there has been relatively little research relating to the significant potential of governments' use of AI having the potential to contravene the Rule of Law. Studies have explored overlapping areas. For example, judicial functions (for example, sentencing decisions – which are explored in ch 3),[48] or the steps necessary to regulate AI itself.[49] Some studies have taken a basic conception of the Rule of Law and looked to either current or future uses of AI.[50] Even amongst the work conducted that is within the sphere of AI and the Rule of Law, the work to date has not sought to conduct the detailed preliminary that is necessary to answer the question answered in this book regarding the way in which our conception of the Rule of Law will need to evolve in order to address the challenges that AI exercising power will bring.

II. Structure and Chapter Arguments

The structure of the book, and the titles of the various chapters, reflects the form and nature of the argument that I make. In chapter two, *The Rule of Law (Past and Present)*, I set out in more detail the meaning of the Past and the Present of the Rule of Law that has been touched upon above. In order to avoid criticisms for over generalising, I detail the various popular conceptions that go into the Past and

[46] For example, AI's use in predicting recidivism or in making parole decisions. Dressel and Farid (n 32); Shillingford et al (n 32).

[47] Particularly in relation to law-making in democratic societies, there are a number of caveats and stipulations that are necessary for this hypothetical to pass other constitutional hurdles relating to accountability and legitimacy. These are addressed in later chapters.

[48] Hogan-Doran (n 33).

[49] N Cristianini and T Scantamburlo, 'On Social Machines for Algorithmic Regulation' (2020) 35(3) *AI & Society* 645.

[50] Zalnieriute, Moses and Williams (n 4); S Greenstein, 'Preserving the Rule of Law in the Era of Artificial Intelligence (AI)' [2021] *Artificial Intelligence and Law*: doi.org/10.1007/s10506-021-09294-4.

the Present ideas. By taking more time to do this, the boundaries of the various conceptions become clearer and the nature of the interrelationships between the ideas becomes apparent.

Chapter three is entitled *AI – What it is, Does, and May Be.* Like chapter two, it expands upon the brief explanations provided above. In addition to detailing the nature of AI and its contemporary limitations, the chapter briefly sets out the hypotheticals that will be used to frame the arguments made in the rest of the book. In this sense, the chapter sets out the reality of AI before illustrating the ways in which AI is expected to impact the way in which power – through decision- and law-making – will be exercised in the future. Together, chapters two and three define and set up the terms of the argument that will be explored in chapters four, five, and six.

In chapters four, five, and six I explore (each in a separate chapter) whether – and how – the Past and Present Rule of Law can operate so as to curb the arbitrary exercise of power of AIs in a future in which the hypothetical extension of AI's capabilities exists. The chapters, respectively, consider the Rule of Law in terms of hypothetical applications that relate to the use of AI in: making administrative decisions; making secondary legislation (through delegated power); and, making laws in the form of primary legislation. In the course of the arguments made in each of those chapters, it becomes clear that across both Past and Present conceptions of the Rule of Law there are considerable shortcomings in the ability of the Past and Present ideas to apply to actions taken by non-humans. However, what also becomes clear is that the relative nature and scope of the problems differ across the hypotheticals and that some ways to consider what the Rule of Law is intended to do provide additional forms of solution.

In the concluding chapter – *AI and the Future of the Rule of Law* – I consider the problems raised in the previous three chapters in a different way. Instead of simply re-stating the conclusions in a way that reflects each of the hypotheticals, I consider the conclusions from the perspective of both the Past and Present forms of the Rule of Law. The different perspective that this affords enables me to detail the nature of the shortcomings and indicate the ways in which the concept of the Rule of Law must evolve – in terms of both the Past and Present ideas – if it is to continue to prevent the exercise of arbitrary power in the future.

III. Why the Answer to the Question is Important

In the first paragraph of this chapter, I posed the question that informs the thesis of this book: how will the concept of the Rule of Law need to evolve in order to account for artificial intelligence being used to exercise public power in the future? Across the course of the book, I analyse the ways in which the most popularly accepted ideas of the Rule of Law may inform the answer to this question in relation to ways in which AI *may* be used to exercise public power in the future.

I conclude that the Rule of Law will need to evolve – or, at least, our understanding of what it is will need to evolve. In identifying the Future Rule of Law, I point to the need to consider the specific problems that AI's exercise of power raises that I identify through the course of this book: explainability, speed, and accountability. I also suggest that, because the problems that the use of AI generates are *different* to the problems that the Rule of Law has previously been deployed to solve, solving these problems means the Future Rule of Law needs to be created on a blank canvas; from a position that does not rely on the previous canonical conceptions of the Past or Present Rule of Law.

2

The Rule of Law (Past and Present)

When considering popular Rule of Law conceptions, there are (at least) two broad ways in which the concept can be conceived. I call these *the Past Rule of Law* and *the Present Rule of Law*. In this chapter, the aim is to detail the content of these two ways to conceive of the concept and to outline how this way of considering the Rule of Law is useful in the context of the rest of this book. This is because I seek to consider the concept in a way that takes account of the concept's contested nature whilst also avoiding conflating or ignoring ideas in a way that renders any conclusions objectionable to either perspective. I use the Past and Present ideas – together with varying levels of abstraction within each – to assess the relative ability of AI's use/deployment to satisfy Rule of Law ideas.

As a preliminary note, it is important to be clear that, by adopting the terms the 'Past' and the 'Present' of the Rule of Law, I do not intend to suggest that either way to view the concept is more – or less – correct than the other. I simply reflect the relevant temporality of the periods in which the various ideas were first authored. Unsurprisingly, the Past conceptions were authored in the past – generally before the 1970s – and the Present conceptions have been authored in more recent decades – generally in the period after the 1970s but they continue to be added to in the current decade. Through this chapter, I will expand upon the nature, form, and differentiating features of the Past and Present ideas of the Rule of Law. However, it is useful to start with some broad overarching features.

To identify the Past and the Present of the Rule of Law, I include some of the most popular, and frequently relied upon, statements of the Rule of Law in the Anglo-American legal tradition. The Past ideas are constituted by the well-known and popularly cited Rule of Law conceptions by Aristotle, Locke, Dicey, Hayek, Fuller, and Raz. These ideas reflect a tradition that opposes the imposition of arbitrary power over individuals by the state. In order to combat this problem, these theorists reflect a thin/formal/procedural solution that constrains the exercise of power by ensuring that new norms are, amongst other things, predictable.[1]

As noted briefly in chapter one, the Present of the Rule of Law can be differentiated from the Past Rule of Law in two distinct ways. For this reason, I distinguish two forms of the Present Rule of Law. In the first – represented by conceptions by,

[1] I have previously identified predictability as one of the common themes that exist across all of these accounts. P Burgess, 'The Rule of Law: Beyond Contestedness' (2017) 8(3) *Jurisprudence* 480.

inter alia, Krygier and King – the Present Rule of Law responds to the arbitrary exercise of power in general (and not merely to the *state-based* arbitrary exercise of power) and includes accounts that see the Rule of Law as operating in a private setting – ie, individual to individual – and not merely in a public setting from the state to an individual. The second form reflects the more traditional distinction of thin/thick or formal/substantive conceptions of the Rule of Law.[2] Popular Present conceptions of the Rule of Law that adopt a substantive view considered in this book are provided by Tom Bingham and the UN.

For anyone that has read this far into this book, many of the names – whether representing the Past or the Present of the Rule of Law – will be familiar. Such is the prevalence of the authors that constitute the Past Rule of Law, I have previously described them as the 'usual suspects' of the Rule of Law.[3] The selection of theorists is largely made for me and is not a result of my cherry-picking conceptions. They represent some of the most frequently deployed conceptions when attempts are being made to illustrate the meaning and conceptual boundaries of the Rule of Law.[4]

In terms of the Present of the Rule of Law, these ideas represent popular conceptions that are also frequently relied upon to illustrate the concept's meaning. The selection of these conceptions could be seen to be arbitrary in comparison to the conceptions representing the Past of the Rule of Law. Unlike the Past of the Rule of Law, the Present ideas have had less opportunity to take-hold. They also have less of a homogenous acceptance in discussions of the Rule of Law as there are a range of thinkers that express different ideas associated with what could be a Present idea of the Rule of Law. (This could include the accounts provided by, for example, Julian Sempill and Sanne Taekema.[5]) Nevertheless, those that are considered here are clearly impactful by virtue of the wide institutional acceptance they hold (for example, the UN's conception), or the prominence of the author and/or the wide interest in the conception (for example, Lord Bingham and Jeff King, respectively). As will be seen and expanded upon later in this chapter, these ideas represent a re-imagining of the meaning and operation of the concept of the Rule of Law from the authors' perspectives. Consideration of *these* Present ideas represents a range of different approaches that encompass the general ideas that are prevalent in the present day.

[2] The classic illustration of this distinction is provided by Paul Craig. P Craig, 'Formal and Substantive Conceptions of the Rule of Raw an Analytical Framework' [1997] (Autumn) *Public Law* 467.

[3] P Burgess, 'The Rule of Lore in the Rule of Law: Putting the Problem of the Rule of Law in Context' (2020) 12 *Hague Journal on the Rule of Law* 333 ('Rule of Lore'); P Burgess, 'Deriving the International Rule of Law: An Unnecessary, Impractical and Unhelpful Exercise' (2019) 10(1) *Transnational Legal Theory* 65 ('Deriving the International Rule of Law').

[4] It is because of their relatively infrequent deployment that a number of important theorists who nevertheless hold well-reasoned ideas of or associated with the Rule of Law are *not* included. These include Harrington, Montesquieu, Rawls, and Finnis.

[5] See, as just two examples, JA Sempill, 'What Rendered Ancient Tyrants Detestable: The Rule of Law and the Constitution of Corporate Power' [2018] *Hague Journal on the Rule of Law* 1; K Bhatt, J Lander and S Taekema, 'Introduction: The Rule of Law in Transnational Development Projects – Private Actors and Public Chokeholds' (2021) 17(1) *International Journal of Law in Context* 91.

As will be seen over the course of the chapter, and as will be apparent from the brief overview provided immediately above, the Past and the Present of the Rule of Law are different. The conceptions that constitute each category are themselves all different to one another, but similarities can be noted across the conceptions that allows them to be seen as falling into the relevant conceptual category. The categorisation is different to other conceptual distinctions that have previously been used. It is, for example, common to place the ideas into thin or thick categories, or formal or substantive categories.[6] Most of the Past Rule of Law conceptions could be described as being thin/formal conceptions of the Rule of Law. This would include the conceptions of Aristotle, Locke, Dicey, Hayek, and Raz. (But, Fuller represents something of an outlier as there is a thick*er* element to his idea.)

Similarly, whilst the Present conceptions each accept the need for some sort of formal base, it is a relative oversimplification to suggest that they are all substantive in the same way. For example, the nature of the UN's approach – in which the Rule of Law is used as a vehicle to achieve other forms of the good, differs to the way in which Bingham or King see the substantive nature of the concept; Bingham sees the Rule of Law as providing an aspirational target to which governments should aspire; King sees the concept as requiring a particular form of action be taken in society. For these reasons, the thin/thick distinction cannot accurately reflect some of the complexities that arise when the wide variety of popular Rule of Law conceptions is taken into account. In addition, the thin/thick way of grouping the ideas fails to highlight the relative significance of the temporal connection.

The differences across the conceptions should, at least to some extent, not be surprising. After all, the Rule of Law is widely accepted to be a contested concept.[7] In circumstances where the concept itself is contested, and where the conceptions that make up either the Past or the Present of the Rule of Law are used to evidence what the Rule of Law *is*, exploring those accounts enables a more precise idea about the nature of the concept to be adopted. Whilst considering a broad conceptual meaning – or even adopting the frequently used thin/thick or formal/substantive approach – can be helpful, the additional nuance I add in this book goes beyond the mere acknowledgement that the Rule of Law is a good thing and facilitates the location of the potential conceptual boundaries of the concept of the Rule of Law.[8] By segmenting the various popular Rule of Law accounts into the Past and Present categories, a more nuanced appreciation of the concept can be gained. What is more, in considering Past and Present ideas I also adopt an approach that

[6] Craig (n 2); Burgess (n 1).

[7] There is a detailed literature that explores the contested, or essentially contested, nature of the Rule of Law as a concept. For a summary of the various positions and debates, see J Waldron, 'Is the Rule of Law an Essentially Contested Concept (in Florida)?' (2002) 21(2) *Law and Philosophy* 137; Burgess (n 1).

[8] The concept is 'an international hurrah term': M Krygier, 'Four Puzzles About the Rule of Law: Why, What, Where? And Who Cares?' in J Flemming (ed), *Getting to the Rule of Law* (New York, New York University Press, 2011) 64, 64. 'Everyone happens to be in favor of the rule of law at the moment' J Waldron, 'Legislation and the Rule of Law' (2007) 1(1) *Legisprudence* 91, 118.

considers different levels of abstraction – thus covering both breadth and depth aspects of the contested concept.

If the purpose is to nuance the broad conceptual meaning that has so far been explored, a little more must be said about the distinctions and connections between the conceptions. Accordingly, to achieve this nuance, and to cut through some of the contest associated with the concept, I consider some of the canonical statements of what the Rule of Law *is* to be solutions to Rule of Law-problems that existed at the time the conceptions were either authored or applied.[9] This approach enables a clear differentiation to be drawn between the Past and the Present ideas.

The remainder of this chapter provides the conceptual/theoretical basis for the analysis in the rest of the book. After I outline hypothetical ways in which AI may be used in the exercise of public power in the next chapter, I bring together the Past as well as the Present ideas of the Rule of Law with the three hypotheticals in chapters four, five, and six. It is only once I have done this, in the final chapter, that I am able to consider how the Rule of Law can curb the potential for arbitrary exercises of power by AIs. Before I do all of this, in the two sections that follow, I first outline the Past and Present ideas of the Rule of Law. Then, I consider the relative differences in these two forms of ideas as well as considering, in a little more depth than in this section, why it is useful to consider the Rule of Law in this way.

I. The Past Rule of Law

Aristotle, Locke, Dicey, Hayek, Fuller, and Raz's Rule of Law ideas constitute the Past Rule of Law. They are well-known. Together, they represent a 'Who's Who?' of Western political thought ….'[10] These thinkers have not been selected for the purpose of this book to illustrate a particular point of view or a particular view of the world. They have not been selected because of any particular preference for *these* thinkers over a raft of others. They are the main body of theorists that are deployed when there is a need to define what the concept of the Rule of Law means. As noted earlier, their prevalence in this definitional space has caused me to describe them previously as the Rule of Law's 'usual suspects'.[11] They are the

[9] For the Rule of Law in problem/solution terms see Burgess, 'Rule of Lore' (n 3). The Rule of Law has been described as a solution concept by Waldron (n 7) 158. See also NB Reynolds, 'Grounding the Rule of Law' (1989) 2(1) *Ratio Juris* 1, 5; M Krygier, 'The Rule of Law After the Short Twentieth Century: Launching a Global Career' in R Nobles and D Schiff (eds), *Law, Society and Community: Socio-Legal Essays in Honour of Roger Cotterrell* (London, Ashgate, 2014) 327, 327.

[10] J Møller and S-Erik Skaaning, *The Rule of Law: Definitions, Measures, Patterns and Causes* (Basingstoke, Palgrave Macmillan, 2014) 2. Waldron provides a similar list. J Waldron, 'The Rule of Law' in EN Zalta (ed), *The Stanford Encyclopedia of Philosophy* (Fall 2016, 2016) plato.stanford.edu/entries/rule-of-law/.

[11] P Burgess, 'You Say It Best When You Say Nothing At All: "[The Rule of Law]"' (2021) 25(1) *Edinburgh Law Review* 1.

thinkers most frequently used to illustrate both the contents and the boundary of the concept in a period loosely described as the past.[12] In this respect, the relative selection of *these* thinkers has been made for me.

The conscious decision that has been made here to describe them as the *Past* Rule of Law should not be seen to reflect a waning or the eradication of their relative popularity as usual suspects. These thinkers remain popular – but it is also clear that the most recently authored account (that is constitutive of the usual suspects' conceptions) was published in 1977.[13] Some of the authors have made subsequent forays refining their conceptual meaning of the Rule of Law, but these have not been as popularly received and, hence, they are not taken to be as constitutive of the relative canonical meaning of the concept provided by the usual suspects in their earlier accounts.[14]

The usual suspects' historical and philosophical diversity – and their conceptions' often very different desiderata – make it difficult to draw exact parallels between their accounts.[15] However, two broad traits can be noted: their Rule of Law solutions were intended to remedy problems associated with *state* arbitrary power; and, their ideas are largely thin/formal accounts relating to the exercise of public power. However, as suggested earlier, the relative thinness/formality is not a completely accurate way to group them (even though some of the Present theorists can be seen as thick/substantive). Again, using the temporal descriptor reflects a simple way to show that all of these ideas were written in the past in conceptions are all at least 45 years' old.

In what follows, in order to clearly illustrate the idea of the Past Rule of Law, I outline the broad brushstrokes of each of the usual suspects' Rule of Law ideas. This allows a clearer and more nuanced appreciation of the contours of the Past Rule of Law. In exploring the usual suspects' accounts, and where there is a massive literature that expands upon and explores each of the thinkers' accounts – either specifically in terms of the Rule of Law or in relation to their work more generally – I provide only a relatively brief summary of each of the Rule of Law

[12] Examples of this approach include: JP Reid, *Rule of Law: The Jurisprudence of Liberty in the Seventeenth and Eighteenth Centuries* (Dekalb, ILL, Northern Illinois University Press, 2004) 5–8; C Sampford et al, *Retrospectivity and the Rule of Law* (Oxford, Oxford University Press, 2006) 14; J Waldron, 'Stare Decisis and the Rule of Law: A Layered Approach' (2011) 111 *Michigan Law Review* 1, 4; Waldron (n 10). For a critique of this approach, see Burgess, 'Rule of Lore' (n 3).

[13] The most recent account was first authored by Raz in 1977, and has been reproduced subsequently. J Raz, *The Authority of Law: Essays on Law and Morality*, 2nd edn (Oxford, Oxford University Press, 2009).

[14] Two prevalent examples of these more recent accounts that have not received as much popular acceptance as earlier accounts are provided by Raz and Hayek. J Raz, 'The Law's Own Virtue' (2019) 39(1) *Oxford Journal of Legal Studies* 1; FA von Hayek, *Law, Legislation and Liberty: Rules and Order* (Chicago, University of Chicago Press, 1979) 4 and 5.

[15] However, they are largely white, frequently bearded, mostly dead, men. This, undoubtedly, impacts our conception of what the Rule of Law is.

aspects of their ideas.[16] There is no possible way to condense all of their work into a single book. However, in providing this outline, notwithstanding its relative brevity, I provide enough detail for an overarching category of the Past Rule of Law to be fleshed out and enable a clearer idea of the way that the usual suspects' accounts integrate into the category.

A. Aristotle

> Therefore he who asks law to rule is asking God and intelligence and no others to rule; while he who asks for the rule of a human being is importing a wild beast too; for desire is like a wild beast, and anger perverts rulers and the very best of men. Hence law is intelligence without appetition.[17]

Aristotle sought to prevent legislative decision-making from being infused with emotion. In order to prevent this, he suggested a form of – what may now be deemed – legislative due process.[18] In providing this requirement, he suggested that there was a need for laws to be expressed in general terms.[19] Notwithstanding the variation in the Past Rule of Law's theorists' ideas, the particular component that is most frequently seen as a core idea of the Rule of Law is predictability.[20]

Aristotle's concern for restraining popular tyranny was put this way: 'We begin by asking whether it is more expedient to be ruled by the best man or by the best laws.'[21] He decries making hasty and emotion-fuelled decisions and refers to a need for laws – expressed generally – that provide for predictability and stability.[22] He puts it this way in terms where the orientation of Athenians was toward the political community and where 'democracy was synonymous for the Athenians with the "rule of law"'.[23] Despite his not using the term 'the Rule of Law', the inclusion of predictability in Aristotle's account of law making could be a fundamental reason that he is frequently cited as the originator of the idea of the Rule of Law.[24]

[16] A more detailed – yet not contradictory – exegesis of each of the thinkers' Rule of Law conceptions can be found in: BZ Tamanaha, *On the Rule of Law History, Politics, Theory* (Cambridge, Cambridge University Press, 2004); Waldron (n 10).

[17] Aristotle, T Sinclair and TJ Saunders, *The Politics* (London, Penguin UK, 1981) 1287a23.

[18] Aristotle, *Rhetoric*, trans W Rhys Roberts (Dover, 2004) 1, ch 1.

[19] Aristotle, Sinclair and Saunders (n 17) 1286A7.

[20] Burgess (n 1); A Bedner, 'An Elementary Approach to the Rule of Law' (2010) 2(01) *Hague Journal on the Rule of Law* 48; G Palombella, 'The Rule of Law and Its Core' in G Palombella and N Walker (eds), *Relocating the Rule of Law* (Oxford, Hart Publishing, 2009).

[21] Aristotle, Sinclair and Saunders (n 17) 1286A7.

[22] ibid.

[23] JW Jones, *The Law and Legal Theory of the Greeks: An Introduction*, 1st edn (Oxford, Clarendon Press, 1956) 90. Cited, in these terms, by Tamanaha (n 16) 7.

[24] This is a common assumption of the Rule of Law. See, eg, P Costa, D Zolo and E Santoro (eds), *The Rule of Law: History, Theory and Criticism* (Cham, Springer, 2007) 75; Burgess, 'Rule of Lore' (n 3). Similarly, Fallon states: 'Some have traced the modern ideal to Aristotle, who equated the Rule of Law with the rule of reason ….' RH Fallon Jr, '"The Rule of Law" as a Concept in Constitutional Discourse' (1997) 97(1) *Columbia Law Review* 1, 1.

Aristotle did not only fear tyranny in a general sense. He was also concerned that democracy could result in a form of tyranny. The legislature in ancient Athens did not operate in the same way as a legislature in most contemporary societies. The *creation* of laws by a legislature was not then accepted as a core function of the institution.[25] Today, across most liberal democracies, it is relatively uncontroversial that law – as a directive or as some form of written statute – can be made. This is seen as the defining characteristic of a legislature. In this respect, the power that the legislature holds is not merely a power to *amend* existing laws or to generate laws that not only marginally effect a change in society. Its power to create a completely new law – where there was previously no law or where legislation did not previously exist in a particular societal sphere – is not doubted. This is different to any particularly constitutionally regulated limits on law making powers; within any constitutional limits modern legislatures are generally taken to have a plenary power to create new laws. Yet, this idea, that law could be *made* is a contemporary invention. Legislative innovation in the ancient world was controlled; a process was undertaken where the 'new' law was contrasted to the existing laws to ensure that there was some level of certainty or consistency. Should there be too substantial a deviation and should the newly proposed law not be compatible with the already existing laws, fines could be imposed (or even a sentence of death for the individual proposing the law).[26] With potential consequences like these, the process of law-making was slowed. The legislature's innovation was controlled in a way that meant the pre-existing/accepted laws acted as a loose anchor on evolution of societal norms. When this ancient context is taken into consideration, Aristotle's suggestion illustrates society's understanding of the form and function of the legislative process: legislative outputs should be controlled. What this demonstrates is that, notwithstanding the frequently made suggestion that the idea of the Rule of Law is ancient and that it originated with Aristotle,[27] Aristotle did not 'create' a Rule of Law idea. Aristotle merely *described* the state of affairs that already existed in the polis. Whilst Aristotle is, in some sense, innovating – as his statement of the descriptive rationale is, itself, useful as some form of benchmark – it is the *community's* view of the existing law, coupled with the legislative limitations, that subject the law-making part of government to some sort of normative force.

Aristotle describes a limitation on the imposition of state power. What we can see from Aristotle's account is that the Rule of Law-related idea that he describes is a norm that constrains the actions of the state; it limits the way that the legislature can act to regulate the lives of its citizens. The way that this operates is by providing some form of procedural check – that the proposed law does not fundamentally

[25] For a detailed survey of conceptions of the Rule of Law in Athens, see EM Harris, *The Rule of Law in Action in Democratic Athens* (New York, Oxford University Press, 2013). See also M Canevaro, 'The Rule of Law as the Measure of Political Legitimacy in the Greek City States' (2017) 9(2) *Hague Journal on the Rule of Law* 211.

[26] B Leoni, *Freedom and the Law*, 1st edn (Springfield, OR, Nash Publishing, 1961) 4.

[27] This is one of the four frequently cited tropes of the Rule of Law. Burgess, 'Rule of Lore' (n 3).

alter the pre-existing law – on the application of power. This avoids the potential for the 'beast' to rule and, instead, means that there is a control operating so as to avoid the arbitrary application of power. In these respects, it becomes apparent why Aristotle's idea can be seen as a thin/formal idea of the Rule of Law. It is also clear that his idea operates so as to control the relationship between the state and the individual. What is important for the categorisation adopted in this book (even if it is obvious and apparent) is that this account can be seen as a Past conception of the Rule of Law.

B. Locke

> For all the power the Government has, being only for the good of the Society, as it ought not to be *Arbitrary* and at *Pleasure*, so it ought to be exercised by *established and promulgated Laws*; that both the People may know their Duty, and be safe and secure within the limits of the Law; and the Rulers too kept within their bounds, and not be tempted by the Power they have in their hands ....[28]

Locke's *Two Treatises* was authored between the English Civil War and the Glorious Revolution. Locke's Past Rule of Law idea remains influential in many contemporary societies. Like Aristotle, his idea is clearly a Past conception of the Rule of Law. As part of his famous thought experiment in which rational actors would move from a state of nature to a civil society to protect their property, Locke suggests: 'the legislative, or supream authority, cannot assume to its self a power to rule by extemporary arbitrary decree, but is bound to dispense *justice*, and decide the rights of the subject by *promulgated standing laws, and known authoris'd* judges'.[29] Even though the original issue related to private property, it is also clear that the problem that Locke saw as resulting from the move from a state of nature was one associated with state-based arbitrary rule.

Locke's quote is drawn from a broader passage that is remarkable for its use of language – including mention of 'absolute arbitrary power', 'established and promulgated laws', 'declared and received laws', 'stated rules', and 'settled standing laws'[30] – that is immediately recognisable to anyone familiar with the contemporary debate regarding the meaning of the concept of the Rule of Law.[31] In what was – originally, but erroneously – seen as a justification for the Glorious Revolution and the subsequent exercise of governmental power in England in the late seventeenth century,[32] Locke outlines the move from a state of nature to

[28] J Locke, *Two Treatises of Government*, ed P Laslett (Cambridge, Cambridge University Press, 1988) II, 137. (Emphasis in the original.).

[29] ibid II 136. (Emphasis in the original.).

[30] ibid II, 137. (Lest we miss their importance, he was even kind enough to emphasise the phrases quoted here by using italics.).

[31] For a summary, see Waldron (n 7); Tamanaha (n 16).

[32] For an excellent outline of this, see ibid 45–66. See also, R Ashcraft, *Revolutionary Politics & Locke's Two Treatises of Government* (Princeton, NJ, Princeton University Press, 1986) 183; R Ashcraft, *Locke's*

a civil society as being one taken by rational humans eager to preserve their – pre-political and naturally accruing – property. He defines the state of nature in these terms: 'Men living together according to reason, without a common superior on earth, with authority to judge between them, is *properly the state of nature*.'[33] This occurs in two stages: first, the people unanimously agree with *one another* to form a civil society; and, second, the people agree, by majority, to institute a government. Through this consensual ceding of only powers – held by individuals in the state of nature – sufficient to enable the government to protect each individual's life, liberty, and property, government legitimacy is, Locke suggests, generated. When the language that Locke used is considered, what becomes obvious is, notwithstanding their historical pedigree, the terms he used remain popular in contemporary Rule of Law discourse.

In the quote above, Locke describes the legislature as being supreme. He references no absolute controls on its sovereignty. Yet, in relation to the nature of the government's powers, Locke states:

> … the Law of Nature stands as an Eternal Rule to all Men, *Legislators* as well as others. The *Rules* that they make for other Mens Actions, must, as well as their own and other Mens Actions, be conformable to the Law of Nature … no Humane Sanction can be good, or valid against it.[34]

Further, as noted above, Locke's government is formed through a limited delegation of power and for limited purposes.[35] Taking these together, it seems both the natural rights *not* surrendered, and the requirement that the government operate in accordance with the Rule of Law-like terms outlined above,[36] act to limit governmental power. Accordingly, under Locke's move from the state of nature, consent, as a series of individuals' pragmatically motivated decisions to protect their (property) interests, is not only the mechanism by which political societies are created, but it is also responsible for the generation of a limitation on the exercise of governmental power as an unintended consequence.

It is this form of limitation on the exercise of governmental power that constitutes what we now call the Rule of Law. The way Locke uses pre-political property as the foundation on which he structures his theory – notwithstanding the hypothetical status of the state of nature – is a change that reflects action and not design. His theory follows a chain of inference something like this: property is natural; labour can be mixed with material things to appropriate property; it becomes possible to accrue more than is needed (via the adoption of currency); as a result,

Two Treatises of Government: Volume 17, 1st edn (London, Routledge, 2012) 291; CD Tarlton, '"The Rulers Now on Earth": Locke's Two Treatises and the Revolution of 1688' (1985) 28(02) *The Historical Journal* 279, 279.

[33] Locke (n 28) II, 19. (Emphasis in original.).

[34] ibid II, 135.

[35] ibid II, 87–89 and 123–4.

[36] MP Zuckert, 'Hobbes, Locke, and the Problems of the Rule of Law' (1994) 36 *Nomos* 63, 72–74; Tamanaha (n 16) 50.

each individual agrees with each other they will enter a social contract to protect their property; each individual agrees to cede only as much power as is necessary to protect their property; and, this results in limited government power.[37] The crucial part – for a discussion about the Rule of Law – occurs in the latter stages of this chain: without any intention to ultimately create a sovereign power, each individual agrees with each other individual (without being directed to do so) to enter the contract. Individuals do so for prudential reasons, not because they want to set up a governmental power. It is in this way that the order is formed by the action – but not design – of the individuals within the society and it is in this way that there is a constraint created on the imposition of governmental power. This results in the broadly stated form of Locke's Rule of Law conception.

The more precise nature of the conception Locke proposes, and the solution that it provides, can be established from both the context of the authorship of his *Two Treatises* and from the language he uses (as extracted above). The problem on which society was focused during the authoring period of the *Two Treatises* relates to the issue of whether the extant sovereign (in the King) or a future sovereign (in Parliament) should be obeyed. For example, pamphlets authored around the same time asked the question how an 'Arbitrary absolute Popish Tyrant' can be a lawful successor to an established and bounded government in circumstances where he 'violently, unlawfully, and tyrannically overruns the due bounds of power'.[38] Where Locke sought to argue that Parliament would be a locus of power that would be subject to limitation (unlike the monarchy), the key point related to the questions regarding the ability of Parliament to function in this way related to its nature as a representative institution.

The argument being put by Locke takes the form: if Parliament cannot be what it suggests it must be to rule, then it should not be obeyed. The contrary position is the Filmerian argument related to the divine authority of Kings: the monarch should be obeyed in consequence of natural law and the authority bestowed by God.[39] Whig responses – that reflect Locke's position – were focused on illustrating reasons why the divine right of Kings was sub-optimal and that, in comparison, Parliament – as an institution created and limited by the consent of the people – represented a far superior option. Locke's solution to the period's problems related principally to the suggestion of, and lobbying for, an alternative in the course of arguing that at least one prominent and popular opposing account is deficient.

In making his argument and in providing an alternative to the tyrannical rule of all-powerful monarchs, Locke propounds a form of limited government in

[37] EP Thompson suggests something like this occurred when, in 18th century England, powerful actors took steps to retain their power, but this power was then used by the less-powerful to protect their own rights and curb the exercise of arbitrary power. EP Thompson, *Whigs and Hunters: The Origin of the Black Act* (Pantheon Books, 1st American, 1975) 264–65.

[38] E Settle, *The Character of a Popish Successour* (printed for T. Davies, 1681) 20.

[39] R Filmer, 'Patriarcha' in JP Sommerville (ed), *Patriarcha and Other Writings* (Cambridge, Cambridge University Press, 1991) 1; R Filmer, *The Free-Holders Grand Inquest* (1648).

which the Parliament is subject to constraints. These constraints, whilst protective of rights that Locke saw as fundamental, meant that a normative force operated on the process of government in a way that ensures laws are, inter alia, certain, predictable, and stable. These ideas form part of what we now call the Rule of Law.

What will be apparent from this account is that Locke's Rule of Law idea, like Aristotle's, imposes the constraints in a way that is 'thin'; the relative outcome of the imposition of the laws is of no consequence; 'good' outcomes are not necessary. In addition, Locke's account is clearly a solution that is focused on constraining the actions of the *state*. It is a control on the law-making powers in a way that a shield is generated that protects the people. (This was a fundamental part of the persuasive value of the theory given the problems in society at the time.) Given its obvious historical origins, this is also a Past form of the Rule of Law.

C. Dicey

> Two features have at all times since the Norman Conquest characterised the political institutions of England … The first of these features is the omnipotence or undisputed supremacy throughout the whole country of the central government … The second of these features, which is closely connected with the first, is the rule or supremacy of law.[40]

Dicey's formulation – originally penned in the late nineteenth century – is frequently cited for popularising the phrase *the Rule of Law*.[41] When the various usual suspects of the Rule of Law are discussed, it is a common assumption that Dicey and the other theorists are joined in a shared endeavour.[42] The error in this assumption is brought to the fore in considering Dicey through the cautionary note by Arndt who stated that the Diceyean form of the concept did not exist until the 1860s and that it meant 'very different things to Bracton, Coke, Locke and Dicey'.[43]

Dicey saw similar state-based problems. He feared that the expanding administrative state in England would destroy the Rule of Law which, for him, had 'three distinct though kindred conceptions'.[44] Dicey formulated these as an inclusive list

[40] AV Dicey, *Introduction to the Study of the Law of the Constitution*, 10th edn (Basingstoke, Palgrave Macmillan, 1979) 183–84.

[41] Terms like 'the empire of laws and not of men' had been invoked in the mid-seventeenth century and, arguably, before. Harrington paraphrases an Aristotelean sentiment in J Harrington, *Harrington: 'The Commonwealth of Oceana' and 'A System of Politics'*, ed JGA Pocock (Cambridge, Cambridge University Press, 1992) 8–9. Jeremy Waldron, too, recognises this. J Waldron, *The Rule of Law and the Measure of Property: The Hamlyn Lectures* (Cambridge, Cambridge University Press, 2012) 7. (Citation omitted.).

[42] I have explored and considered this view of the theorists here: Burgess, 'Rule of Lore' (n 3).

[43] HW Arndt, 'The Origins of Dicey's Concept of the "Rule of Law"' (1957) 31 *Australian Law Journal* 117, 121.

[44] Dicey (n 41) 187–88.

stating: 'When we say that the supremacy or the rule of law is a characteristic of the English constitution, we generally include under one expression at least three distinct though kindred conceptions.'[45] The first is associated with the absence of arbitrary power in which he contrasts the Rule of Law with 'every system of government based on the exercise by persons in authority of wide, arbitrary, or discretionary powers of constraint';[46] the second relates to the equal application of the law where 'every man, whatever be his rank or condition, is subject to the ordinary law of the realm and amenable to the jurisdiction of the ordinary tribunals'.[47] Together, these two form the backbone of the Diceyean Rule of Law. They are the aspects frequently relied upon when a Diceyean idea of the Rule of Law is adopted. Notwithstanding its frequently forgotten application,[48] Dicey's third kindred conception – that 'the general principles of the constitution (as for example the right to personal liberty, or the right of public meeting) are with us the result of judicial decisions determining the rights of private persons in particular cases brought before the courts'[49] – epitomises the problem-focused nature of his Rule of Law conception. It is here that the relative difference between Dicey's conception and the other theorists becomes clearest.

Throughout his account Dicey sees the rise of the administrative state in England as being destructive of the idea of the Rule of Law as he sees it. It is the Rule of Law's decline, and the accompanying rise in the welfare state that motivates Dicey. He sees the Rule of Law as being something that is inherent in the English constitutional system and not as something that can be manufactured or decided by individuals making administrative decisions – it is for this reason that he prefers the decisions of the courts. (It is this aspect that has particular resonance with the first hypothetical: the use of AI in administrative decision-making.)

In referencing work by Mill – in which Dicey takes Mill to be suggesting it is 'absurd' to suggest the idea that 'the constitution has not been made but has "grown"'[50] – Dicey suggests the English Constitution is so intertwined with the idea of spontaneous growth it makes no sense to treat it as the product of human will.[51] He also suggests it arose as the 'fruit of contests carried on in the courts on behalf of the rights of individuals'.[52] By doing so, albeit in a different way to the previous two thinkers, he acknowledges growth within the courts that avoids the application of arbitrary rules.

Recall the quote opening this section. Notwithstanding the threat he sees, Dicey is working under the impression that the Rule of Law – at least as he conceives

[45] ibid.
[46] ibid 188.
[47] ibid 188, 193.
[48] For the perils of neglecting origins and conceptions' meanings, see P Burgess, 'Neglecting the History of the Rule of Law: (Unintended) Conceptual Eugenics' (2017) 9(2) *Hague Journal on the Rule of Law* 195.
[49] Dicey (n 40) 195.
[50] ibid 196; JS Mill, *The Collected Works of John Stuart Mill*, ed JM Robson, vol XIX 374.
[51] Dicey (n 40) 196.
[52] ibid.

it – had, in the late nineteenth century, already existed in England for over 800 years. Dicey is attempting only to describe an existing system that he sees as being eroded by contemporary institutions. In the first two of his Rule of Law components – relating to preventing arbitrary power and legal equality – the importance of his descriptive endeavour is clear. He relies on the extant nature and operation of the Rule of Law to illustrate the value in retaining the system as it is (or was) as a purposive bulwark against the growth of the administrative state. The account is clearly descriptive of a societal reality that is either extant but under threat or has been recently lost. Dicey's Rule of Law idea is built on the operation of common law courts' decisions in a societal structure that was hundreds of years old.

Even though the Rule of Law account that is posed by the three thinkers explored so far is similar, the accounts can be differentiated based on the problems to which they respond.[53] The fear that Dicey has, and the problem to which he is responding is *different* to the problems to which Aristotle and Locke are responding. For Aristotle, the problem is the potential for the tyranny that could follow from the democratic process or in allowing 'the beast' to make any laws unchecked. For Locke, the problem was convincing the populous that Parliament was less likely to make arbitrary decisions than a monarch. Dicey's fear related to the potential of arbitrary decisions resulting from an expanding administrative system.

Dicey's account is temporally closer to the present day than either Aristotle or Locke. However, being originally authored in the late-nineteenth century, it remains obviously a Past Rule of Law conception. Dicey's ideas, nevertheless, remain a staple in many discussions of the Rule of Law.[54] As we will see in the remaining Past conceptions of the Rule of Law, the anti-arbitrariness connection that has been seen so far does still remain – but so too does the relative difference in the problems to which each theorist responds. Once all of the usual suspects (Past) conceptions have been outlined, I will come back to this point and also illustrate other connections between the Past conceptions that makes this categorisation appropriate for this book.

D. Hayek

> Nothing distinguishes more clearly conditions in a free country from those in a country under arbitrary government than the observance in the former of the great principles known as the Rule of Law. Stripped of all technicalities, this means that government in all its actions is bound by rules fixed and announced beforehand – rules which make it

[53] Burgess (n 11).

[54] See, eg, LB Crawford et al, *Public Law and Statutory Interpretation: Principles and Practice*, 2nd edn (Alexandria, NSW, Federation Press, 2021); M Elliott and R Thomas, *Public Law*, 4th edn (Oxford, Oxford University Press, 2020).

> possible to foresee with fair certainty how the authority will use its coercive powers in given circumstances and to plan one's individual affairs on the basis of this knowledge.[55]

Hayek's most influential Rule of Law conception – formed, in part, from the extract above – was written in the mid-twentieth century. After Dicey had popularised the phrase 'the Rule of Law', Hayek adopts it but also specifically points out that they have different ideas about what it means.[56] Yet, whilst the solutions may superficially be seen to be similar, the *problems* to which they respond are very different. Yet, in common with Dicey, Locke, and Aristotle, Hayek provides a solution to a problem that is created by the exercise of power by the state.

The notion of predictability pervades his various Rule of Law works;[57] for Hayek, state coercion can be tempered only by the actions of a limited government being predictable.[58] In this respect, Hayek's solution is singularly focussed on the potential for the state to force the hand of individuals in society. He says: '*government* in all its actions is bound by rules fixed and announced beforehand … under the Rule of Law the *government* is prevented from stultifying individual efforts by ad hoc action'.[59] Where the state is constrained in this way, coercion can be avoided as individuals are able to plan (around) the state's acts.[60]

The differences between the problems that the usual suspects address in their Rule of Law ideas are important to note. As noted above, Hayek sees his project as being different to Dicey's.[61] For Hayek, the Rule of Law-related problem is the issue of totalitarian rule and the associated nationalisation of state assets – this is borne of the context of the period in which he is writing – amidst the horrors of World War II. Hayek's fear is that a too-powerful state would coerce individuals. For this reason, the solution that Hayek proposes constrains the state in order to ensure that its actions are predictable. Whilst the solution is superficially similar, this differs considerably to the authoring contexts for Aristotle, Locke, and Dicey. Contrary to the problems detailed above that Aristotle, Locke, and Dicey address, Hayek's work can be seen as an attack on socialism. He suggests state power can be curtailed by allowing individuals to plan around state action and, therefore, avoid coercion. Whilst Hayek's fears of a coercive state also relate to arbitrary actions being taken, the specific problem that gives rise to this fear is *different* to the other usual suspects.

[55] FA von Hayek, *The Road to Serfdom*, ed B Caldwell (Chicago, University of Chicago Press, 2007) 112.

[56] bid. (At fn 2.).

[57] Hayek (n 55); FA von Hayek, *The Constitution of Liberty* (Chicago, University of Chicago Press, 1960); FA von Hayek, *Law, Legislation and Liberty: The Political Order of a Free People*, vol 3 (1973) ('*Law, Legislation and Liberty*').

[58] Hayek (n 55) 112.

[59] ibid. (Emphasis added.).

[60] Predictability, is the clearest and most consistent idea within his various Rule of Law ideas. ibid; Hayek, *The Constitution of Liberty* (n 58); Hayek, *Law, Legislation and Liberty* (n 57).

[61] Hayek (n 55) 112. (At fn 2.).

Hayek's Rule of Law-problem relates, at the most fundamental level, to the operation of the state. By requiring that the state operate in a predictable way, he seeks to ensure private actors are able to combat the state's central power. Whilst Hayek's Rule of Law ideas were modified in his more recent writings, his older work – reflected in the passages above – is most frequently held out as being reflective of the concept of the Rule of Law.[62] Yet, throughout his writing, and given the fundamental relationship to state power, there is no indication that an extension to non-state actors was conceived by him in responding to the state-centric Rule of Law-problem. (This contrasts to some of the Present accounts explored later in this chapter.)

The same state-centric focus can be seen in the ideas' association with Aristotle, Locke, and Dicey. Each of them conceives the state as being the actor responsible for the generation of arbitrary laws. In this respect, the broad and general idea that the Rule of Law is about anti-arbitrariness shines through. Hayek's particular state-centric focus brings into sharper focus than the other thinkers explored thus far another element of the usual suspects' Past Rule of Law accounts: state-centricity. This sharper focus will also become apparent in the next two accounts from Fuller and Raz. Once we consider those accounts together with the earlier ones, the thin/procedural aspect that unites the accounts will also become apparent. Although these conceptual similarities echo popular ways to segment and identify the accounts, I will illustrate after the final two usual suspects why categorisation in terms of the 'Past' Rule of Law represents a more effective way to conceive of the accounts.

E. Fuller

> Certainly there can be no rational ground for asserting that a man can have a moral obligation to obey a legal rule that does not exist, or is kept secret from him, or that came into existence only after he had acted, or was unintelligible, or was contradicted by another rule of the same system, or commanded the impossible, or changed every minute.[63]

King Rex – Fuller's hypothetical ruler – fails to make law in eight different ways. He fails due to an absence of generality, publicity, prospectivity, intelligibility, consistency, practicability, stability, and congruence. These ideas, described in the allegory of King Rex, reflect Fuller's inner morality of law.[64] These are frequently taken to be desiderata of the Rule of Law – even though Fuller does not adopt or deploy the phrase 'the Rule of Law'.[65] The nature of the desiderata themselves – as formal

[62] For examples, see Burgess, 'Rule of Lore' (n 3).
[63] LL Fuller, *The Morality of Law* (New Haven, Yale University Press, 1964) 39.
[64] ibid 33–39.
[65] For an example of a statement of this conception's popularity, see J Waldron, 'The Rule of Law and the Importance of Procedure' in JE Fleming (ed), *Getting to the Rule of Law* (New York, New York University Press, 2011) 3, 5.

constraints on the way that effective laws should be made – provides some guide and provides a point of connection to the other usual suspects. Fuller's account brings together the ideas associated with the arbitrary application of power and that power being wielded by the state in a way that also illustrates another connecting thread: the procedural nature of the Rule of Law.

The hypothetical nature of King Rex's tale makes identifying a single problem to which Fuller directs his solutions difficult. As the focus is on the *making* of the laws, this demonstrates that the problem to be addressed can be construed as broadly relating to the state's exercise of power. This aspect illustrates a broad connection to the other usual suspects. However, Fuller's account differs in consequence of the hypothetical nature of the account that he provides. The accounts by Aristotle, Locke, Dicey, and Hayek each are grounded in a particular – identified and real – issue that existed in society at the time that the conception was authored. Fuller's account is not *specifically* couched in terms of a real societal problem – though, as I note below – there are some clear parallels.

Fuller provides a list of factors that must be present in a functioning legal system. Each desideratum need not be perfectly realised for a legal system to exist; however, a total failure to satisfy any one results in something that is not properly called a legal system.[66] The extracted quote reflects Fuller's formal idea of reciprocity between the ruler and the ruled. In circumstances where the inner morality itself represents a morality of aspiration – and not of duty – in which the 'primary appeal is to a sense of trusteeship and to the pride of the craftsman',[67] observation of and adherence to the rules is grounded on the assurance that only those rules so made will be applied to conduct.

The formal requirements of Fuller's desiderata reflect the way in which effective legislation – as law – should be made. Where this endeavour relates to what is required in order for what has been described – by HLA Hart, in his review of Fuller's work – as 'the efficient execution of the purpose of guiding human conduct by rules', it seems that 'they are essentially principles of good craftsmanship'.[68] Fuller's principles 'are independent of the law's substantive aims just as the principles of carpentry are independent of whether the carpenter is making hospital beds or torturers' racks'.[69] Whilst this reflects a valid criticism of any formal rule of law (or bare legality), Fuller's reciprocity element reflects – if only a little – more than merely crafting something and sending it out into the world without consideration of subsequent effects. Contrary to what could be seen as 'ethically neutral'

[66] Fuller (n 63) 39.

[67] ibid 43.

[68] HLA Hart, 'Book Reviews: The Morality of Law by Lon L. Fuller' (1964) 78 *Harvard Law Review* 1281, 1284. Raz – perhaps, more famously – argued that law, like a knife which can be used potentially for evil means, is morally neutral. J Raz, 'The Rule of Law and Its Virtue' in *The Authority of Law: Essays on Law and Morality*, 2nd edn (Oxford, Oxford University Press, 2009) 210, 225. For an extension of this idea, see Burgess (n 1).

[69] Hart (n 68) 1284.

demands,[70] laws conforming with Fuller's desiderata are more likely to reflect, what may otherwise be deemed, good laws or at least be less likely to reflect bad ones.[71] Further, law made this way could be seen as a moral good as it enhances individual dignity or autonomy.[72] The emptiness of formal legality may, however, run contrary to the Rule of Law's traditional focus regarding the prevention of tyranny; for example, where the focus relates to limits that were 'substantive, based upon natural law, shared customs, Christian morality, or the good of community'.[73] This characterisation by Tamanaha appears, in some not insignificant way, to reflect the basis on which the earlier thinkers highlighted based their accounts; each describes an accepted practice related directly to the context in which each theorist was writing. As noted previously, the same cannot be said – or cannot so easily be seen – in relation to Fuller.

Fuller illustrates his idea by relaying the ways in which Rex *fails* to make law. Whilst this may simply be a pedagogical device, the negative portrayal – and abject failure – is important to reflect on. This does not illustrate Fuller's societal context. Fuller's account is not intended to reflect any particular historical or factual context. He simply uses the tale to more clearly illustrate *his* thinking. The lack of a practical point of reference that could – directly – relate to reality seems to differ from the – albeit hypothetical – state of nature portrayed by Locke. Locke's state of nature, whilst not necessarily intended as being reflective of any particular existing state (despite Locke's references to the conditions of native American society) seems to be based on an idea of the society that *could* have existed in some way. This is not to say Fuller does not consider real-world applications. He explores, inter alia, Nazi laws, apartheid, and specific case law in his work. However, his Rule of Law-relevant account and allegory, is clearly a stipulated hypothetical.[74]

Fuller's account differs from those already examined in another way: it has no descriptive element; it is aspirational. Whilst the introduction of morality could be seen as injecting some form of substantive sense (as a reflection of society's views), it is clear his *inner* morality relates to the element of trusteeship that exists between the governor and the governed and does not relate to an *external* sense of morality as any form of societal reflection. There appears to be no immediate human action on which he builds his theory as it is *all* his design. Accordingly, Fuller's account does not reflect a completely substantive idea – and can therefore be contrasted to the Present Rule of Law conceptions that I detail below.

The same form of similarities and differences that have already been identified between Fuller's account and the other usual suspects' Rule of Law accounts can be highlighted. They all respond to a problem that broadly relates to the arbitrary application of power with a procedural check on state-based actors. Fuller's

[70] Raz (n 68) 225.
[71] Fuller (n 63) 157–59.
[72] ibid 157–59.
[73] Tamanaha (n 16) 96.
[74] Fuller (n 63) IV.

account is the first to provide a checklist of items that require specific desiderata to be satisfied. In his account, the broad ideas of predictability and procedural clarity – that can also be seen across the other accounts[75] – remain obvious features. The relative point of difference can be seen in the nature of the proposed solutions; Fuller provides a fictional account that illustrates his aspirational solution imposing procedural limits on the state's law-making ability; the other usual suspects provide procedural limits on states' law-making abilities that are based in real-life scenarios. The final usual suspect will bolster these connections and differences.

F. Raz

> The rule of law is a political ideal which a legal system may lack or may possess to a greater or lesser degree. That much is common ground. It is also to be insisted that the rule of law is just one of the virtues which a legal system may possess and by which it is to be judged. It is not to be confused with democracy, justice, equality (before the law or otherwise), human rights of any kind or respect for persons or for the dignity of man.[76]

After he acknowledges Hayek's definition as 'one of the clearest and most powerful formulations of the ideal of the rule of law', Raz uses his critique of Hayek as a springboard into his own formulation of the idea.[77] The account that Raz provides has proved popular. The account, that is now more than four decades old, remains the Razian Rule of Law account that is included in the usual suspects' list despite Raz's provision of a newer form of the account in 2019.[78] In his earlier and more popular account, Raz provides a simple rule: that people should obey the law and be ruled by it – which has been seen in political theory as meaning that the *government* shall be ruled by the law.[79] Even on the basis of this simple recognition of state-centricity and control, it becomes clear why Raz's account – notwithstanding it being the newest of the usual suspects' accounts – is a Past formulation of the Rule of Law.

The state-centricity is partially lost when Raz further illuminates the rule into two aspects: that people should be ruled by the law and obey it; and, that the law shall be such that people will be able to be guided by it.[80] But, the relevance and centrality of the state in his wider idea becomes more obvious when he sets out a non-exhaustive list of the most important principles of the Rule of Law in society (that must be interpreted in light of the basic idea).

[75] Burgess (n 1).
[76] Raz (n 68) 211.
[77] Raz (n 13) 210. For Hayek's definition, see Hayek (n 55) 112.
[78] Raz (n 14).
[79] Raz (n 13) 212. (Emphasis added.).
[80] ibid 213.

He provides eight Rule of Law principles (that differ to Fuller's eight).[81] He includes: prospectivity, stability; law-making guided by rules; judicial independence; natural justice; courts' review powers; accessible courts; and, discretions should not pervert the law.[82] Initially, Raz's desiderata cover similar ground to the other usual suspects – particularly in relation predictability's key role; however, the end of the list has marked differences – as there are requirements that relate to the functional nature of the legal system more broadly.[83]

Notwithstanding these differences, it seems clear that the problem that Raz seeks to address is both one centred on the state *and* one that details a thin/formal conception of the Rule of Law. He specifically notes that he provides the principles 'to illustrate the power and fruitfulness of the formal conception of the rule of law'.[84] In addition, Raz also seeks to contrast his conception of the Rule of Law with a mere opposition to arbitrary power – and acknowledges that there are ways in which arbitrary power can be exercised that do not necessarily fall foul of the Rule of Law.[85]

As will be apparent from the quote that opens this section, in addition to providing particular desiderata related to the content of the Rule of Law, Raz also seeks to differentiate the concept from other political concepts. In consciously recognising the contest relating to the content of the Rule of Law, and in seeking to distinguish the concept from other potentially virtuous concepts, Raz provides a clear and precise account of what the Rule of Law is in its position as 'just one important virtue that legal systems should possess'.[86] In doing so he famously illustrates – through analogising the concept to a knife, which is neither good nor bad *of itself*, but can result in good or bad ends – that the Rule of Law should not be considered in terms of the good or bad laws that follow from a Rule of Law-system.[87]

At this stage in the outline of the various usual suspects' conceptions, the various points of commonality between the conceptions will be apparent. In this respect, little more needs to be said. Raz's laundry list of desiderata echoes this common procedural function by requiring that the *making* of laws be guided by clear and transparent rules and that natural justice is to be observed within courts that are easily accessible.[88] In this basic sense, his list-based formula does not only reflect Fuller (and his similar number of desiderata). The ways that Raz fits within the thin/state-based/anti-arbitrariness function of the Rule of Law that has been

[81] Raz (n 68) 214–19.
[82] ibid 210, 214–19.
[83] These ideas – like natural justice and in the independence of the judiciary – can be seen to be components that are necessary to allow a legal system to operate in a way to enable the Rule of Law to exist; without these things, the idea or promise of the Rule of Law is vacant.
[84] Raz (n 13) 218.
[85] ibid 219.
[86] ibid 211.
[87] ibid 225.
[88] ibid 214–17.

seen in the other usual suspects is clear. (This remains the case where Raz does not see the Rule of Law as opposing *all* and *any* forms of arbitrariness – a distinction that will become important when considering the Present Rule of Law.) Raz covers similar territory to the other usual suspects that are included within the Past Rule of Law.

G. Summary – The Past Rule of Law

This very brief summary of the usual suspects' accounts as reflecting problems to which they directed a Rule of Law solution illustrates a broad similarity relating to the need for the (arbitrary) actions of the state to be controlled. Later in the book, in chapters four, five, and six, I use this broadly stated idea of the Rule of Law to provide a high-level/abstract view of the Rule of Law. Any similarities or connections beyond this broadly stated Rule of Law idea may be difficult to parse from the relatively disparate discussion. Accordingly, in this brief sub-section, I summarise and bring together the common threads that may be seen in the ideas mentioned above.

The Past Rule of Law is constituted by conceptions that remain vitally important in defining the conceptual boundaries of the Rule of Law. Frequent recourse is had to one, several, or all of these accounts when attempts are made to define the Rule of Law.[89] This much is clear as the group of accounts – authored by what I called the usual suspects – was based on this collective principle. More than this is, however, needed to unite the group in a meaningful way for the remainder of this book. Collectively, the ideas put forward by the usual suspects – relating to a state-centric (public) idea and solutions that are thin/formal solutions to a series of problems relating to arbitrary exercises of power – will be taken to be the '*Past Rule of Law*'. The categorisation of these accounts as the Past Rule of Law – notwithstanding the commonly used descriptors in which they fit – is justified when held in contrast to the Present Rule of Law conceptions that are outlined in the section that follows. Each of the usual suspects of the Rule of Law that I have outlined above achieve this through thin/formal means.[90] Other broad similarities related to the solutions posed to different problems can also be identified. For example, there is a focus on procedural solutions – related to the way the laws are made. This general idea relating to the way that the arbitrary exercises of power seen/feared by each of the usual suspects will provide a key point of difference to the Present forms of the Rule of Law explored below.

The ideas of predictability and procedural clarity could be seen to be core elements of the legislative process across the usual suspects' conceptions. If any desiderata can be identified as being common across the different accounts put

[89] Burgess, 'Rule of Lore' (n 3).
[90] Craig (n 2).

forth by the usual suspects, these would represent the prime candidates.[91] The Present ideas of the Rule of Law that follow are generally built on a foundation that requires a thin/formal base to be adhered to in order that the *additional* requirements of the Present Rule of Law theorists can be satisfied. In this respect, many of the Present Rule of Law ideas – as explored below – would not disagree with the identification of these core/elemental desiderata. It is for this reason that I adopt these ideas as an *additional* point of analysis when considering the application of AI in the hypotheticals in chapters four, five, and six. This provides a mid-point between the highly abstract notion explored at the start of this sub-section and the specific consideration of the individual Past Rule of Law ideas.

The thin/formal nature of the accounts and the common desiderata affording a more nuanced idea of the conceptual boundaries is a relatively common observation or categorisation. Yet, as I have already suggested, this is not the categorisation that is adopted for this book. When these conceptions are considered in contradistinction to the Present Rule of Law ideas presented below, a more nuanced way to understand the concept – and to think about *change* in the concept – emerges.

By embracing the multiple similarities across the conceptions – and whilst acknowledging the differences that stem from the different problems that each thinker was trying to solve – it is possible to see the category of conceptions in more temporal terms. The Past Rule of Law reflects some of the most popular series of ideas in today's discourse regarding the Rule of Law; it reflects a series of – broadly connected – conceptions that were posited in the past (with the most recent being around half a century old). The relative thinking in those times is reflected in those works. By considering the Past Rule of Law as having these constituent parts it can be clearly differentiated from the ideas that reflect the Present of the Rule of Law.

II. The Present Rule of Law

As suggested earlier, the Present of the Rule of Law is not to be taken as being a *more* correct idea of the concept of the Rule of Law than the Past Rule of Law simply because of its chronological proximity to the point at which this book is being written. 'Present' simply reflects trends in the meaning of the concept that have arisen – and that differ to the Past Rule of Law – in recent years. In illustrating what the Present Rule of Law is, the same approach has been used as with the Past Rule of Law to identify illustrative authors' conceptions that are frequently used to illustrate the idea's nature and scope.

Unlike the Past Rule of Law, where a readily apparent homogenous classification was apparent, two different forms of the Present Rule of Law are identified. Whilst both the Past and Present ideas share some fundamental ideas, the core

[91] For similar suggestions, see Burgess (n 1).

differentiating aspects relate to the Present Rule of Law being a thick (substantive) idea and being one that does not necessarily relate to only the arbitrary exercise of *state* power. In the first difference, the Present Rule of Law relates to an aim to achieve substantively good *outcomes* – if laws that are made attain a particular end, the Rule of Law satisfies its function.[92] In the second, it is the *source* of the arbitrary application of power is what differs. In the Present Rule of Law, the source does not necessarily need to be from the state (it can be from a private source). These differences in the two forms of the Present Rule of Law relate and contrast – each in a different way – to the Past Rule of Law's characteristics. I describe them as being outcome- or source-based ideas.

In what follows, I consider both of these ideas and expand on what this means. I will use four key examples to illustrate the Present of the Rule of Law. These are conceptions provided by the UN, Tom Bingham, Jeff King, and Martin Krygier. The first two provide a version of the Present Rule of Law that seeks to attain a substantively good outcome. The second two see the Rule of Law in a way that impacts and relates to the potential source of power (and not just the public exercise of power). As the Present conceptions of the Rule of Law have not had as much time to be considered authoritative – even though each has attained significant support – the selection of *these* conceptions is not as easy to achieve in a way that avoids bias. For this reason, in this chapter I will also rely upon several other core conceptions that also illustrate other trends that reflect the way some see the concept in the Present. As with the Past Rule of Law, I outline the basics of each idea providing key examples in a separate sub-section before briefly bringing them all together in a summary at the end of this section.

A. The Present Rule of Law (Outcome-based): The United Nations

An example of the thick/substantive form of the Rule of Law is provided by the UN. Whilst the UN does not have a single form of the Rule of Law, the popular definitions explored here provide sufficient detail to illustrate its substantive nature.[93]

As with other thick/substantive conceptions, the UN's idea of the Rule of Law incorporates the thin ideas included in the Past Rule of Law – that laws be publicly promulgated, equally enforced, and independently adjudicated.[94] These ideas

[92] The classic statement of the thin and thick ideas of the Rule of Law is provided by Craig. Craig (n 2).

[93] Secretary General, *Delivering Justice: Programme of Action to Strengthen the Rule of Law at the National and International Levels* (No A/66/749, 16 March 2012). Paragraph 2 of that report provides a definition of the Rule of Law that – relevantly for the second Present form, below – encompasses 'all persons, institutions and entities, public and private, including the State'. In addition, it also cites ideas – in near identical terms – to the quote cited immediately below.

[94] Thick/substantive ideas of the Rule of Law are built on a thin/formal base. Burgess (n 1) 485.

provide a necessary foundational base on which thicker conceptions are structured. In other words, the thicker ideas could not operate without the thinner ideas providing a conceptual core. By including additional aspects, the UN's conception, as with the other Present Rule of Law conceptions, goes *beyond* these ideas. This includes 'fairness in the application of the law, separation of powers, participation in decision-making, legal certainty, avoidance of arbitrariness and procedural and legal transparency'.[95] The UN's conception is intended to be deployed for specific purposes that include, for example, the achievement of Human Rights.[96] This conception is a clear reflection of both the nature of the UN and the problems in the world that it seeks to address.

What is apparent is that the form of the Present Rule of Law that is exemplified by the UN's – thick/substantive – definition goes *beyond* the – thin/formal – solutions provided in the Past ideas. The substantive function of the Rule of Law, for the UN, relates to the attainment and protection of human rights;[97] it sees the Rule of Law as a vehicle to achieve the substantive aim of rights protection.[98] Even on the brief account provided of Raz's view above, it will also likely be clear that a Razian objection could be raised in circumstances where the Rule of Law is used to encompass these other potentially virtuous concepts that a legal system can or should possess. The UN's thick Rule of Law conception is not, however, the only example of this form of the outcome-based Present Rule of Law.

B. The Present Rule of Law (Outcome-based): Tom Bingham

Lord Bingham's conception is included in his popular text: *The Rule of Law*. Bingham's book includes a list that is a reflection of his contemporary idea of what the Rule of Law should be. In some sense, it is derived from other contemporary ideas – including those of the UN. He describes several 'historical milestones on the way to the rule of law *as we know it today*', and, in introducing his own eight principles, states he has tried to 'identify what the rule of law really means to us, *here and now*'.[99] In this respect, Bingham's idea of the Rule of Law is clearly tethered to the present – it is intended to go beyond the ideas of the Rule of Law that had previously been proposed and seeks to provide an account of what the Rule of Law requires in a *contemporary* Rule of Law-adhering society – as a direct contrast

[95] UN Security Council, *The Rule of Law and Transitional Justice in Conflict and Post-Conflict Societies – Report of the Secretary-General* (No UN doc S/2004/616, 23 August 2004) 6: www.un.org/ruleoflaw/files/2004%20report.pdf.

[96] ibid.

[97] United Nations General Assembly, *Universal Declaration of Human Rights* (No Resolution 217 A, 10 December 1948) Preamble.

[98] United Nations General Assembly, *Strengthening and Coordinating United Nations Rule of Law Activities – Report of the Secretary-General – Addendum* (No A/68/213/Add.1, United Nations, 11 July 2014).

[99] T Bingham, *The Rule of Law* (London, Allen Lane, 2010) 10, 37. (Emphasis added.).

to ideas that could be categorised by him and are in this book, as Past ideas of the Rule of Law.

In detailing the requirements of the Rule of Law, Bingham includes – as with Fuller and Raz's conceptions – eight sub-rules: laws should be accessible, clear and predictable; issues regarding legal rights/liability should be decided through the application of law; the law should apply equally to all; public officials should exercise their powers in good faith (and act within those powers); the law must protect fundamental rights; resolution of civil disputes should be provided for (at reasonable costs); adjudicative procedures must be provided and be fair; the state must comply with its obligations under international law.[100] Whilst the first two of Bingham's sub-rules cover similar ground – making it clear that Bingham structures his thick/substantive idea on a formal base – the rest are substantive ideas that are focussed on achieving particular or 'good' outcomes.

The extended list Bingham provides is very different to the conceptions provided by the thinkers in the Past Rule of Law. He uses contemporary sensibilities to recognise the idea that (in relation to human rights, for example) the Rule of Law can only be satisfied in circumstances where human rights enhancing outcomes follow; he uses Raz's conception – that the Rule of Law is a thin notion that does not require the attainment of substantive outcomes – as a foil and says '[a] state which savagely represses or persecutes sections of its people cannot in my view be regarded as observing the rule of law'.[101] In this sense, Bingham's idea is unabashedly optimistic and aspirational. He sets out Rule of Law desiderata that would be difficult, if not impossible, for many states to achieve. His account is clearly distinguishable from Past Rule of Law accounts due to its substantive nature. Its authorship by the UK's most preeminent jurists of the modern age demands attention and sets out a clear and compelling argument for a contemporary view of the Rule of Law.

C. Present Rule of Law (Source-based): Jeff King

In only the last few years, Jeff King has suggested a different form of the Rule of Law that brings together a substantively 'good' outcome, together with the suggestion that the Rule of Law should not only operate so as to limit the arbitrary exercise of power by state entities. King's *social dimension* of the Rule of Law argues that 'the best conception of the rule of law would require the provision of a legally structured welfare and regulatory state'.[102]

[100] Bingham (n 99). (This is a somewhat simplified version of the list.).
[101] ibid 67.
[102] J King, '"Constitutional Boundaries" – The Social Dimension of the Rule of Law', *I·CONnect* (2018) www.iconnectblog.com/2018/04/i-connect-symposium-on-constitutional-boundaries-the-social-dimension-of-the-rule-of-law/; J King, 'The Rule of Law' in R Bellamy and J King (eds), *The Cambridge Handbook of Constitutional Theory* (2024) papers.ssrn.com/abstract=4487306.

King specifically rejects the dominant – thin – theories, with specific reference to those of Raz and Fuller, because they are based on the fundamental assumption that the dominant idea on which the Rule of Law is based (as a procedural account) is for the law to be able to guide behaviour. He also does not think that the worry – expressed most prominently by Raz – that the Rule of Law would be conflated with justice is falsified in practice.[103] Instead, King's suggestion is that the Rule of Law has a historical legacy influenced by libertarian thinking that does not acknowledge the potential regulatory way in which the concept may be conceived. For him, in identifying the social dimension that exists within this regulatory idea, the taming of the exercise of arbitrary power is what is key; the relative *source* of this power is not determinative of the protection that the concept should offer.[104] King's premise sees the Rule of Law in a different light – he sees a tradition in which the state has a duty to protect people through law and that this duty extends to creating regulation in both the public and private spheres.[105] This means that the Rule of Law does not only act so as to prevent the state from acting in arbitrary ways, but also creates a duty for the state to prevent various forms of arbitrary power through positive actions. This duty-creating idea renders King's approach both unique and appealing.

King, unlike many, sees the potential for a historical disjoint between his own idea (as well as Bingham's and the UN's). He suggests that this is not simply 'a historical reboot',[106] and points to Julian Sempill's work in ideas akin to that which he puts forward can be found within the works of historical authors like Locke.[107] King is not the only one to suggest that the Rule of Law should operate in the private sphere. An entire edited collection was dedicated to this project and there have been wider suggestions by others including Martin Krygier (detailed in the following subsection) and Sanne Taekema.[108] Whilst the idea of the private application of the Rule of Law is not without its critics,[109] the idea has gained some relative popular support in recent years. But, what we see across the accounts is the suggestion that for a state to claim that it is a Rule of Law state, then actions to prevent the arbitrary application of power – whether in the private or the public

[103] King, '"Constitutional Boundaries" – The Social Dimension of the Rule of Law' (n 102). For the Razian idea, see Raz (n 68).

[104] King, 'The Rule of Law' (n 102).

[105] King cites Sempill's work as a comparable project. JA Sempill, 'Ruler's Sword, Citizen's Shield: The Rule of Law & the Constitution of Power' (2015) 31 *Journal of Law & Politics* 333.

[106] King, '"Constitutional Boundaries" – The Social Dimension of the Rule of Law' (n 103).

[107] Sempill (n 105).

[108] LM Austin and D Klimchuk (eds), *Private Law and the Rule of Law* (Oxford, Oxford University Press, 2014). This has also been suggested by Sempill. JA Sempill, 'The Lions and the Greatest Part: The Rule of Law and the Constitution of Employer Power' (2017) 9(2) *Hague Journal on the Rule of Law* 283. A special issue of *International Journal of Law in Context* introduces this position. Bhatt, Lander and Taekema (n 5).

[109] P Burgess, 'Googling the Equivalence of Private Arbitrary Power and State Arbitrary Power: Why The Rule of Law Does Not Relate to Private Relationships' [2021] *International Journal of Law in Context*.

sphere – should be prevented. This provides a fundamental point of difference to the way that most see the conceptions that make up the Past Rule of Law.

D. Present Rule of Law (Source-based): Martin Krygier

Martin Krygier has been writing on the Rule of Law for several decades. His work is wide and varied. His contribution is clear and apparent through the breadth and depth of sentiment expressed in the two-issue special issue (encompassing 35 articles authored by some of the world's greatest authorities on the Rule of Law) in the *Hague Journal on the Rule of Law* dedicated to his work.[110]

What is clear across Krygier's period of academic endeavour is that the ideas that he has explored in relation to the Rule of Law have not remained stagnant. As with any ongoing and genuine academic endeavour, the ideas Krygier has put forward have themselves evolved. His ideas developed a form of sociological jurisprudence that commenced with thoughts on rules which led to further thoughts on the Rule of Law.[111] The idea that is represented here is drawn from Krygier's more recent view of the Rule of Law: the Rule of Law is a concept that opposes arbitrary power *in whatever form that arbitrary power takes*.[112] This is summed up in Jeremy Waldron's sentiment regarding Krygier's contribution: 'Krygier has often insisted that the question "What is the rule of law?" needs to be displaced in favor of a more teleological understanding: "What is the rule of law *for*?"'[113] This theme, also explored in depth in Jeff King's contribution to the special issues,[114] differentiates Krygier's focus from the 'anatomical' views of the Rule of Law – that consider only what the concept *is* or, more precisely, what it is made up of – from most others. By considering this *telos* of the Rule of Law, Krygier arrives at the conclusion that the Rule of Law is for countering arbitrary power and the source of that power is not determinative of whether the Rule of Law can or should intervene. This means that, for Krygier, the Rule of Law does not only operate so as to prevent arbitrary exercises of power by the state and, instead, protects against the arbitrary exercise of power in both public and private settings.[115]

The potential for the private exercise of power to be Rule of Law-protection-worthy, as noted in the previous sub-section, is a view not exclusive to Krygier.

[110] J Waldron, 'Preface' (2019) 11(2) *Hague Journal on the Rule of Law* 251. The Preface to the special issues provides an invaluable starting point and entry into the rest of the pieces.

[111] L Rodak, 'From Rules of Life to Rules of Law. An Account of M Krygier Approach to Sociological Jurisprudence' (2019) 11(2) *Hague Journal on the Rule of Law* 283.

[112] Krygier (n 8); M Krygier, 'Tempering Power' in M Adams, EH Ballin and A Meuwese (eds), *Constitutionalism and the Rule of Law: Bridging Idealism and Realism* (Cambridge, Cambridge University Press, 2017).

[113] Waldron (n 110) 251.

[114] J King, 'Martin Krygier and the Tempering of Power' (2019) 11(2) *Hague Journal on the Rule of Law* 363.

[115] M Krygier, 'The Rule of Law: Legality, Teleology and Sociology' in G Palombella and N Walker (eds), *Relocating the Rule of Law* (Oxford, Hart Publishing, 2009).

It is also present in the work of Sempill and Taekema (and others).[116] Krygier's teleological route to the solution is, however, notable. In each of these accounts what is also notable is the relative recency of the ideas. The Present ideas have all been refined and presented in the period that comes after the last of the Past Rule of Law conceptions. They have gained wider appreciation in only the last decade. And, they have done so and garnered support despite the fundamental differences they represent when contrasted to the Past Rule of Law.

E. Summary: The Present Rule of Law

The UN and Bingham provide influential and important examples of the substantive turn. They both address problems regarding the non-achievement of certain ends. Yet, through their suggestions that the Rule of Law should achieve substantive ends, they both illustrate only one form – an outcome-based form – of what I have called the Present Rule of Law. Another form – a source-based form – of the Present Rule of Law is reflected through a point of difference to the Past Rule of Law's view on state-based arbitrariness. The broad conceptual meaning of the Rule of Law relates to the operation of arbitrary power; Past Rule of Law accounts focus exclusively and specifically on solving a problem related to arbitrariness in the *public* sphere. However, in this second form of the Present Rule of Law, the location of arbitrariness in the *state* is not necessary; arbitrariness itself – in whatever sphere it arises – is seen as being able to be solved by the Rule of Law.[117] This idea has become popular in recent years,[118] but it is not new.[119] The shift is both subtle and significant; the application of arbitrary power is retained, the usual suspects' state-only focus is abandoned.

What follows from this is that that the Present Rule of Law can be seen to take two forms. They each reflect different differences to the Past Rule of Law. The first outcome-based form differs from the Past in its substantive application of the Rule of Law; the second source-based form differs in its non-state-centric concern with the application of arbitrary power. What has, however, also been seen in this section is that there are similarities between the Past and the Present ideas. For example, both forms largely agree on the need for certain common principles like predictability. In this respect, the Present ideas frequently adopt and accept, yet go beyond, ideas included in Past conceptions. These briefly stated connections will be explored in more detail in the next section.

[116] Sempill (n 108); Sempill (n 5); Bhatt, Lander and Taekema (n 5); Austin and Klimchuk (n 108). For my own objections to this view, see Burgess (n 109).

[117] Krygier (n 8); Sempill (n 5); Sempill (n 108); King, '"Constitutional Boundaries" – The Social Dimension of the Rule of Law' (n 102). This idea has been criticised. See, eg, Burgess (n 109).

[118] Austin and Klimchuk (n 108). For a critique of the extension of the Rule of Law in this way, see Burgess (n 109).

[119] See, eg, P Selznick, *Law, Society, and Industrial Justice: 50th Anniversary Edition* (New Orleans, Quid Pro, 2020).

III. The Past and Present Rule of Law – Differences and Similarities

A clear difference can be seen between the Past and Present of the Rule of Law. I highlight the nature of this difference in this section. It is, however, important to acknowledge there are also some similarities. In brief, the similarities can be identified as being related to either the content or the function of the Rule of Law.[120]

There is a similarity in terms of the *content* of the ideas; the thin ideas of the Past are used as a base on which to construct the thick/substantive ideas of the Present. In effect, as noted earlier, substantive ideas are built using formal foundations.[121] This content-based idea means there are desiderata similarities. As previously noted, the need for *predictability* or *procedural clarity* are common elements across the Past conceptions. Yet even these common ideas can be differentiated if the problems that underlie the conceptions are used to nuance those ideas.[122] This has the effect of ensuring that any similarities in relation to content can only be drawn at relatively broad levels of abstraction.

There is also a similarity in terms of the broad functional goals. The Past Rule of Law is focused on preventing the exercise of arbitrary power; this *function* is replicated and expanded – from only the public exercise of power to include the private exercise – in the Present Rule of Law. As with content, deeper consideration of the function of the Rule of Law results in similarities between conceptions being lost. That nature of the way that non-state arbitrary power is prevented is different. In relation to the Present Rule of Law, there also seems to be no immediate connection to either the substantive protection of rights or other values or a suggestion that there is an exercise of arbitrary power from any other source.

Consideration beyond these *general* ideas of similarity is, however, appropriate. When considered in this way, the superficial similarity of the forms can be distinguished because there is little *actual* similarity. These two ideas seem to be pulling in different directions. Whilst there is clear common ground – where the Present conceptions require a conceptual foundation premised on Past conceptions – the demands on those holding power are fundamentally different. It is for this reason that the examination that takes place through the remainder of this book does not try to bring these ideas together. Instead, it holds them apart and considers what the Future of the Rule of Law may look like in circumstances where the Past or the Present of the Rule of Law evolves.

In order to consider the ways in which either the Past or Present ideas of the Rule of Law will need to evolve in order to face challenges in the future, I must first detail what some of these problems may be. In the following chapter, I set out the challenges that may come in the form of AI. More specifically, I detail ways

[120] Of course, this reflects the distinction that Krygier has made that was illuminated by King, above.
[121] Burgess (n 1) 485.
[122] Burgess, 'Rule of Lore' (n 3).

in which AI may be used in the exercise of power. To do this, I spend some time explaining the nature of AI (and differentiating it from other technologies) before I pose some hypothetical applications of AI in order to illustrate the ways in which AI-exercised power may, in the near future, prove to be arbitrary. These can be categorised in terms of AI's role in: administrative decision-making; the creation of secondary (delegated) legislation; and, the creation of primary legislation. The hypotheticals represent the ways in which AI is expected to impact the way in which power – through decision- and law-making – will be exercised in the future. Those hypotheticals will then frame the discussion in the remainder in the book. When considered together, in the final chapter of the book, they will lead to the conclusion that the current ways in which the Rule of Law is conceived – through both the Past and Present ideas – render the use of AI in the ways contemplated to be contrary to the Rule of Law; yet, notwithstanding this pessimistic conclusion, the potential for the concept of the Rule of Law to (continue to) evolve will facilitate the ever-expanding use of AI in the exercise of public power.

3

Artificial Intelligence – What it is, Does, and May Be

In this chapter I expand upon the very brief explanation of AI provided in chapter one. I explain both the reality of the current technology and the contemporary applications of AI. I set out the way that AI has already been used in administrative, legal, and judicial decision-making in jurisdictions around the world and, from these things I consider how it may be used in the future. The chapter plays an important part in setting the parameters of the discussion that will follow; both in the consideration of a non-dystopian use of AI (that avoids both dystopian fears of AI propagating the end of humanity) and an overt utopian view that cannot be sensibly realised and in establishing the actual capability of AI in the present as a reality check.

The non-dystopian (yet realistic) future-looking approach I adopt plays an important role in delineating what aspects of the subsequent discussions are real, possible, and speculative exercises. By doing this, science fiction-type discussions of the use of AI will be avoided and, instead, the parameters are set for a grounded set of hypotheticals. The chapter projects forward to hypothesise three ways that AI could be used in the future: first, in administrative decision-making; second, in the creation of secondary (delegated) legislation; and third, in the creation of primary legislation. The hypotheticals represent the ways in which AI may impact the way in which power – through decision- and law-making – may be exercised in the future. In circumstances where this exercise may be arbitrary, ideas of the Rule of Law are enlivened. Together, chapters two and three define and set up the terms of the argument that will be explored by considering the Past and Present of the Rule of Law in terms of the three hypotheticals in chapters four, five, and six.

As part of the conclusions to the chapter, I also consider whether the Rule of Law *must* give way to technology. This includes considering *why* it is that the Past and Present of the Rule of Law illustrate that a change or evolution of the Rule of Law in the future does not merely mean that the Rule of Law is giving way to the change in technology. Instead, I illustrate that the Rule of Law may need to change *because of* another idea – the change in the problems that the exercise of power raises when AI is used. In other words, I will start the argument that will be developed across the remainder of the book that there will need to be a necessary evolution of the Rule of Law.

This chapter covers a lot of ground. It provides the most technical consideration of AI, machine learning, and algorithms (and provides an explanation and overview of these terms) in the book. It is, however, written for a non-technical audience. The book, and the chapter, is not intended as a technical manual. It presents a view of the technology both as it is, and how it may be, in a way that is intended to be considered by constitutional theorists, lawyers, and others that are interested in the way that power – and, in particular, state power – can be exercised in the future. It is not for those that are interesting in the precise technical make up or limitations of the technology.

As noted above, where the aim of the non-dystopian (yet realistic) future-looking approach plays an important part in avoiding subsequent chapters falling into speculative science fiction-type discussions, the exposition of the ideas in this chapter takes some time. The structure of the chapter is such that there are distinct sections that can be digested relatively discretely depending on a reader's background knowledge or expertise.

In the section immediately following this introduction, I set out what AI *is*. I do this in more detail than in chapter one in order to identify precisely what it can do at the moment. This section operates so as to anchor the rest of the chapter (and book) in reality. It is vital that in considering AI, machine learning, algorithms, and the other technologies discussed in this book, a clear understanding is provided as to what these things are and how they are different to, similar to, or related to one another. In doing this the actual real limitations of those technologies in the present is set out. This contrasts with the picture that is often presented in the popular media regarding the use of AI – even if blatant science fiction is put to one side – that seems to frequently over-inflate the technology's capabilities.

After setting out the contemporary reality of the technology, I set out what AI *does*. I illustrate in the third section practical ways in which AI has been and is being used by various states and in various functions around the world. This includes the use of AI in courts, administrative decisions, and in state decision-making more broadly as well as in legal practice. The discussion across the third section is geared toward demonstrating that AI has been increasingly used in making ever-more important decisions in the exercise of public power. The suggestion is that the use of technology in this way is likely to both continue and increase in scope and importance. Setting out these contemporary applications and realities is essential as, without an appreciation of what AI is and how it is currently being used, it would not be possible to consider what it may be.

It is in the fourth section of the chapter that I set out what the use of AI *may be*. By building off the contemporary practical applications explored in the third section focus shifts toward future applications of AI. I hypothesise three ways that AI could be used in the future: first, in administrative decision-making; second, in the creation of secondary (delegated) legislation; and third, in the creation of primary legislation. The hypotheticals represent the ways in which AI is expected to impact the way in which power – through decision- and law-making – will be exercised in the future. In considering these hypotheticals, I also clarify the role that AI – as a tool for the making of human decisions – fundamentally plays. The delineation of these hypotheticals is intended to form the basis for their expansion and consideration in chapters four, five, and six.

The fifth and final section of the chapter serves several purposes. It provides a summary of the previous sections and places them into a context that enables them to be used as a springboard for the discussions in the remainder of the book. It also serves as a place to raise a distinction that will become important to consider through the rest of the book: the difference between the future use of AI in data-driven decisions and the more complex decisions that are made by a machine exercising a form of judgment.[1] As part of the concluding section, I consider whether the Rule of Law *must* give way to technology and *why* it is that the past and present of the Rule of Law illustrate that a change or evolution of the Rule of Law does not merely mean that the Rule of Law *has* given way to the change in technology and, instead, illustrate that the Rule of Law must change *because of* another idea: the problems raised by the use of AI in exercising power are *different* to those to that framed the solutions provided by the Past and Present Rule of Law ideas.

I. What AI Is

By 2023, 'we will have the technological means to create superhuman intelligence. Shortly after, the human era will be ended'.[2] This statement, and this vision of the future, was made only three decades ago by Vernor Vinge – the professor and popular science fiction author. Vinge proposed a 'singularity'; a time when the growth and expansion of technology becomes unstoppable and results in a fundamental (and irreversible) change to civilization. Whilst AI is not essential to the idea of the singularity, it is difficult to imagine this occurring without some form of intelligence that surpasses human intelligence. Vinge and other prominent authors see AI as being an essential component of this event – even if they are less optimistic (or pessimistic, depending on your viewpoint) as to the date of the event. Kurzwiel, for example, suggests the date would be 2045.[3]

The inevitability of a singularity, as an event where intelligent machines could design even more intelligent machines is challenged by Toby Walsh – who notes that most proponents of the technological singularity are not AI researchers.[4] Walsh suggests – based on a median prediction from a 2017 poll of more than 300

[1] This was an important distinction that was raised by some of the anonymous reviewers of the book. I thank them for this suggestion as well as all of the others made.

[2] V Vinge, 'The Coming Technological Singularity: How to Survive in the Post-Human Era' (1993) mindstalk.net/vinge/vinge-sing.html.

[3] In addition to Vinge, see also R Kurzweil, *The Singularity Is Near: When Humans Transcend Biology* (London, Penguin Books, 2006).

[4] T Walsh, *2062: The World That AI Made* (Melbourne, La Trobe University Press, 2018) 36.

researchers in AI – that 2062 would be the date at which a machine – and Artificial General Intelligence (AGI) – can outperform humans in a broad range of tasks.[5] (A more detailed explanation of AGI is provided in the sub-sections that follow.) It is important that this distinction is drawn. Here, AGI is contrasted to a machine being better than humans in *specific* tasks – because, in specific tasks, for example, playing games like chess or in completing computations, machines can already outperform humans.

Whilst the practical and technological reality of AGI – never mind the singularity – are far from being imminent, popular fiction and movie portrayals frequently suggest the singularity or AGI are far closer than even Walsh's assessment. (Which, of course, represents only the middle point of those surveyed.) The 1984 movie *The Terminator* and its sequels suggested that a non-human intelligence called *Skynet* would become self-aware – and would commence a military campaign to eradicate humans – in 1997. The 1999 movie *The Matrix* (and its sequels) suggest a similarly apocalyptic end – this time occurring in the early twenty-first century – resulting from intelligent machines' war on humans. These fictional portrayals have done much to colour the perception of those *not* involved in AI research and have popularised the idea that AGI is just around the corner.

This book is not about AGI. It is also not about apocalyptic scenarios in which humanity is destroyed following a singularity. It is about the use and application of AI in exercising power. But, given the broad popular impact and perception about the potential for AGI, the relative distance from AGI does not, however, prevent forms of AI from having an impact *now*. In adopting the non-dystopian approach – between utopian and dystopian extremes – the hypotheticals that are posed later in this chapter, and explored through the rest of the book, do not necessitate AGI. They are grounded in the use of AI in relatively specific narrow applications. Even though some of the applications are not yet possible, they are posed in such a way so as to be possibilities in the future; but, they are not intended to be science fiction. This provides a reality-grounded view to this book that falls short of adopting a purely utopian view of the future yet also avoids an apocalyptic sci-fi dystopia.

Before considering the day-to-day realities of the vital ways that AI impacts our daily lives that are explored in the next substantive section of the book, it is important to consider precisely what AI – and related terms – mean. Accordingly, in the sub-sections that follow, I provide a brief description of some of the terms that will be used throughout the rest of this book.

A. Artificial Intelligence

As noted in the first chapter, 'AI' can cover a vast range of technologies. This can include driverless cars, Siri and Alexa, and a raft of other applications. AI can be

[5] ibid 35–37. Walsh's poll and suggested date reflects others that have been conducted. See, eg, C Dilmegani, 'When Will Singularity Happen? 995 Experts' Opinions on AGI' (3 February 2022) research.aimultiple.com/artificial-general-intelligence-singularity-timing/.

seen to assist decision-making, automate and simplify tasks, and improve accuracy across a vast spectrum of processes. On this basis, a definition of AI could be equally broad. The term 'AI' has no single agreed definition. There are core ideas of what AI would be accepted to be and there are instances that may be more marginal. This book does not seek to define a new category or advocate for an idea of AI that is novel. There is also little benefit for this project in drawing a specific or narrow definition of what constitutes AI; and, there is little to be lost in adopting a broader view of AI. Accordingly, I adopt a broad meaning of AI that will, hopefully, be relatively uncontroversial. I consider AI to include any machine that acts intelligently – as one that can make correct decisions in a given circumstance.[6]

Within this broad definition, other sub-fields – for example, machine learning (explained below) or predicting an outcome – are encompassed. This means that a range of processes – like chess-playing AIs where humans are readily outperformed in limited tasks, to artificial general intelligence as an as yet unrealised form of AI that can think (or simulate what we consider to be thinking) in a way that is indistinguishable from human intelligence – are encompassed within the definition.[7] The definition also includes various forms of data acquisition, storage, and processing in ways that emulate human intelligence like natural language processing, knowledge representation, decision-making and reasoning, and learning.[8]

Ryan Abbott states that AI is 'an algorithm or machine capable of completing tasks that would otherwise require cognition'.[9] This, of course, requires an understanding of what 'cognition' is – which Abbott states is the process of acquiring knowledge and understanding through thought.[10] (This could, of course, continue with consideration of what 'thought' is.) This clearly wide understanding of what AI is provides another way to understand the nature of the wide definition that I provide in the paragraph above. Both of the definitions serve the purpose of casting the net suitably wide for the purposes of the arguments raised in later chapters.

[6] For weak AI see Y LeCun, Y Bengio and G Hinton, 'Deep Learning' (2015) 521(7553) *Nature* 436. For strong AI see W Naudé and N Dimitri, 'The Race for an Artificial General Intelligence: Implications for Public Policy' (2020) 35(2) *AI & Society* 367, 367–68. Y Hermstrüwer, 'Artificial Intelligence and Administrative Decisions Under Uncertainty' in T Wischmeyer and T Rademacher (eds), *Regulating Artificial Intelligence* (Scham, pringer International Publishing, 2020) 199, 201: doi.org/10.1007/978-3-030-32361-5_9.

[7] In these respects, and as will be apparent from what follows, I bring a more specific – old fashioned – idea of AI, big data, and machine learning together under my single umbrella term. This sort of approach is not unique. For example, big data and AI have been brought together in the past. See, eg, MC Elish and danah boyd, 'Situating Methods in the Magic of Big Data and AI' (2018) 85(1) *Communication Monographs* 57. Whilst not ideal, taking a broad approach adds a level of simplicity to the examination conducted herein.

[8] These ideas replicate the form of Turing Test that is seen as 'acting humanly' by Russell and Norvig. S Russell and P Norvig, *Artificial Intelligence: A Modern Approach*, 4th edn (Harlow, Pearson, 2020) 20.

[9] R Abbott, *The Reasonable Robot: Artificial Intelligence and the Law*, 1st edn (Cambridge, Cambridge University Press, 2020) 22.

[10] ibid.

The use of the sort of hypothetical extension that I adopt in relation to the technology is useful.[11] By taking this approach, I unashamedly have one foot in the present and one in the – potential – future whilst simultaneously adopting a non-controversial definition. The breadth of the definition of AI adopted encompasses technology that has existed for some decades as well as a technology that does not exist. The use of such a wide definition that includes an idea of AI that is not yet possible could be criticised; however, in circumstances where a non-dystopian yet realistic approach is being taken to the potential of AI in the future, the aim is not only to encompass an idea of what AI *is* or may be in the immediate future. Given the realistic constraints that are adopted to the nature of the technology – as will become apparent through the examples in this chapter and even in the ways in which the hypotheticals are used in later chapters – the definition achieves this aim.

B. Algorithm

The term 'algorithm' is frequently used and not always clearly defined or understood. It forms a part of Abbott's definition above but is easily glossed over. It is, however, important to bring some clarity to what this is and how it can be differentiated from some of the other terms defined here.

An algorithm is a finite and organised sequence of defined instructions that is used to perform a calculation or function or to solve a problem.[12] Whilst the definition is often provided in conjunction to a reference to the word's origins,[13] this does not bring the term's contemporary use into any sharper focus. Focus on the critical elements – as a process that includes a finite number of steps/calculations that produce a result – provides the ideal insight into the potential benefit of algorithms and their essentiality to AI. It is the algorithm that is the driver of any AI – it is the algorithm that allows these digital machines to work. What is more, it is the speed at which the steps/calculations that form part of the algorithm can be carried out that facilitates some of the real advantages of AI; by being able to perform millions of calculations per second and in dealing with vast pools of data to come to a result, an AI can – in limited or specific respects – far outperform a human.

[11] J Chen and P Burgess, 'The Boundaries of Legal Personhood: How Spontaneous Intelligence Can Problematise Differences between Humans, Artificial Intelligence, Companies and Animals' (2019) 27(1) *Artificial Intelligence and Law* 73; N Bostrom, *Superintelligence: Paths, Dangers, Strategies*, illustrated edn (Oxford, Oxford University Press 2014).

[12] This definition is inspired by the statement provided by Deakin and Markou: S Deakin and C Markou (eds), *Is Law Computable?: Critical Perspectives on Law and Artificial Intelligence* (Oxford, Hart Publishing, 2020) 286; G Fares, 'Artificial Intelligence in Social and Health Services: A New Challenge for Public Authorities in Ensuring Constitutional Rights' in Dr M Belov (ed), *The IT Revolution and Its Impact on State, Constitutionalism and Public Law* (Oxford, Hart Publishing, 2021) 276.

[13] Including references to Muhammad ibn Musa al-Khwarizmi's use of the term. Russell and Norvig (n 8) 27; Fares (n 12) 276.

C. Artificial General Intelligence

AGI was touched on earlier. After exploring the meaning of both 'AI' and 'algorithm', it is useful to reconsider AGI in order to identify the relationship between the terms. As noted immediately above, AI can outperform humans in terms of raw processing power in specific limited respects. Whilst enabling this narrow victory, the nature of the algorithm is also a limiting factor. As the algorithm is a finite and organised sequence of defined instructions that is used to perform a calculation or function or to solve a problem, that finite set of instructions can limit what can be achieved. The idea of narrow AI relates to systems that use artificial cognitive functions in a *specific* task – like playing specific games, recognising handwriting, or reading X-rays – in relation to which AI can outperform humans.

Popular science fiction is generally not centred around narrow forms of AI. They are often inspired by AGI. The *Terminator* franchise, *2001: A Space Odyssey*, and a number of Isaac Asimov's stories describe intelligent machines that not only outperform humans in narrow or specific tasks, but also can perform *any* task that a person could perform. AGI remains a hypothetical idea that exists only within the realms of science fiction. Although, this has not stopped discussions of its potential dangers,[14] or discussions regarding how the potential for its achievement may require a change in our conception of AI.[15] The use of the non-dystopian hypotheticals in this book allow the potential realities that may follow from further steps toward AGI to be considered without becoming bogged in concerns regarding both utopianism or dystopianism.

D. Machine Learning

Understanding machine learning – as a sub-set or technique within artificial intelligence and in terms of its connections to algorithms – is essential to considering the ways that technologies are currently being implemented as well as the ways that they may be implemented in the future. It is also crucial to ground the discussions that follow in terms of the way in which AI can enhance human decision-making in ways that impact the Rule of Law. Machine learning relates to the design and use of an algorithm that automatically alters the way in which it works in order to improve output. Crucially, this means that performance can be improved *without* this being specifically programmed. This normally would occur through the ability of the algorithm to identify and extrapolate patterns in the data provided to it. In short, machines can 'learn from examples and generate their own rules'.[16]

[14] Bostrom (n 11); R JM Boyles and JJ Joaquin, 'Why Friendly AIs Won't Be That Friendly: A Friendly Reply to Muehlhauser and Bostrom' (2020) 35(2) *AI & Society* 505. See also discussions of what may happen if an intelligence spontaneously generated and how it would be treated: Chen and Burgess (n 11).

[15] Russell and Norvig (n 8) 51.

[16] Abbott (n 9) 30.

The process by which machine learning takes place can be either supervised or it can be unsupervised. This represents a form of control over the way in which a machine can generate its answers or own rules. This can be thought of as having a human 'in-the-loop', 'out-of-the-loop', or 'over-the-loop'. Respectively, this involves the operation of the process taking place: with human decision-making being *supported*; *without* human intervention; or, with human *oversight*. These distinctions will become critical in later chapters where the nature of the use of algorithms in the exercise of power by the state is considered as the three hypotheticals explored in this book represent varieties of these forms of control. As will be seen, especially in terms of certain forms of the Rule of Law, controlling the way in which machine learning is regulated provides a vital mechanism of control over outputs or decisions. It may be seen as being critical to have human involvement in the decision- or law-making process.

E. Algorithmic Decision Making

Algorithmic Decision-Making (ADM) systems use machine learning in order to replicate the human decision-making process. Whilst this may seem like an attractive idea that enables greater efficiencies, there are some considerable problems that may also be imported. Some of these are discussed here. (More are expanded upon through the rest of the chapter.)

A point of clarification is that ADM does not necessarily require AI or machine learning. Whilst AI and machine learning may be part of ADM, it is possible to have forms of ADM that are more linear. In reflecting on the meaning of algorithm – as a finite and organised sequence of instructions – it is possible to create a sequence of instructions that does not involve AI – as a process in which a machine acts in a way that would otherwise require cognition. For example, ADM may simply include a process that states: if condition A is met, then decision B should result. This requires no cognition on the part of the machine, and it does not involve any machine learning. The decision-making process is wholly defined and created by the person creating the algorithm. Processes like this – albeit on a larger scale – resulted in the 'Robodebt' scandal in Australia where automated debt notices were erroneously sent by a government department in consequence of a poorly designed algorithm.[17] Whilst this sort of process is properly ADM, the scale and relative complexity of the systems may make it appear to be an AI that being used and not the human-based programming.

[17] C Holmes AC SC, *Royal Commission into the Robodebt Scheme* (2023) robodebt.royalcommission.gov.au/publications/report; J Townsend, 'Better Decisions? Robodebt and the Failings of Merits Review' in J Boughey and K Miller (eds), *The Automated State: Implications, Challenges and Opportunities for Public Law*, 1st edn (Alexandria, NSW, Federation Press, 2021) 52: federationpress.com.au/product/the-automated-state/.

In the context of a book that is focused on the concept of the Rule of Law – which, in its simplest sense, reflects a concept that opposes the arbitrary application of state power – the process of power being exercised through an ADM process has clear relevance. This is reflected in Pasquale's statement that 'authority is increasingly expressed algorithmically'.[18] The ability of the concept of the Rule of Law to exercise some form of control over power that is exercised with humans either 'in-the-loop', 'out-of-the-loop', or 'over-the-loop', becomes a core consideration. These ideas will be expanded upon in both the examples later in this chapter as well as through the deeper consideration that follows in the chapters after this one. For the moment, it is sufficient to note that ADM is increasingly seen as an important and, crucially, an incredibly *efficient* way in which power can be exercised.[19]

F. The Black Box

Notwithstanding the potential benefits related to efficiency, there are considerable fears that relate to the lack of transparency of – especially complex – ADM processes. The 'black box' aspect of decisions made by an AI that has not been specifically programmed in order to reach a form of answer is a clear and obvious point at which concerns arise.[20] The idea of the black box means there may be no way to see or understand how the decisions that have ultimately been made.[21] In other words, the nature of the algorithm and the steps that an AI system takes in coming to an answer is so complex that there is no way in which the processes through which the decision has been made can be identified or stipulated.

The problems that the black box aspect presents for the Rule of Law will form a persistent refrain throughout this book. The problems are relatively clear; core ideals often associated with the Rule of Law – including transparency, fairness, and accountability – are placed at risk.[22] In addition, there is considerable scope for systems that train themselves to *not* be completely unbiased decision-making systems and, instead, to exhibit considerable bias. The problem with bias – especially when decisions are made within a black box – in terms of ADM

[18] F Pasquale, *The Black Box Society: The Secret Algorithms That Control Money and Information*, reprint edn (Cambridge, Mass, Harvard University Press, 2016) 8.

[19] M Oswald, 'Algorithm-Assisted Decision-Making in the Public Sector: Framing the Issues Using Administrative Law Rules Governing Discretionary Power' (2018) 376(2128) *Philosophical Transactions of the Royal Society A: Mathematical, Physical and Engineering Sciences* 20170359; M Whittaker et al, *AI Now 2018 Report* (AI Now, December 2018) 18: ainowinstitute.org/AI_Now_2018_Report.pdf.

[20] Pasquale (n 18).

[21] ibid; T Wischmeyer, 'Artificial Intelligence and Transparency: Opening the Black Box' in T Wischmeyer and T Rademacher (eds), *Regulating Artificial Intelligence* (Cham, Springer International Publishing, 2020) 75: doi.org/10.1007/978-3-030-32361-5_4.

[22] S Greenstein, 'Preserving the Rule of Law in the Era of Artificial Intelligence (AI)' [2021] *Artificial Intelligence and Law*: doi.org/10.1007/s10506-021-09294-4.

is well-known. Bias and racism have been shown to follow from the application of certain algorithms.[23] In circumstances where decisions are being made by algorithms, and where bias may be known to be a possibility, there is an increased need for those decisions to be truly transparent. Yet, the complexity of the code means that decision-making becomes, and remains, opaque. The result is that those subject to decisions will be unable to understand the way in which those decisions are being made. When considered in terms of the possibility of bias creeping into the equation, this may cause considerable doubt relating to the ability of algorithms to make decisions in the right way and based on the right powers – especially decisions where humans are 'out-of-the-loop'. (A comparison of this form of opacity with human opacity will take place in the chapters that follow.)

In the consideration immediately below of *What AI Does*, these issues will be explored in a little more detail and they will be placed into the context of the realistic yet non-dystopian approach that I adopt in this book. When taken together, the discussion above and the section immediately below will provide a sufficient dose of realism to ground the section III discussion of *What AI May Be*.

II. What AI Does

In this section, the aim is to illustrate some ways in which AI has been and is being used by various states and in various functions around the world. The overarching purpose to this section is to demonstrate that AI has been increasingly used in making ever-more important decisions in the exercise of public power and to explore the relative scope (and nature) of those uses. By doing this, I suggest that the use of technology in this way is likely to both continue and increase in scope and importance. This is not to say these are the only ways in which AI is being used. AI is increasingly used in many aspects of modern life that go far beyond Alexa and Siri in areas like new drug development. The increasing availability of AI tools is seeing institutional change across the world. For example, AI, especially in the form of generative AI, is also the source of reform in the educational sector due to concerns that the technology will be used to facilitate academic cheating. The speed and nature of these changes seems set to continue.

In this section, after a brief overview relating to the history of AI in public decision-making, I consider four different state-based spheres where AI is used: in legislative decision-making (broadly construed); in courts; in administrative decisions; and, in legal practice. (These spheres do not precisely map onto the

[23] C Sandvig et al, 'When the Algorithm Itself Is a Racist: Diagnosing Ethical Harm in the Basic Components of Software' (2016) 10 *International Journal of Communication* 4972; M Spielkamp, 'Inspecting Algorithms for Bias', MIT Technology Review (12 June 2017) www.technologyreview.com/2017/06/12/105804/inspecting-algorithms-for-bias/; E Nissan, 'Digital Technologies and Artificial Intelligence's Present and Foreseeable Impact on Lawyering, Judging, Policing and Law Enforcement' (2017) 32(3) *AI & Society* 441.

hypotheticals explored in later chapters – they are presented here to illustrate the relative scope and impact of AI in law more generally.) The first three, broadly, map onto the familiar tripartite categories that reflect the Montesquieuian separation of powers of the legislature, the judicial system, and in the executive.[24] The fourth represents the location at which the other three may be seen to come together and overlap. Accordingly, the fourth sub-section is also used as a brief summary and conclusion to the section and a way to link to the idea of what AI may be in the next section.

A. The Use of AI in Public Decision-Making

Given the potential for AI to speed up decision-making processes, increase accuracy, and to process vast amounts of data far faster than a human, the reasons for the increased use and integration of AI in the exercise of public decision-making seem to be reasonably evident.[25] In circumstances where western liberal democracies function in a way that takes account of a considerable amount of data in order to come to any given policy decision or in order to promote the welfare of the state, having access to more efficient ways to process that data and come to conclusions is an attractive proposition.

Some of the benefits of the use of AI in public decision-making that have been noted in a recent report by the New South Wales Ombudsman include: efficiency and cost saving; improved accuracy; improved consistency; and a better customer experience.[26] A particularly surprising point that was made in that report – that was instituted to address a particular situation, but was still broad in scope within a relatively small state government – is the admission that 'we do not know how many other NSW Government agencies are using, or developing, machine technology to assist them in the exercise of their statutory functions'.[27] This relative inability of a powerful and important state-based entity to identify the scope and nature of the use of AI within a particular (relatively small) state government

[24] C de Secondat Montesquieu, *The Spirit of the Laws* (New York, Hafner Pub. Co., 1949) archive.org/details/spiritlaws01montgoog.

[25] A data-driven government may be more effective and more efficient through being more responsive. S Goldsmith and S Crawford, *The Responsive City: Engaging Communities Through Data–Smart Governance*, 1st edn (San Francisco, CA, Jossey-Bass, 2014). There may be significant efficiency gains – but with existing technology, they may not necessarily result in benefit without human input. H Mehr, *Artificial Intelligence for Citizen Services and Government* (Harvard Kennedy School, 2017) 19. This desire is – generally speaking – one that is applied to the way in which AI is currently being deployed in the public sphere. P-Adrien Hanania and A-Laure Thieullent, 'Perform AI for Public Sector: Public Goes AI!', Capgemini Worldwide (4 March 2020) www.capgemini.com/2020/03/perform-ai-for-public-sector-public-goes-ai/.

[26] NSW Ombudsman, *The New Machinery of Government: Using Machine Technology in Administrative Decision-Making* (NSW Ombudsman, 29 November 2021) 2: www.ombo.nsw.gov.au/news-and-publications/publications/reports/state-and-local-government/the-new-machinery-of-government-using-machine-technology-in-administrative-decision-making.

[27] ibid 3.

illustrates the extent to which the use of AI and associated technologies have been integrated into the state-system. It also serves to illustrate the increasing extent to which the lines between human and algorithmic/automated decision-making lines are blurred.

There are a number of other recent studies that consider the role of AI in terms of constitutional democracy and state-based decision making.[28] The scope of the impact that the involvement of AI in decision-making could have is already vast and, as noted by the report referred to in the previous paragraph, is difficult to track and identify. AI is involved in automated decision-making and in providing information that is used to make data-driven decisions in a vast number of different fields across the entire scope of state decision-making.[29] This can include areas as diverse as facilitating decisions regarding who may be released from prison via predicting recidivism or, alternatively, in reading lips.[30] What is also clear is that given the potential benefits of the increased integration of AI and ADM, the ways in which the technologies are used in public decision-making is only likely to increase. But, in considering the current state of decision-making it is clear – and will become clearer in the sub-sections immediately below – that the use of AI and ADM plays an important role in the exercise of public power.

B. The Use of AI in Legislative Decision-Making

The ways in which AI is involved in specific state-based functions range across, and in some sense overlap, areas related to administrative decision-making as well as decisions that are made in the public sector more broadly.[31] In consequence

[28] Notable examples are M Zalnieriute, LB Moses and G Williams, 'The Rule of Law and Automation of Government Decision-Making' (2019) 82(3) *The Modern Law Review* 425; P Nemitz, 'Constitutional Democracy and Technology in the Age of Artificial Intelligence' [2018] *Philosophical Transactions of the Royal Society A: Mathematical, Physical and Engineering Sciences*: royalsocietypublishing.org/doi/abs/10.1098/rsta.2018.0089.

[29] Here construed to be a decision that is made by automated means without the involvement of a human actor in the decision. For a similar definitional structure, see the General Data Protection Regulation (GDPR) 2016. In relation to the use of AI to guide (human) decision-making generally, see S Newell and M Marabelli, 'Strategic Opportunities (and Challenges) of Algorithmic Decision-Making: A Call for Action on the Long-Term Societal Effects of "Datification"' (2015) 24(1) *The Journal of Strategic Information Systems* 3.

[30] J Dressel and H Farid, 'The Accuracy, Fairness, and Limits of Predicting Recidivism' (2018) 4(1) *Science Advances* eaao5580; B Shillingford et al, 'Large-Scale Visual Speech Recognition' [2018] *arXiv:1807.05162 [cs]*: arxiv.org/abs/1807.05162.

[31] In relation to administrative decision-making: C Coglianese and D Lehr, 'Regulating by Robot: Administrative Decision Making in the Machine-Learning Era' [2017] (105) *Georgetown Law Journal* 1147; D Hogan-Doran, 'Computer Says "No": Automation, Algorithms and Artificial Intelligence in Government Decision-Making' [2017] *Judicial Review: Selected Conference Papers: Journal of the Judicial Commission of New South Wales*, search.informit.org/doi/abs/10.3316/INFORMIT.173260757765464. In relation to public sector decisions: Oswald (n 19); Hanania and Thieullent (n 25). See also, Zalnieriute, Moses and Williams (n 28).

of the current state of the technology, there are certainly many hurdles that would need to be overcome before any utopian idea of the use of AI can be achieved. These are hinted at below – as they will be explored in more detail in the chapters that follow. But, this is not to trivialise the issues that go hand in hand with the potential for AI systems to exacerbate bias, for decisions made by AI to be opaque (within a black box), or for human agency to be lost completely.[32] However, if we look to the potential future application of AI, and if we retain a realistic yet non-dystopian approach, some real benefits are possible. This includes the ability for more objective transparency to occur, for decisions to be truly uniform and equally applied, and understandable.[33] As with the drawbacks, these are hinted at below and explored further in future chapters.

The nature of legislative decision-making will play a principal role in the chapters that follow. As the branch of government that is responsible for making the laws that govern society, the role and function of the legislature impacts citizens' lives in a modern democracy in a myriad of different ways. The legislative function in democratic states has traditionally been one that relies on *human* decision-makers.[34] As Rule of Law constraints operate most conspicuously in terms of the making of laws, consideration of alternative forms of decision-making by the legislature will form a fundamental part of the future-facing hypotheticals later in this book. Yet, as has been illustrated in the previous sub-section, the use and integration of AI as a way to *aid* the state – and the legislators that form part of it – is increasingly prevalent and important.

The role of the legislator has traditionally been seen in two ways. The first involves a Burkean trustee ideal in which legislators bring their own agency and critical assessments to bear on making decisions on behalf of their electors.[35] In contrast to Burke's trustee idea of representation, the delegate model of the representative function – often attributed to Madison – sees representatives merely following the preferences of their constituents.[36] In both of these functions, it is not difficult to see how AI can be used to assist. In the trustee form, assistance is provided directly to the legislator in making decisions. The legislator is aided by having access to the fruits of consideration of data via the identification of patterns that they – as a human – could not hope to identify. In the delegate form, AI can be used to better understand, collate, and present electors' preferences and identify trends, needs, and patterns not previously identifiable. Accordingly, regardless of the way in which the role of the legislator is seen to operate has the potential to enhance the function.

[32] This is expanded upon in the following section.

[33] P Burgess, 'Algorithmic Augmentation of Democracy: Considering Whether Technology Can Enhance the Concepts of Democracy and the Rule of Law Through Four Hypotheticals' [2021] *AI & Society*.

[34] For an alternative view, see ibid.

[35] E Burke and I Hampsher-Monk, *Revolutionary Writings: Reflections on the Revolution in France and the First Letter on a Regicide Peace* (Cambridge, Cambridge University Press, 2013) 115.

[36] S Dovi, Metaphysics Research Lab, Stanford University, *The Stanford Encyclopedia of Philosophy*, Edward N Zalta (ed) (online at 23 March 2022).

As noted, AI is already used to assist in making decisions that impact humans in a way that is more efficient and takes account of a greater volume of data than could be achieved by a human alone. This can create a data-driven 'technocracy' that may outperform the human-only decision-making processes in a way that avoids opaque motivations.[37] However, for this benefit to be fully realised, this requires existing issues related to the explainability of AI (the black box) and the issues relating to bias in AI to be overcome. This reflects the fact that authority is increasingly being expressed algorithmically.[38] The increased use and dependence on algorithms in the processes of making laws can lead to an algocracy – as 'a system in which algorithms are used to collect, collate and organise the data upon which decisions are typically made and to assist in how that data is processed and communicated through the relevant governance system'.[39] This precise idea, provided by Danaher, in broad terms reflects a system of governance that is organised and structured on the basis of computer-controlled algorithms. It will hopefully be apparent that this could, if exercised appropriately, result in real benefits; but, substantial problems can also be readily imagined given the state of the current technology.

If democracy is a system of government that pays some form of attention to electors' preferences or needs – and, hence, encompasses both the delegate and trustee modes of representative government – the use of AI to come to *some* conclusions about the data that is available, especially where society increasingly generates vast quantities of data, in order to make 'good', 'effective', or 'beneficial' legislative decisions appears increasingly attractive. AI can save time, money, and effort and, potential, can come to better decisions through the examination of more data. For these reasons, it is no surprise that a move toward AI or algorithm-centric modes of governance can be seen in several states' plans for the future in recent years.[40]

Given the massive potential benefits to both society and to the democratic and legislative processes, what starts to become problematic is identifying the ways in which humans can (or should) remain part of the process. Here the parallel

[37] Khanna provides a compelling argument for a similar position: P Khanna, *Technocracy in America: Rise of the Info-State* (CreateSpace Independent Publishing Platform, 2017); B Lepri et al, 'Fair, Transparent, and Accountable Algorithmic Decision-Making Processes' (2018) 31(4) *Philosophy & Technology* 611. In some senses, people may prefer algorithmic judgment: JM Logg, JA Minson and DA Moore, 'Algorithm Appreciation: People Prefer Algorithmic to Human Judgment' (2019) 151 *Organizational Behavior and Human Decision Processes* 90. See also PB de Laat, 'Algorithmic Decision-Making Based on Machine Learning from Big Data: Can Transparency Restore Accountability?' (2018) 31(4) *Philosophy & Technology* 525.

[38] Pasquale (n 18) 8.

[39] J Danaher, 'The Threat of Algocracy: Reality, Resistance and Accommodation' (2016) 29(3) *Philosophy & Technology* 245, 247.

[40] Treasury Board of Canada Secretariat, *Digital Operations Strategic Plan: 2018–2022* (13 May 2021) www.canada.ca/en/government/system/digital-government/government-canada-digital-operations-strategic-plans/digital-operations-strategic-plan-2018-2022.html; UK Cabinet Office, *Government Transformation Strategy 2017 to 2020*: www.gov.uk/government/publications/government-transformation-strategy-2017-to-2020.

that is readily recognisable is in driverless car technology. It can be imagined that at some point in the near future an AI will represent a driving option that is *so* much safer than a human that it becomes not a question of what the AI should be allowed to do safely but, instead, what the *human* should be allowed to do. If a machine becomes objectively better at a task than a human, the consideration becomes one focused on the relative shortcomings of the human approach and not the benefits of the AI approach. What is certainly clear is that AI is set to play an ever more important role in state and legislative decision-making in the years to come. Concerns have been raised regarding the relative opacity of algorithms' decision-making, or for the potential for bias to enter into the decision-making process (which cannot then be 'seen' due to the opacity of the decision-making process), which have caused some to suggest that humans should remain in the loop regarding decisions.[41] Through the discussions in this book, attempts will be made to identify some limits at which humans should remain in the loop and the relative benefits of doing so. The hypotheticals in chapters four, five, and six will illuminate these issues and the relative benefits and drawbacks – relating to the Rule of Law – of the use of AI in the creation and application of laws.

C. The Use of AI in the Courts

In many respects, the court system operates like an algorithm. It will be recalled that earlier in the chapter, algorithm was defined in these terms: a finite and organised sequence of defined instructions that is used to perform a calculation or function or to solve a problem. The court system operates so as to solve (legal) problems through an organised system of rules (being the rules of civil procedure, legislation, and precedent from prior cases). Within that system, discreet legal decisions are required to be made following the input of particular facts. This form of decision-making – following a simple form of decision-matrix – formed a first wave of AI technologies. However, AI has become increasingly sophisticated through machine learning and predictive technologies. With these similarities in mind, it is of no surprise that various aspects of the judicial function, and courts' functions more generally, have been impacted by the use of AI.

Arguments have been made against the use of AI in the core business of judicial determinations,[42] and arguments have been made as to hurdles that must be overcome before AI can have an *independent* role in these settings,[43] but these arguments have not been sufficient to deter many extended uses of AI in the court

[41] Pasquale (n 18) 8; Danaher (n 39) 266.

[42] J Boughey et al (eds), 'Public Law Limits on Automated Courts' in *The Automated State: Implications, Challenges and Opportunities for Public Law*, 1st edn (Alexandria, NSW, Federation Press 2021) federationpress.com.au/product/the-automated-state/.

[43] K Brennan-Marquez and S Henderson, 'Artificial Intelligence and Role-Reversible Judgment' (2019) 109(2) *Journal of Criminal Law and Criminology* 137.

system – many of which could be seen to impinge on courts' core business. The benefits, and possibilities, of a more electronic form of court decision-making has been mooted for some time.[44] Many of these benefits were realised during the COVID-19 pandemic and enabled the judicial system to continue functioning. However, a simple shift online does not, of itself, necessitate an increase in the use of AI in making decisions. (Although being online may be a useful precursor.) The core issue, regarding the automation of decisions is raised in the question of whether AI can replace a judge in the judicial function (or part of it). As has been noted by Sourdin, the integration of technology (broadly construed) into the justice system can be of three forms: using technology to inform and support those in the system (supportive technology); replacing functions and activities previously carried out by humans (replacement technologies); and, changing the way that the system operates so as to provide a different form of justice (disruptive technologies).[45] It is useful to touch on each.

Supportive technology is already in place. As noted, this came to the fore in many justice systems during the COVID-19 pandemic. Hearings and other dispute resolution processes were moved online.[46] This was assisted through the fact that electronic filing of documents had been in place in many jurisdictions for several years. However, as noted above, these processes do not necessarily involve the use of AI. (Although, to function many will have some sort of AI assisting the applications to run.) There is one supportive technology that has been used that goes far beyond simply replacing paper-based systems: COMPAS. This system is used to predict the likely risk of recidivism. In this instance, the algorithm provides a judge with a score for an individual that can be used in determining whether an individual should receive a custodial sentence.[47] COMPAS is supportive. It provides information that the judge can take into account in making a decision. Whilst it can support the judicial function, criticisms have also been raised because the way in which the score is derived by the algorithm is opaque (as it is proprietary software). This opacity is problematic as it does not replicate in a transparent way a judicial function that requires a reasoned approach. The need for transparency is a key component of the Rule of Law. Discussions later in the book will return to this crucial aspect in decision-making. After all, in many respects the judicial system is based not only on the principal that the right decision is arrived at, but that the right decision can be *seen* to have been arrived at.[48]

[44] A Sela, 'Streamlining Justice: How Online Courts Can Resolve the Challenges of Pro Se Litigation' (2016) 26(2) *Cornell Journal of Law and Public Policy* 331.

[45] T Sourdin, 'Judge v Robot? Artificial Intelligence and Judicial Decision-Making' (2018) 41(4) *University of New South Wales Law Journal* 1117: www.unswlawjournal.unsw.edu.au/article/judge-v-robot-artificial-intelligence-and-judicial-decision-making/.

[46] JM Baldwin, JM Eassey and EJ Brooke, 'Court Operations during the COVID-19 Pandemic' (2020) 45(4) *American Journal of Criminal Justice* 743.

[47] Chesterman provides a useful overview: S Chesterman, *We, the Robots?: Regulating Artificial Intelligence and the Limits of the Law* (Cambridge, Cambridge University Press, 2021) 63–65.

[48] This does not mean that courts do not rely on 'black box' decisions. Juries provide a decision and are not required to provide any form of justification.

The supportive technologies outlined above are not really the focus of this book. Many of the technologies merely facilitate easier decisions. Although, some systems (like COMPAS) do raise some considerable questions relating to the nature of a decision that will be considered later. At the other extreme, disruptive technologies are also not the concern of this book. They necessarily fundamentally change the form of justice.

Completely disrupting the judicial function and changing the form of justice is not the focus of this book. Whilst there seems the potential for AI to do this, the non-dystopian approach to looking toward the future does not seek to examine a completely new judicial order. Instead, the use of AI as part of the core judicial function is a clearer example of a replacement technology. This form of technology will anchor this book. In this respect, and has been noted by others, the use of technology becomes fundamental to the maintenance of the Rule of Law (in the general sense).[49]

In replacing the judicial function, there have been some instances where aspects of the judge's previous role have been replaced through some form of AI. One aspect already noted above, that was previously a judicial function, is in predicting recidivism.[50] Through the use of COMPAS the previous function requiring the judge to evaluate the risk of recidivism (on an individual basis) before making a determination has been replaced by an AI.

Outcomes of particular questions can already be suggested in forms of AI that use decision trees.[51] More sophisticated forms of AI can also be used to predict outcomes of judicial determinations.[52] Yet, this predictive function is not precisely what judges do in their role; they determine an answer to a legal problem; they do not merely predict what the outcome could or should be. Judges also play a fundamental role in the broader administration of a matter and to educating and participating in a society.[53] In this sense, AI's current ability to replicate the judicial function remains limited.[54] For the moment, at least, the ideal of automated decisions in complex legal matters in the court room, without human intervention in any way, remains the stuff of science fiction. Yet, it remains important to consider what that sort of future may hold. By taking a realistic approach to the potential use of AI in replacing the judicial function, this book seeks to explore some of those issues.

[49] D Harvey, 'From Susskind to Briggs: Online Court Approaches' (2016) 84(5) *Journal of Civil Litigation and Practice* 12, 95.

[50] Dressel and Farid (n 30).

[51] KD Ashley, *Artificial Intelligence and Legal Analytics: New Tools for Law Practice in the Digital Age* (Cambridge, Cambridge University Press, 2017) 4 www.cambridge.org/core/books/artificial-intelligence-and-legal-analytics/E7D705EEF392501A1DB180645917E7E0.

[52] NB Chaphalkar, KC Iyer and Smita K Patil, 'Prediction of Outcome of Construction Dispute Claims Using Multilayer Perceptron Neural Network Model' (2015) 8(33) *International Journal of Project Management* 1827.

[53] These points are echoed by Sourdin (n 45) 1124.

[54] RE Susskind, 'Detmold's Refutation of Positivism and the Computer Judge', MJ Detmold (ed), (1986) 49(1) *The Modern Law Review* 125.

D. The Use of AI in Administrative Decision-Making

Administrative decisions in modern western states represent a fundamental and common way in which individuals interact with the state apparatus. This may represent a decision regarding a benefit payment, a fine or penalty, or any other instance where any form of decision is made by an agent acting on behalf of the state. Given the considerable number of interactions that individuals have with their state, it is of no surprise that governments have been keen to introduce AI and ADM to these transactions in order to take advantage of the efficiencies that they offer.

At present, there are certain decisions that cannot be made by a non-human entity. For example, the need for decisions to be made by an 'officer of the Board' in the Taxes Management Act in England.[55] Yet, there are decisions being made – at least relatively simple decisions – that are placed in the hands of an AI.[56] Some suggestions have been raised that an AI judge would, for example, be appropriate in (relatively) small claims.[57] In situations where participants may both agree to an AI decision-maker and, for example, where both wish to have a quick and cost effective decision, it is conceivable that AI decision-makers would be both feasible and attractive.

The 'Robo-debt' programme in Australia is one instance where attempts to replace the manual review of individual cases with an automated system – that, ultimately, failed to take into account all relevant details and resulted in a substantial and significant number of errors.[58] The process was intended to collect debts that stemmed from an overpayment of welfare. The system involved collating and assessing data from several agencies and automating the process of sending letters to individuals that were determined as owing money as a result of overpayments. The system was not, as noted earlier in the chapter, an AI system. It was a process related to the analysis of data that resulted in an automated outcome. As a consequence of the poor design of the system, debt letters were sent to individuals that did not owe any money.[59] Other jurisdictions have had similar problems with automating public agencies' decisions.[60] However, at least for the moment, problems like those outlined above decrease the public's faith in automated systems

[55] Taxes Management Act 1970, s 8.

[56] M Perry, 'Administrative Law: IDecide: Administrative Decision-Making in the Digital World | Westlaw AU' (2017) 91 *Australian Law Journal* 29.

[57] Niiler, 'Can AI Be a Fair Judge in Court? Estonia Thinks So' (25 March 2019) *Wired*: www.wired.com/story/can-ai-be-fair-judge-court-estonia-thinks-so.

[58] Catherine Holmes AC SC (n 17).

[59] Commonwealth Ombudsman, *Centrelink's Automated Debt Raising and Recovery System* (No 02/2017, April 2017) www.ombudsman.gov.au/__data/assets/pdf_file/0022/43528/Report-Centrelinks-automated-debt-raising-and-recovery-system-April-2017.pdf.

[60] Examples in Sweden and China also exist. For a useful summary, see Zalnieriute, Moses and Williams (n 28) 438–39.

and may play a part in ensuring the need for a human to be involved in, at least, reviewing decisions.[61]

E. The Use of AI in Legal Practice

Lawyers are seen by some as being resistant to change – or, at least, resistant to change caused by external agents.[62] As will be seen, this does not describe the change in a lawyers' role and function over an extended period or even in more recent times. Whilst some uses of technology may have been seen as inappropriate – for example, lawyers using generative AI to generate submissions to court[63] – the widespread adoption of technology has revolutionised and made possible the process of discovery in large litigation matters where tens or hundreds of millions of documents may be involved. The instances of technological change are explored in more detail in the following pages.

The common law system is ancient and has its own form of artificial reason. In arguing that the King lacked the ability, skill and practice to determine the law, Chief Justice Coke said, in 1607, 'legal determinations are not to be decided by natural reason but by the artificial reason and judgment of law, which law is an act which requires long study and experience, before that a man can attain to the cognizance of it'.[64] The idea of an *artificial reason* in determining the law has, for the last several hundred years, created a traditionalist profession that adheres to particular ways of creating and determining the law. However, in an age of AI, where long study and experience can be achieved in moments by a machine in a true form of *artificial* reason, the Chief Justice's words can be seen in a new light.

As noted above, legal practice was able to rapidly pivot during the pandemic.[65] Some are already considering the future for law and lawyers in an era of AI.[66] But, in many respects, the *way* in which legal practice is conducted has been changing in consequence of technology for much longer. Whilst the 'long study and experience' that Coke describes is still necessary to become a lawyer, the practice of being a lawyer has fundamentally changed. In Coke's era, very few court

[61] Perry (n 56); J Townsend, 'Better Decisions? Robodebt and the Failings of Merits Review' in J Boughey and K Miller (eds), *The Automated State: Implications, Challenges and Opportunities for Public Law*, 1st edn (Alexandria, NSW, Federation Press, 2021) 52, 69: federationpress.com.au/product/the-automated-state/.

[62] C Brooks, C Gherhes and T Vorley, 'Artificial Intelligence in the Legal Sector: Pressures and Challenges of Transformation' (2020) 13(1) *Cambridge Journal of Regions, Economy and Society* 135, 148.

[63] 'ChatGPT: US Lawyer Admits Using AI for Case Research', *BBC News* (online, 27 May 2023) www.bbc.com/news/world-us-canada-65735769; *Mata v Avianca, Inc* (United States District Court – Southern District of New York, 22 June 2023).

[64] Prohibitions, Case of [1607] EWHC KB J23 (EWHC (KB), 1 November 1607).

[65] Baldwin, Eassey and Brooke (n 46).

[66] R Susskind, *Tomorrow's Lawyers: An Introduction To Your Future*, 2nd edn (Oxford, Oxford University Press 2017).

proceedings were reported upon – the *Prohibitions* case report cited above was authored by Coke himself. Today, live broadcasts of superior court proceedings are commonplace and full transcripts can be obtained almost immediately. Heavy tomes – published yearly – were replaced by more readily updatable looseleaf publications. But these have also been replaced by alternative media that can be updated immediately and accessed from anywhere. Case reports are available from numerous sources online for free or through specialist publishers – like LexisNexis or Westlaw – that provide additional services and commentary to the legal profession. In this respect, the volume of material produced by courts (putting aside any increase in the number of cases determined each year) has exponentially increased. Any ability to 'attain to the cognizance of [the law]' now involves the application of several substantial technological innovations.

Technological innovations in the legal sector are now a burgeoning business. The legal-tech sector now provides a huge potential for the development of the services that law firms provide. During large scale litigation matters, a vast number of documents that relate to the proceeding may need to be examined to determine whether they are either the subject of legal professional privilege or whether they can be disclosed to the other party or parties in the litigation. Whilst technology assisted document review has existed for more than 20 years,[67] systems, such as the proprietary software Relativity,[68] have changed the way that discovery operates. After initial steps that enabled simple duplication identification, more complex AI systems now thread, categorise, and continually learn from the discovery process in order to automatically add or remove the vast proportion of documents from the need to be manually considered. This means that large scale litigation that involves many millions of documents is now possible as a human lawyer may never see the majority of the documents. (The corollary to this technological innovation is that the courts are also willing to accept that a lawyer's duty to the court can be discharged in this way.)

Other innovations have enabled forms of legal advice to be provided by an AI. The website donotpay.com describes itself as the 'world's first robot lawyer' and offers a service that enables individuals to engage the system to commence and conduct legal matters without having to pay the level of fees that are necessary when dealing with big law firms. In this respect, the use of AI has enabled legal practice to be conducted by or for individuals with no prior legal knowledge – moving beyond Coke's requirement for 'long study and experience'. The nature and role of the lawyer is changing.[69] In consequence of the technology and AI tools that are now available, today's lawyer would not only be fundamentally unrecognisable to Coke, but also (given the relative pace of development), would likely be unrecognisable to a lawyer from 30 years ago.

[67] A Kershaw, 'Automated Document Review Proves Its Reliability' (2005) 5(11) *Digital Discovery & e-Evidence* 10.

[68] See Relativity.com.

[69] Susskind (n 66).

These innovative technologies in legal practice exist at the junction between the systems (and technologies) of legislative, judicial, and administrative decision-making. The use of these technologies is consequent on the structures – either implicit or explicit – that allow them to operate. This could include courts allowing the use of e-discovery tools that use AI to sift documents knowing that there has not been a human inspection of *every* document, or it could relate to the administrative decision-making processes that operate so as to allow submissions to be made by systems like donotpay.com. Yet, none of this means that we are any closer to completely replacing lawyers than we are to completely replacing judges. AI has been adopted across all areas of legal practice – as it has across the legislative, judicial, and administrative decision-making processes – as a fundamental tool that facilitates the more effective and efficient provision of a service. It has and, as will be seen in the next section, will likely continue to change the way that society interacts with the law.

III. What AI May Be

I have previously considered the ways in which AI has been used. That exploration was necessarily grounded in reality. In this section, I engage in speculation – but, as noted in previous sections, I do not wish to delve fully in the world of sci-fi. This is not the place to consider hyper-futuristic uses of AI in a utopian or dystopian world. Instead, my non-dystopian consideration of what AI *may* be uses the present uses of AI – plus the feasible achievable uses of the technology – as a reality check. In this respect, whilst the hypotheticals that follow are necessarily future-looking, the suggestions relating to the way that AI may be used are potentially realisable. In this sense they provide a foundation for the extended consideration of the hypotheticals in the following three chapters.

The three hypothetical scenarios are each addressed in a separate subsection. Respectively, they relate to the use of AI in: administrative decision-making; creating secondary (delegated) legislation; and, creating primary legislation. Whilst not exclusively related to these things, each of the hypotheticals enables the foregrounding of a particular level of human intervention in the process: humans in the loop; humans over the loop; and, humans out of the loop. Each sub-section represents a progressively more hypothetical extension of our current AI technology. Once I have set these out, I provide an overview/summary of the chapter in the final section.

A. Hypothetical One: The Use of AI in Administrative Decision-Making

The modern administrative state in most democratic states – especially those with well-developed social welfare systems – is necessarily constituted by the rendering of a vast number of administrative decisions. Each time the executive arm of the government (normally via an agency or department) makes a determination – by making a decision, taking an action or failing to take an action – regarding the rights and interests of others, this would constitute an administrative decision. As these actions are made on behalf of the government, these inherently involve the exercise of state power and discretion.

An entire body of law – Administrative Law – is concerned with the regulation of these types of decisions. Exploring the nature and scope of that body of law is, however, not necessary for this chapter or for this book. These decisions can relate to, for example, whether an individual is able to receive a particular benefit or, alternatively, whether a particular organisation or body is granted a licence or authority to do something. A frequently made form of decision would relate to the grant of a travel visa. Many thousands of decisions of this kind may be made by any department on any given day. For example, the relatively small nation of Australia made decisions relating to almost 3 million temporary visa applications in 2021–22; prior to the pandemic, there were three times this number of decisions made about temporary visas – representing an average of approximately 25,000 decisions being made per day of the calendar year.[70] This staggering number of decisions represents *one* form of decision-making function of just *one* department in the Australian Federal government. Given the substantial number of decisions, and given the fact that there is often a requirement to assess and consider various data, the benefits of AI in the sphere are apparent. In this respect, there has been an ongoing discussion regarding the appropriateness of using AI or algorithms to aid in administrative decision making.[71] The consideration in this section relates to how these administrative processes may adopt AI in the future. Whilst it would be relatively simply to imagine a future in which, for example, *all* Australian visa applications were received and processed by an AI, this hypothetical will be less extreme and will retain a human in the loop. The use of AI will enable the decisions but will not be the final or unilateral form of decision.

The hypothetical constructed here involves an AI system learning from current practices of decision-making, identifying the relevant patterns therein and, as a result, making its own decisions relating to new applications. These decisions, themselves, are then presented as 'recommendations' to a human decision-maker for sign off/authority. This example is intentionally couched in broad and general terms – with the suggestion that this could be applied to almost any form of decision that is required to be made by any particular department or agency. This is a simple process that does not extend the technology – in general – beyond what we already have. It does, however, go beyond basic decision trees or automated decision-making that follows a pre-determined or pre-programmed path.

[70] Department of Home Affairs, *Department of Home Affairs 2021–22 Annual Report* (30 June 2022).

[71] J Boughey and K Miller (eds), *The Automated State: Implications, Challenges and Opportunities for Public Law*, 1st edn (Alexandira, NSW, Federation Press, 2021) federationpress.com.au/product/the-automated-state/; M Oswald, 'Algorithm-Assisted Decision-Making in the Public Sector: Framing the Issues Using Administrative Law Rules Governing Discretionary Power' (2018) 376(2128) *Philosophical Transactions of the Royal Society A: Mathematical, Physical and Engineering Sciences* 20170359.

From what has been stated before, we already know of issues that may arise in this hypothetical. For example, in circumstances where the process of learning and decision-making occurs in a relative black box, there are issues of transparency and, further, based on current limitations of AI systems, there may also be the real potential for bias to creep into the decision-making system.[72] These issues, and several others, will be explored in relation to the Past and Present ideas of the Rule of Law in the next chapter. What becomes apparent is that the fundamental need for explainability renders the use of AI in this sort of scenario contrary to the Rule of Law.

B. Hypothetical Two: The Use of AI in Creating Secondary Legislation

This hypothetical is a stretch for both the current technological abilities and, in circumstances where the human input is one step removed, for our trust in the technology. In this scenario, AI is used to assess the appropriateness of and implement secondary legislation without human input. This is not a fully unsupervised process, however, as the creation of secondary legislation still requires laying before the legislature – which means there is the potential of a form of veto. In this respect, this hypothetical represents a human-in-the-loop scenario.

Secondary legislation is a form of binding rule that is not directly passed by the legislature but, instead, is created by another body to which authority to create that rule has been delegated through the passage of a piece of primary legislation. In parliamentary systems, Parliament will frequently delegate limited powers to the Executive arm of the government within certain acts. This means that the legislature retains some form of ultimate authority or oversight in terms of the creation of the rule, yet the many hundreds of rules or regulations that are necessary for the functioning of the modern state can still be accomplished. In this respect, secondary legislation satisfies a necessary trade-off in the modern state; because the legislature cannot hope to consider and pass all of the pieces of legislation necessary for a modern state to function, some level of authority is delegated to another body to make rules and regulations on its behalf in a way that ensures a level of accountability and scrutiny is retained.

A relevant example that comes from the UK – that will be used to frame the hypothetical in chapter five – can be seen in the Misuse of Drugs Act 1971. This Act includes, in section 2(2), the delegation that:

> Her Majesty may by Order in Council make such amendments in Schedule 2 to this Act as may be requisite for the purpose of adding any substance or product to, or removing any substance or product from, any of Parts I to III of that Schedule, ...

[72] See also, Oswald (n 71).

This has the effect that the list of Schedule 2 drugs – which is a list of controlled drugs contained within the legislation – can be amended or augmented by an 'order in council'. The effect of sub-section 2(5) of the Act is that an order in council requires, first, a recommendation by an advisory council and, second, that a draft of the order be laid by the Secretary of State before – and approved by way of resolution by – each House of Parliament. Once this has happened, the Schedule can be amended. This has the effect that, where a substance has been added, it makes it an offence for a person to possess that substance.

The second hypothetical replaces two parties in this process with a single AI system. The first party to be replaced is the advisory council. Section 1(1) of Schedule 1 states that the council: 'shall be appointed by the Secretary of State after consultation with such organisations as he considers appropriate'. This broad ambit provides no specific guidance on the make-up of the body – although section 1 of the Act implies that the members should have sufficient expertise in relation to the potential for drugs to be subject to misuse. The other party to be replaced is the Secretary of State in the role of laying the draft order before both houses of Parliament. In this hypothetical, an AI would both identify a drug as being potentially subject to misuse *and* be the entity responsible for laying the draft order – recommending that drug be added to the schedule – before both houses.

It is not suggested that the actual terms of the Misuse of Drugs Act would facilitate the delegation of power to an AI in the way suggested. However, at least on the face of the legislation – and given the UK Parliament's position as being legally sovereign – there is no reason why any necessary amendments could not be made. In this sense, the legislative formulation provides a useful basis on which to ground the hypothetical. The framework of delegated legislation – and, in particular, the supervisory check by Parliament having to ostensibly scrutinise the recommendations before they are added to the Schedule – also provides a structure that facilitates a direct comparator to the AI-based idea of having humans over the loop.

As with the first hypothetical, and as will be explored in chapter five, a number of caveats relating to the AI's robustness and accuracy must be accepted in order for the hypothetical to provide any benefit. Once these are accepted, it is possible to consider the relevant Rule of Law-relevant consequences of an AI creating delegated legislation. This second hypothetical does go, much more clearly than the first, beyond the current uses of AI systems. Whilst the process of evaluation that an AI system would need to undertake in order to replace the roles outlined above is not technically a fundamental stretch, the relative acceptance of an AI system being able to act in this way would be a considerable stretch for a government to adopt. In this sense, the second hypothetical does remain a future-facing vision of what AI *may be*. What is found in chapter five is that, similar to the first hypothetical, the absence of explainability is a problem for Rule of Law compliance; however, the hypothetical also illuminates problems associated with both accountability and the speed of decision-making that occur when AIs make these sorts of decisions.

C. Hypothetical Three: The Use of AI in Creating Primary Legislation

This third hypothetical not only extends (in quite an extreme way) the potential for the acceptance of what an AI system may be allowed to do, but it also extends the current technical ability of an AI system to achieve a result that would be both accepted and acceptable. The suggestion in hypothetical three is relatively simple: the elected (human) individuals that constitute the legislature are each replaced by elected algorithms.

In modern democratic systems the legislature is composed of one or two houses that are responsible for making or amending the laws that operate within its jurisdiction. The function of the legislature in this sense is simple and this remains the same regardless of whether the representatives in those houses can be elected or appointed to their positions and it is the same regardless of the system of government that operates. This is even so where a constitution may limit the extent or nature of the laws that can be passed. Where a constitution exists, for example in the US, it may be the case that laws that are made within the legislature can be challenged for their conformity with the powers granted under the constitution itself. However, there are instances where the law-making power is not subject to any such constraint. A prime example of this is the UK Parliament which is, pursuant to what is described as the orthodox view, said to be sovereign.[73]

All of the legislatures that do exist share one common thread: they are populated by humans. Or, in other words, it is a particular group of humans within the legislature that decide – through whatever processes may be particular to that institution – what laws operate and exist within a particular jurisdiction. It is this idea that the third hypothetical upsets. It imagines a system where there are still elections held in order to elect legislators – and those elections are held across a nation in particular electorates for seats in the legislature – for set periods of time before the elected members may then seek re-election. But, the difference is that it is not humans that are being elected as representatives; it is particular AI systems. Once elected, those AI systems come together in order to make laws. They make the laws in exactly the same sort of way that the human-legislators with which we are familiar make laws: they debate the pros and cons and the impact and effect and then they vote the Bills into law. In this sense, the *only* real change is that the law-makers are no longer human.

Constituting a legislature with AIs has a number of Rule of Law-related impacts that will be addressed in full in chapter six. However, it is useful to note some of them briefly here. The first relates to the relative speed at which debates

[73] AV Dicey, *Introduction to the Study of the Law of the Constitution*, 9th edn (Basingstoke, Macmillan, 1939); M Elliott, 'Parliamentary Sovereignty in a Changing Constitutional Landscape' in *The Changing Constitution* (Oxford, Oxford University Press, 2019) 29: www.oxfordlawtrove.com/view/10.1093/he/9780198806363.001.0001/he-9780198806363-chapter-2.

can take place. Hundreds of debates could take place in a fraction of a second. Another relates to the information that can be used to inform those debates. Machines can process considerably more than even the most enlightened or well-staffed human. There also arises a natural question as to who is actually in control of the law-making – especially where systems are created that seek to achieve/promote particular outcomes? How is the AI system programmed, how does it make decisions, is there a way to 'understand' what it will do and why it will do it?

Providing a certain form of answers to these questions may require a deep technical or philosophical analysis; however, that is not the focus of this book. Instead, whilst the potential for this sort of institution treads very close to sci-fi-territory and whilst the potential for this sort of institution to be accepted by any given society is (at least at the present) unlikely, I ask only that these issues be suspended for the purpose of considering the terms of the hypothetical itself. The key aspect relating to this hypothetical relates to the legislative power that is then placed in the hands of machines. It is posed in order to consider which, if any, aspects of the Rule of Law are enlivened in circumstances where the entity that is wielding the power of the state is *not* a human. The conclusions that follow from this – that are explored in full in chapter six – demonstrate that whilst issues related to a lack of explainability, accountability, and speed of decision-making (seen in earlier hypotheticals) remain, the more extreme nature of this hypothetical does not necessarily mean there are no potential Rule of Law-enhancing aspects. The use of AI in this way does also illustrate a *different* aspect to the speed-related problem; this relates to the effect of increased speed on *subjects* of the law and not on law-makers.

IV. AI and the Rule of Law

The three hypotheticals set out in the previous section progressively move further away from our contemporary reality and our technological capability. In doing so, they also progressively represent less and less human control of the AI entities. In the first hypothetical – the use of AI in administrative decision-making – the technology is used to apply the law and represents only a small step beyond the way in which technology is currently used. The function of AI is used in partnership with humans; humans are in the loop. In the second hypothetical – the use of AI in creating secondary legislation – the legislators retain a level of control over the rule-making function of the AI. Whilst the AI can make rules, the law-makers can veto the decisions or can revoke the AI's power to make rules. In this respect, humans are over the loop. The third hypothetical is intentionally extreme. In this instance – the use of AI in creating legislation – humans are completely removed from the law-making process. The AIs exercise law-making power without any input or veto potential from humans. Humans are out of the loop.

Each of the hypotheticals relates to the potential impact of law – through application or creation – on society. In these circumstances, and where even the most generally accepted version of the concept of the Rule of Law relates to a concept that is opposed to the *arbitrary* application of power, the potential for the hypotheticals to relate to the Rule of Law is apparent; there is clearly the potential for there to be an exercise of power (in relation to the way that the laws are applied or made) and, as with any exercise of power, there exists the potential for this to be arbitrary. The question that is raised in the remainder of this book relates to the nature and scope of that potential and how the Rule of Law may need to evolve if the protections that it purports to offer may continue into the future.

The structure of this chapter is intended to provide – in conjunction with chapter two – all of the necessary detail (theoretical, definitional, and hypothetical) for the two substantive chapters that follow. This chapter has expanded on the definition of AI initially provided in chapter one and has sought to explain both the reality of the current technology and the contemporary applications of AI. There are a several broad observations that are useful to re-state at this point. The first is that the potential benefits of AI – especially in relation to its ability to process vast amounts of data quickly – mean that its use and operation in the world is only likely to increase. This leads to the second observation: the extended use of AI in the public sector – as applied by governments – is also likely to increase. It is this second observation that is extended by the hypotheticals. Whilst I do not claim that these are the *only* ways that the technology may be used in the future, they provide a variety of points in a continuum of application. In this respect, and as the hypotheticals clearly involve the potential exercise of arbitrary power, they are relevant to consider through a Rule of Law-lens.

What will be clear from chapter two, however, is that there cannot be a simple analysis of whether the Rule of Law is or is not contravened by the use of AI as set out in the hypotheticals. As the Rule of Law is a contested concept, it becomes analytically difficult to identify a singular idea to then apply to the question and come to a conclusion. It is for this reason that the broad aggregations explained in chapter two – the Past Rule of Law and the Present Rule of Law – will be applied to each of the three hypotheticals (in each of the following three chapters) in order to identify whether the Rule of Law, in the form provided by either the Past or Present conceptions, can continue to provide a protection against the arbitrary application of power by AI systems. The concluding chapter will then consider the form that the Rule of Law would need to have if it is to respond to the problems that the use of AI in hypotheticals reveals.

A. Does the Rule of Law Give Way to Technology?

It is in briefly raising and answering the above question that I will close this chapter. The broad thesis of this book relates to the ways in which the Rule of Law must necessarily change in order to account for the wider use of AI in the exercise of power in the future. In this final sub-section, I consider whether the Rule of Law must give way to technology. I will illustrate that a change or evolution of the Rule of Law does not merely mean that the Rule of Law *has* given way to the change in technology and, instead, suggest the Rule of Law has changed *because of* another idea.

The Rule of Law has not remained static over time. This much will be clear and apparent from the way that conceptions of the Rule of Law have been bifurcated for the purpose of this book; the temporal split between differing ideas in from the past and the present require that there has been a different form of the Rule of Law that has been broadly accepted over time. The way that the Past and Present Rule of Law conceptions we delineated in chapter two was premised on broad levels of acceptance of the ideas. The Usual Suspects of the Past Rule of Law were so described based on their frequent deployment to illustrate the meaning of the concept.[74] Whilst the Present thinkers are less easy to identify on this basis, the accounts that make up that more recent form of the Rule of Law are also popular. In this respect, there has been a clear shift or a difference – at least by some – as to what the Rule of Law does or, at least, should mean.

The change in the conceptions of the Rule of Law can be seen to be in reaction to the circumstances in which the relative conceptions were posed. This was explored in chapter two through identifying the problems to which each of the Past conceptions' thinkers were responding; their ideas of the Rule of Law were designed to provide a solution to the arbitrary application of power but the specific nature of that power – as a problem – coloured the specific nature of the solutions that were proposed. At some point, the problems that were sought to be addressed under the wide umbrella of the Rule of Law were expanded. (And this expansion was, at least by some, broadly accepted.) It is in this respect that the Present ideas of the Rule of Law encompass substantive ideas like the protection of human rights, or they include the private exercise of power, or even challenging power's arbitrary exercise in any of its forms.

It is possible here to identify that there has been a clear and apparent shift to an acceptance (by some) of a more substantive view or a wider view of the application of the concept. (This can be seen in the outcome- and source-based Present Rule of Law ideas identified in chapter two). It is one thing to recognise that there has been a change, it is another completely to identify precisely *why* that change has occurred. One could speculate, for example, that this relates to shifts in what is required by governments or as to the role that the Rule of Law should play in being a concept that is a useful tool to shape national development. A discussion of the potential viability of either of those ideas must await its own separate project; however, in the context of this book, it is possible and sensible to consider whether the change – at least as it has been seen from the Past to the Present – has been a process of giving way.

[74] P Burgess, 'Neglecting the History of the Rule of Law: (Unintended) Conceptual Eugenics' (2017) 9(2) *Hague Journal on the Rule of Law* 195.

The change does not relate to the Rule of Law giving way. The idea of what it means to give way is common to many nations' driving conventions. For example, in Victoria in Australia, 'give way' is defined as meaning that a vehicle 'slow down and, if necessary, stop to avoid a collision'.[75] I do not suggest that there is going to be a collision between the Rule of Law and technology. What I do suggest – in particular in relation to the nature of the necessary change in the Rule of Law that this book explores in the final chapter – is that there is merely an adaptation of the Rule of Law to account for differing conditions. There is a change that reflects a response to changing circumstances that does not fundamentally change the project. This is nothing to do with needing to stop to avoid a collision but would be more akin to putting on snow chains/tyres as the road conditions have fundamentally altered.[76]

The shift by some to encompass the substantive view of the Present Rule of Law is of this kind. The problems that are being addressed by some of the Present Rule of Law thinkers relates to things like the failure for governments to act in order to satisfy basic human rights,[77] or the wide instantiation of instances of arbitrary power between individuals.[78] These things are of a different register to ideas associated with the Past Rule of Law problems relating to the exercise of absolute power or the totalitarian horrors of the second world war, for example.[79] This shift regarding positive and negative requirements of government can be seen – at least broadly – as analogous to the change between civil and political rights and instances of economic, cultural and social rights. In this sense, it is not the use or application of a new technology – per se – that means there must be a necessary change in the concept of the Rule of Law. But the acceptance and use of that technology – should that acceptance occur – may result in very different instances of the exercise of power. And it is the exercise of power that has been a common Rule of Law-thread from the Past to the Present.

On this basis, I suggest here that the Rule of Law has not given way but has, instead, changed *because of* another idea. The nature of that other idea has, between the Past and the Present, related to one thing – potentially the different demands placed on the exercisers of power – and this may occur again in the future when the environment in which the Rule of Law exists changed. I will return to this idea in the final chapter where I will come to the conclusion that there are substantial

[75] *Road Safety Road Rules 2017* Dictionary.

[76] This example does, of course, need to gloss over the fact that it is necessary to stop in order to put on snow chains. Nevertheless, hopefully objections to the driving example can be parked.

[77] T Bingham, *The Rule of Law* (London, Allen Lane, 2010); J King, '"Constitutional Boundaries" – The Social Dimension of the Rule of Law', *I·CONnect* (2018) www.iconnectblog.com/2018/04/i-connect-symposium-on-constitutional-boundaries-the-social-dimension-of-the-rule-of-law/.

[78] M Krygier, 'Four Puzzles About the Rule of Law: Why, What, Where? And Who Cares?' in J Flemming (ed), *Getting to the Rule of Law* (New York, New York University Press, 2011) 64; JA Sempill, 'The Lions and the Greatest Part: The Rule of Law and the Constitution of Employer Power' (2017) 9(2) *Hague Journal on the Rule of Law* 283.

[79] J Locke, *Two Treatises of Government*, P Laslett (ed), (Cambridge, Cambridge University Press, 1988); FA von Hayek, *The Constitution of Liberty* (Chicago, University of Chicago Press, 1960).

Rule of Law problems associated with the use of AI in exercising power in the ways contemplated in this book. For different reasons, notwithstanding the form or level of abstraction at which the Rule of Law is considered, where states seek to remain a Rule of Law-adherent state, there are fundamental reasons why AI cannot be used by states in exercising public power. In order to get to this conclusion, in the following three chapters, I bring together the ideas that have been raised most fundamentally across this chapter and the preceding chapter and I consider whether the Past and Present Rule of Law can provide protections against the forms of power that are described in the three hypotheticals introduced in this chapter.

4

The Rule of Law and the Use of AI in Administrative Decision-Making

As noted in the conclusion to the previous chapter, this chapter considers the first of the three hypothetical applications in terms of the Past and Present ideas of the Rule of Law. I consider whether – and how – the Rule of Law can curb the arbitrary exercise of power in circumstances where an AI is exercising administrative decision-making powers. I do this by considering a number of Rule of Law ideas across a range of levels of abstraction from the broad-brush idea of the Rule of Law to both the Past and the Present ideas of the concept. I conclude that, in circumstances where the power exercised by an AI posed in the hypothetical cannot be effectively explained, a Rule of Law state that adopts a Past Rule of Law conception cannot exercise power in this way if it seeks to remain a Rule of Law state. A similar conclusion is reached for the Present Rule of Law; however, as will be seen across the chapter, the nature of the problems that arise varies when the Rule of Law is considered at different levels of abstraction. These conclusions, and the ramifications of them, will be considered with the conclusions from the other hypotheticals in the final chapter of the book.

To arrive at these conclusions, and in order to consider as many different ideas of the Rule of Law as possible, I both use and also disaggregate aspects of the Past and Present ideas of the Rule of Law that I set out in Chapter 2. This does not mean that the aggregative approach is pointless. It is, in fact, essential for ensuring that as broad a range of ideas as possible is applied to the consideration of the hypotheticals. By adopting a view of the Rule of Law that considers the broadest idea of the concept, together with intermediate aggregations, as well as individual (disaggregated) conceptions, I conduct several levels of analysis near-simultaneously in order to address criticisms associated with cherry-picking only one or a few ideas where the Rule of Law is a contested concept. After I adopt a similar approach in the next two chapters, I bring together the various conclusions in the final chapter in order to consider what this means, collectively, for the Future Rule of Law.

It is possible to conduct an analysis based on the broad-brush strokes of the Past Rule of Law category – and this is exactly how I commence the consideration of the hypothetical. By looking at the Rule of Law in its broadest and most unobjectionable conception – as a concept that opposes that arbitrary application of power – I seek to identify the most abstract possible conclusions that would fit with both the Past and Present conceptions. However, this form of analysis can take us only so far. In order to make anything more than a superficial argument, a more nuanced consideration of the inability of the Rule of Law to provide protections against the exercise of power by AIs is necessary. For this reason, after considering the hypothetical in broad-brush terms, I consider increasingly nuanced ideas of the Rule of Law in each of the Past and Present ideas. In this way, the consideration of the hypothetical starts broadly and then progressively narrows – to each of the Past and Present ideas – before ending at the most nuanced consideration of particular thinkers' views. In other words, after taking a wide view of the hypothetical based on the Rule of Law most generally, I delve into some of the details by considering aspects of various conceptions within that category. By taking this approach, I hope to provide a clearer and more substantive thread to the overall argument.

The approach noted above means that the chapter adopts a simple structure. There are five substantive sections after these introductory comments. The first expands upon the hypothetical to fully frame the chapter. The second, considers the hypothetical in terms of the broad-brush idea of the Rule of Law. The third and fourth narrow the consideration of the hypothetical and consider the Past and Present ideas of the Rule of Law. The final section provides a summary and conclusion to the chapter and enables me to reflect on the relative impact of the Past Rule of Law being unable to protect against the exercise of power as contemplated in the hypotheticals.

This same approach and structure will be adopted for each of the chapters that focuses on each of the three hypotheticals. As the hypotheticals become more extreme, the issues raised scaffold and present different problematics but, wherever possible, I do not re-tread ground that has been dealt with in previous chapters. (This has the effect of making latter chapters somewhat shorter than this chapter.)

I. The Use of AI in Administrative Decision-Making

As will be recalled from the last chapter, the use of AI in administrative decision-making relates to using AI as a *tool* for humans to more effectively/efficiently make administrative decisions. Administrative decisions in modern western states represent a fundamental and common way in which individuals interact with the state. Administrative decisions in this book will be construed as occurring in circumstances where any form of decision is made by an agent acting on behalf of the state. Common examples of administrative decisions would be an entity or agency's decision to pay or not pay a kind of benefit, or whether to revoke a particular penalty or to confer a particular licence. For this reason, as expanded below, the hypothetical in this chapter will relate to a very common form of administrative decision: the decision as to whether, and in what circumstances, to issue a travel visa.

Administrative decisions can be subject to review. Further, the decision may not be made specifically by one individual – it may be a team that conducts an investigation or even conveys the message, but responsibility for the decision itself may rest with a particular person – for example, a minister of state. This hypothetical does not seek to change this. Whilst an AI will be seen as being integral to the gathering of information and coming to a conclusion, it will be the case that the ultimate entity responsible for the decision will remain an actual human. In this respect, the use of AI simply to assist in a process – as with using any technology as a tool – maintains a human-in-the-loop at all times.

Given the massive potential efficiencies that may accrue should technology of this sort be introduced, the scale and scope of AI's use in administrative decisions seems only likely to increase. AI's use in state-based decision-making has been the subject of considerable debate and discussion in recent years.[1] The rise in the number and scope of administrative decisions, and the potential of these decisions to contravene the Rule of Law, is not, however, a new phenomenon. As far back as the late nineteenth century, Dicey – as one of the Past Rule of Law usual suspects – feared the erosion of the Rule of Law in England because of the rise of administrative decision-making. His two most well-known Rule of Law desiderata relate to the need for legal equality and the need to avoid arbitrary decisions by government; but his third is a clear reflection of his fear of the rise of administrative decisions in England at that time. He said: 'the general principles of the constitution (as for example the right to personal liberty, or the right of public meeting) are with us the result of judicial decisions determining the rights of private persons in particular cases brought before the courts'.[2] As noted in chapter two, it is the Rule of Law's decline, and the accompanying rise in the welfare state that Dicey sees as a fundamental problem due to its erosion of the Rule of Law. The welfare and administrative state that currently exists in England – as well as administrative states in many other western democratic nations in which Dicey's Rule of Law may be seen to be relevant – has far exceeded the size of the administrative state that Dicey saw as being problematic for the Rule of Law. In this sense, it could be seen as an irreconcilable notion to apply his Rule of Law idea in the present day. This may be one reason why his third desiderata is less well-known and less frequently deployed than the other two which, absent the context of their authorship, may be seen to provide a 'cleaner' application to modern states without the relative incongruity that comes with the exponentially expanded administrative state in modern

[1] J Boughey and K Miller (eds), *The Automated State: Implications, Challenges and Opportunities for Public Law*, 1st edn (Alexandria, NSW, Federation Press 2021) federationpress.com.au/product/the-automated-state/; M Oswald, 'Algorithm-Assisted Decision-Making in the Public Sector: Framing the Issues Using Administrative Law Rules Governing Discretionary Power' (2018) 376(2128) *Philosophical Transactions of the Royal Society A: Mathematical, Physical and Engineering Sciences* 20170359; *Pintarich v Deputy Commissioner of Taxation* [2018] Cth Federal Court of Australia – Full Court 79.

[2] AV Dicey, *Introduction to the Study of the Law of the Constitution*, 10th edn (Basingstoke, Palgrave Macmillan, 1979) 195.

times.[3] Yet, what is clear is that there is a longstanding connection between the Rule of Law and administrative decisions.

To consider the broad-brush idea of the Past Rule of Law in relation to the use of AI in making administrative decisions I will put aside this incongruity – at least for the moment. Whilst I have set out this hypothetical in general terms, for ease of consideration I adopt a single form of example throughout this chapter. The intent in doing this is not to limit the discussion to *only* this form of administrative decision – as a sufficiently generalisable example has been selected that enables the comments made here to extend to any form of administrative decision. The example relates to the state's administrative decision to issue a travel visa.

As will be recalled, the issuance of a travel visa is a form of decision that is made millions of times per year even in small states like Australia.[4] In the US, in 2018 (to use a pre-pandemic figure), over nine million non-immigrant visas were issued.[5] These figures represent only the issued visas in only *one* visa class. In the same period, more than 3.5 million non-immigrant visa applications were refused – most of which were based on the assessment that the applicant had failed to establish an entitlement to non-immigrant status.[6] This means that in 2018, just in relation to the issue of this single visa class, more than 12.5 million decisions were made. This equates to more than 34,000 decisions being made per day. It is safe to say that this form of decision is very common both in terms of the number of decisions that need to be made and in terms of the fact that this sort of decision is made in states across the entire world. It is also common as it is a familiar decision-making process as it is a form of administrative decision that has impacted many of us at one time or another. For all of these reasons, it is an ideal candidate to use as an example of the application of AI.

Unsurprisingly, given the number of decisions that are required to be made in granting a visa, the suggestion that there should be some form of AI – or, at least, automated decision-making – in immigration is not new.[7] The use of any form of technology – even basic automated processes – does, however, seem to attract controversy.[8] The controversy and the issues raised often go to issues like accountability or the impact on justice.[9] Several different states have been

[3] P Burgess, 'The Rule of Lore in the Rule of Law: Putting the Problem of the Rule of Law in Context' (2020) 12 *Hague Journal on the Rule of Law* 333.

[4] Department of Home Affairs, *Department of Home Affairs 2021–22 Annual Report* (30 June 2022).

[5] US Department of State – Bureau of Consular Affairs, 'Visa Statistics': travel.state.gov/content/travel/en/legal/visa-law0/visa-statistics.html.

[6] ibid.

[7] A Beduschi, 'International Migration Management in the Age of Artificial Intelligence' (2021) 9(3) *Migration Studies* 576.

[8] 'Home Office under Fire for Using Secretive Visa Algorithm', *Financial Times* (9 June 2019); H McDonald, 'AI System for Granting UK Visas Is Biased, Rights Groups Claim', *The Guardian* (online, 29 October 2019) www.theguardian.com/uk-news/2019/oct/29/ai-system-for-granting-uk-visas-is-biased-rights-groups-claim.

[9] F Gualdi and A Cordella, *Artificial Intelligence and Decision-Making: The Question of Accountability* (2021) hdl.handle.net/10125/70894; J McLean and R Mackenzie, 'Digital Justice in Australian Visa Application Processes?' (2019) 44(4) *Alternative Law Journal* 291.

exploring the use of technology to make the immigration process more efficient. A recent report from the European Migration Network – an organisation within the EU – includes the suggestion that:

> Six EU Member States and most non-EU OECD countries currently use AI for migration management, including for language identification and assessment; for detecting identity document fraud; for case management; and for interacting with clients. In addition, 10 EU Member States and Georgia are implementing pilot projects, or planning initiatives to use AI for, inter alia, chatbots, migration forecasting and tracing document fraud.[10]

This statement and the remainder of that report does include reference to the use of AI in relation to some aspects of immigration management – in particular relating to asylum seekers or in relation to the use of AI for facial recognition at borders to verify identities. It does not include the suggestion that AI is being used specifically to make decisions regarding the issue of a visa in a particular circumstance. But especially where algorithmic decision-making approaches are already adopted in places like Canada, it seems to only be a matter of time before AI's potential to provide efficiencies in managing migration will mean that this form of administrative decision is made or, at least, heavily assisted, by an AI system.[11]

The basic process of issuing a visa – as with many forms of administrative decision-making – does lend itself to automated decisions. At a basic level the most popular reason for the rejection of visa applications in America – the applicant had failed to establish an entitlement to non-immigrant status[12] – could be imagined to be reduced to a form of algorithmic conditional: *if the applicant has not evidenced [condition a], [condition b], and [condition c], then they have failed to establish an entitlement to non-immigrant status.* Setting out the algorithmic conditional in this way would mean applicants that fail to establish the necessary conditions can be immediately rejected. Those that do establish the necessary conditions may ultimately be rejected for another reason (and this decision may be made by another algorithmic conditional or by a human). This would not be an application of AI – but would be an instance of automated decision-making. A process like this could be used as a form of triage for a human agent to then review applications that pass this first hurdle requirement. This already occurs in places like Australia, Canada, Chile, New Zealand, Turkey and the UK.[13] The application of AI that is to be considered in this hypothetical goes beyond this processed-based form of automated decision making by way of an algorithmic conditional.

Recall from chapter three the definition of AI that I have adopted for the purpose of this book: AI includes any machine that acts intelligently – as one

[10] European Migration Network, *The Use of Digitalisation and Artificial Intelligence in Migration Management: Joint EMN-OECD Inform. Brussels: European Migration Network.* (February 2022) www.oecd.org/migration/mig/EMN-OECD-INFORM-FEB-2022-The-use-of-Digitalisation-and-AI-in-Migration-Management.pdf.

[11] Beduschi (n 7).

[12] US Department of State – Bureau of Consular Affairs (n 5).

[13] European Migration Network (n 10).

that can make correct decisions in a given circumstance.[14] This means that the parameters of the decision-making are not set in a rigid form as in the example of the algorithmic conditional set out above. The AI system may answer a question about an applicant's entitlement to non-immigrant status or the issuance of the visa by going *beyond* the simple criteria of [condition a], [condition b], and [condition c]. In saying this, the suggestion is not that the AI system is creating its own laws or policy – only that it may find and apply, for example, an exception that applies that enables a visa to be issued in circumstances where only one of the conditions is satisfied. This may be the sort of evaluative check or additional step process that would, outside of the automated process, have been carried out by the human agent. In this sense, the form of AI system that is imagined in this hypothetical would be one that has been tasked to simply determine whether a visa should be issued to a particular person and, in consequence of being given this task, is using all of the data available to it – both about the applicant as well as the relevant policies or laws – in order to come to a correct decision in that circumstance.

The remainder of this chapter will answer a simple question: what, then, is the Rule of Law's problem with the AI system operating in this way? By considering, first, the most abstract idea of the concept before considering the Past and Present ideas of the Rule of Law, the conclusion I draw – that administrative decision making by an AI contravenes the Rule of Law – can be seen across the may broadly accepted conceptions of the concept as well as across varying levels of abstraction.

II. The (Broad-Brush) Rule of Law

The Rule of Law, in its most uncontroversial state, reflects a concept that is opposed to the arbitrary application of power. Anywhere beyond this broad-brush level of abstraction differences arise. The Past Rule of Law would see the locus of the arbitrary power as being the state; however, some Present Rule of Law conceptions do not limit the locus to the state and see the concept as being about arbitrary power wherever that source may lie. Accordingly, even the broad-brush approach to the Rule of Law described in this section can be augmented with some nuance.

An immediate reaction to idea that the Past Rule of Law prevents the arbitrary exercise of power through imposing procedural requirements on the law-making process may simply be that the hypothetical does not relate to the *making* of laws. This would mean that this idea of the Past Rule of Law would have no relevance

[14] For weak AI see Y LeCun, Y Bengio and G Hinton, 'Deep Learning' (2015) 521(7553) *Nature* 436. For strong AI see W Naudé and N Dimitri, 'The Race for an Artificial General Intelligence: Implications for Public Policy' (2020) 35(2) *AI & Society* 367, 367–68. Y Hermstrüwer, 'Artificial Intelligence and Administrative Decisions Under Uncertainty' in T Wischmeyer and T Rademacher (eds), *Regulating Artificial Intelligence* (Cham, Springer International Publishing, 2020) 199, 201: doi.org/10.1007/978-3-030-32361-5_9.

to this hypothetical. After all, it is by limiting the *way* in which laws are made that the Past Rule of Law seeks to limit the arbitrary application of power by the state. Whilst the decision-maker's decision will have a real and tangible impact on the subject of the decision, their decision does not *create* new law. In this sense, it remains the case that it is difficult to conceive of how constraints on the way that laws are being made would be a Rule of Law concern. However, in the broadest statement of what the Rule of Law does – which is to limit the arbitrary application of power – and where there does appear to be an application of state power in the hypothetical situation in which an AI makes a determination regarding a visa (or any other administrative decision), it seems that there should be *some* relation to the Rule of Law. Accordingly, I do not want to simply dismiss the potential application of the Rule of Law without consideration of how there may be some relevance.

If the broad-brush idea of the Rule of Law is that it opposes the arbitrary application of power, and the hypothetical relates to the application of state power, then (at least for this sub-section) the hypothetical does relate to the Rule of Law. In this functional sense, the concept itself seems to be enlivened, but without more it is difficult to get beyond a statement that simply suggests both that the concept is relevant, and it would oppose the arbitrary application of power. Here, the *function* of the Rule of Law is evident from the broad-brush description. In considering the Present Rule of Law in the next section, particularly in considering Martin Krygier's views, a purposive approach to the Rule of Law will be considered in more detail. I differentiate that discussion relating to *purpose* from this one by adopting the term *function* although both stem from a common position that both ideas relate to the Rule of Law being seen as a concept that opposes the arbitrary application of power – although, crucially, in Krygier's teleological view it does not only relate to the exercise of power by the state.[15]

We can, then, consider the function of the Rule of Law, in the broad-brush sense as being to limit the arbitrariness application of state power. This does conform with the tenets of the Past Rule of Law. The question then becomes one related to whether the application of power is arbitrary. Even at this stage of the book, there has been scant exploration of the meaning of arbitrariness. In a technical legal/political theoretical sense, a dictionary definition would be of little assistance. But, in the context of this examination in which an aggregated approach is taken to the idea of the Rule of Law, an idea about what may constitute arbitrariness for the Past Rule of Law theorists may be seen reflected in the common goals that each of the usual suspects sought to pursue.

If we consider this broadest idea of the concept – as a concept that opposes the arbitrary application of power – the question in this section is whether the use of AI in making administrative decisions is itself arbitrary. In a more particular

[15] M Krygier, 'The Rule of Law: Legality, Teleology and Sociology' in G Palombella and N Walker (eds), *Relocating the Rule of Law* (Oxford, Hart Publishing, 2009).

sense, the consideration could be put in terms of the comparison with the current non-AI-based form of administrative decision-making: is the use of AI in making administrative decisions *more* arbitrary than the current form? At this most abstract level, it seems that the consideration of a non-dystopian form of AI does not necessarily lead to arbitrary outcomes. But, as will be seen when less-abstract ideas are considered in the following sections, there are fundamental problems with the technology being imagined that may render decisions arbitrary and, hence, contrary to the Rule of Law. I will not dwell on the ideas here, as they are better explained in more depth in the less abstract accounts that follow, but it will become clear, for example, that a failure to be able to explain decisions – in a way that a human may be able to do so – will represent a fundamental Rule of Law problem for the use of an AI to make administrative decisions.

III. The Past Rule of Law

The conceptions that make up the Past Rule of Law relate to the state-centric (public) arbitrary exercise of power. The usual suspects that make up this category each provide thin/formal solutions to this problem;[16] to provide a check on the arbitrary exercise of power by the state, they each suggest procedural steps that limit and constrain the way in which laws are made. In this sense, as will be recalled from chapter two, the Past Rule of Law provides a particular form of opposition to a particular form of arbitrary power. It is an aggregated idea of the Rule of Law that is constituted from a group of thinkers I describe as usual suspects of the Rule of Law.[17] I have not formed this group simply for the purpose of this book or for my argument. The list reflects a group of thinkers that are frequently deployed when attempts are made to define the Rule of Law;[18] their names and conceptions will be well known to anyone that has considered the content and meaning of the Rule of Law in any depth. The thinkers that make up this category are: Aristotle; Locke; Dicey; Hayek; Fuller; and, Raz. They are aggregated under a banner of the *Past* of the Rule of Law not because their ideas have been superseded in the present – although, the authors of Present Rule of Law ideas and their supporters would, of course, suggest otherwise – but simply because the usual suspects' conceptions that are deployed for the purpose of illustrating the content of the Rule of Law were all authored more than four decades ago. In no way should the 'past' aspect be taken to be a pejorative or as an indicator of something *better* now existing; the Past and Present monikers are purely a descriptive shorthand.

[16] P Craig, 'Formal and Substantive Conceptions of the Rule of Raw an Analytical Framework' [1997] (Autumn) *Public Law* 467.

[17] P Burgess, 'Neglecting the History of the Rule of Law: (Unintended) Conceptual Eugenics' (2017) 9(2) *Hague Journal on the Rule of Law* 195.

[18] Burgess (n 3).

In addition to this very general way in which the usual suspects' account can be aggregated, similarity can also be seen in terms of the individual desiderata or elements of the conceptions. For example, the ideas of predictability and procedural clarity could be seen to be core elements of the legislative process across the usual suspects' conceptions.[19] These ideas can be seen to represent common goals across the accounts of the usual suspects. Across the following sub-sections I move from the broad to narrow assessments of the issues raised in the hypothetical. I first use the elemental ideas as a mid-way point between the general idea of the Rule of Law explained above to consider the hypothetical's implications. Then, to take an even more nuanced view, I assess individual usual suspect's conceptions.

A. Past Rule of Law Elements

These common elements of the Rule of Law exist across the usual suspects accounts that make up the Past Rule of Law. These are the requirements for predictability and procedural clarity.[20] These ideas are evident across the usual suspects' accounts as they can be conceived as what I have described before as a 'need behind the need' inherent in Rule of Law conceptions.[21] What is meant by this is that the various Past Rule of Law thinkers are aiming to achieve these things – sometimes through stating or listing numerous other desiderata – on the way to avoiding the arbitrary application of power. In other words, there are numerous levels of abstraction. At the most abstract level, all seek to avoid the arbitrary application of power – this is a universally agreed idea amongst the thinkers. At the least abstract level, there are various desiderata or requirements that each thinker states as being important (in preventing the arbitrary application of power) – there is an evident and recognised contest between the usual suspects as to these desiderata. In between the two are the two elements that – as generalised statements that reflect what the thinkers seek to attain through the desiderata – are common across the thinkers.

Predictability is the desiderata most conspicuously held in common across the various usual suspects' conceptions. It is specifically named in several conceptions – for example, in Locke's, Fuller's and Raz's ideas – and it provides the fundamental principle on which Hayek's conception is built.[22] It can be seen to reflect the idea that action by the state must be predictable in order to avoid being arbitrary. In terms of this chapter's hypothetical, this would require that the

[19] P Burgess, 'The Rule of Law: Beyond Contestedness' (2017) 8(3) *Jurisprudence* 480.

[20] ibid.

[21] ibid.

[22] J Locke, *Two Treatises of Government*, P Laslett (ed), (Cambridge, Cambridge University Press, 1988); LL Fuller, *The Morality of Law* (New Haven, Yale University Press, 1964); J Raz, 'The Rule of Law and Its Virtue' in *The Authority of Law: Essays on Law and Morality*, 2nd edn (Oxford, Oxford University Press 2009) 210; FA von Hayek, *The Road to Serfdom*, B Caldwell (ed), (Chicago, University of Chicago Press, 2007) 112; FA von Hayek, *The Constitution of Liberty: The Definitive Edition* (London, Routledge, 2011) 210.

use of AI in making decisions about an applicant's eligibility for a visa would need to apply the relevant laws in a way that is predictable. This raises and relates to one of the most obvious problems associated with the use of AI: explainability. As noted in chapter three, the relative black-box of any complex AI's decision-making means that explainability is, at best, a hard to achieve standard; the way in which some decisions are made by an AI may not be possible to see or even describe.[23]

A lack of explainability would result in the absence of predictability. The element of predictability in this situation may require, for example, that the AI is arriving at the decision through an application of the law and not through some other pattern in the data related to applicants. It is conceivable that an AI could identify a pattern that allows it to come to a conclusion regarding the eligibility of applicants that is not based on the application of the law – but where the *outcome* of that non-law-based decision-making process is practically indistinguishable. To give a very basic and unsophisticated example, an AI may have been trained on data in which all 20 applicants named 'Paul' from Wales are rejected for a visa. The reason for the rejection was that they all failed to satisfy some other criteria related to the relevant law; but, the AI treats the name and geographical region as being determinative of an outcome. The 21st Welsh Paul is then rejected by the AI *because* of these two factors and not in consequence of the fact that he also fails to satisfy the legal criteria. If the AI's decision-making process is not explainable, even though the *outcome* is correct, and is made for the wrong reasons, this represents unpredictability. (If the 22nd Welsh Paul does satisfy all legal criteria, but is still rejected, this could be seen as being *more* obviously unpredictable.)

It is a need for *predictability in the application of power* that underlies the common element of predictability in the Rule of Law. As long as there is an element of un-explainability in the use of an AI algorithm, the element of predictability will be difficult to satisfy; there will always be some prospect that a decision is being made in the wrong way and is, therefore, unpredictable. Because of its central importance to the concept of the Rule of Law, I will consider predictability more in both the next subsection and the next sections, as well as in the next chapters.

Procedural clarity is the other common element across Past conceptions of the Rule of Law.[24] This element relates directly to the procedural ideas relating to law making noted earlier. However, it could also be seen to relate to the decision-making process itself. When viewed in this way there is a need for decisions to be made in the right way. The problems related to the explainability of an AI's decision-making explored immediately above can then be seen to be a problem for the Rule of Law. If there is an inability for the decision-making process to be explained, it is hard to conceive of that process as being clear.

[23] F Pasquale, *The Black Box Society: The Secret Algorithms That Control Money and Information* (Cambridge, Mass, Harvard University Press, Reprint edition, 2016).

[24] Burgess (n 19).

In considering the broad-brush approach to the Past Rule of Law – both in terms of the Rule of Law's general opposition to the arbitrary exercise of power by the state and in terms of elements of predictability and procedural clarity that are common across Past Rule of Law conceptions – the use of AI in administrative decision-making presents significant problems. This has been illustrated through considering the example of using an AI to make decisions regarding the issuance of a visa; however, it will also be clear that the discussion above is not exclusive to that sphere of operation. In circumstances where the fundamental problem stems from the fact that the current state of AI technology is plagued by an inability to explain the exact processes by which an AI comes to its decisions, satisfaction of the Rule of Law in an AI making these decisions appears to be impossible.

Two further questions stem from this conclusion. The first relates to whether the absence of explainability in an AI's decision-making is any worse (or better) than the relative inability to properly identify a human's decision-making process. The second relates to how the conclusion may be different in circumstances where an AI's decision-making *is* able to be explained. I deal briefly with each in turn.

I have previously considered the differences that may be seen between an AI's decision-making and a human's in the context of the Rule of Law.[25] In that consideration, in caveating away many of the technical realities associated with the use of AI, I argued that the use of AI in relation to law-making may be Rule of Law-positive. As part of that argument, I also explored the idea that human decision-making is far from transparent. There is reason to believe that, even in the absence of a conscious un-truth, humans may not be able to communicate the actual reasoning behind their decision.[26] In this circumstance, where AI's have problems associated with explainability in their decision-making processes, the question may be seen as a relative one: should an AI or a human decision-maker be preferred?

One way to answer this question is to acknowledge that there may be something inherently human about humans making decisions that impact humans. (Arguments in these terms – that will be returned to in detail later in this chapter – have been made in relation to the judicial decision-making process.[27]) A thought experiment may reveal this intuitive preference. If all other things are equal – relating to the accuracy, process followed, speed, appealability, etc of decision-making – my preference may be for a *human* to make decisions relating to me. However, as soon as all other things are not equal, this intuitive position shifts into one that may be more closely related to particular preferences. Where all

[25] P Burgess, 'Algorithmic Augmentation of Democracy: Considering Whether Technology Can Enhance the Concepts of Democracy and the Rule of Law Through Four Hypotheticals' [2021] *AI & Society*.

[26] T Miller, 'Explanation in Artificial Intelligence: Insights from the Social Sciences' (2019) 267 *Artificial Intelligence* 1.

[27] J Boughey et al (eds), 'Public Law Limits on Automated Courts' in *The Automated State: Implications, Challenges and Opportunities for Public Law*, 1st edn (Alexandria, NSW, Federation Press, 2021) federationpress.com.au/product/the-automated-state/.

other things may be equal, I may be inclined to prefer the form of decision-maker that better meets a particular preference. For example, if an AI's decision is non-appealable, I would likely prefer the human; or, if the AI's decision was faster, but all other factors were the same, and time is of the essence for me, I would likely prefer the AI. It is, however, also conceivable that, for certain people there may be a preference for an AI decision-maker due to a perception of bias in human decision makers. Notwithstanding the controversies – and currently very real issues – related to inherent bias in artificial intelligences, in certain circumstances a machine may be more trusted to make an impartial decision.[28]

What we can draw from this is that in considering whether an AI or a human decision-maker be preferred, there are any number of potential and real issues that exist in relation to artificial intelligences making decisions that relate to the exercise of power. There are also any number of ways that could render those decisions as being arbitrary. Yet, there are also various ways in which an AI making decisions may be preferable. With regard to the wider question – of whether the absence of explainability in an AI's decision-making is any worse (or better) than the relative inability to properly identify a human's decision-making process – the answer, where it is *currently* not possible to see behind a complex decision-making process made by an AI, is that this does impact the relative arbitrariness of the decision.

For this reason, I turn to the second question posed earlier: would the conclusion – that the inability of an AI to explain its decision-making means it cannot satisfy ideas of the Past Rule of Law – be different if the AI could explain its decision-making? As stated on several occasions, this book is not an exercise in science-fiction – but it is future-facing. In this respect, whilst the technology does not yet exist, it is important to consider the potential of a machine that *can* explain its decisions. This consideration goes beyond the relative terms of merely weighing the potential for a machine to be *more* explainable than a human decision-maker. Instead, the consideration is whether an (explainable) AI's explanation could satisfy the Past Rule of Law. It is this approach that I will adopt for the remainder of this sub-section and the next.

The question relating to the (broad-brush) Past Rule of Law's relation to the hypothetical can now be properly considered. In other words, does the function of the Rule of Law – reflected in the elements of the Rule of Law detailed above – limit the arbitrariness application of state power when an AI makes legislative decisions that *are* explainable? In terms of the common element of predictability, the relative explainability of an AI's decision-making (as with a human's) *does* aid predictability. If the rationale behind prior decisions can be clearly stated and seen, this can indicate how future decisions will be made. If it is assumed that a similar rationale would be applied in the future – as no change is made to the AI's underlying programming – the explainability of a prior decision will enable a *stronger* form of prediction relating to future decisions.

[28] JM Logg, JA Minson and DA Moore, 'Algorithm Appreciation: People Prefer Algorithmic to Human Judgment' (2019) 151 *Organizational Behavior and Human Decision Processes* 90.

Predictability may also be enhanced in this hypothetical particularly as the relative explainability of an AI's decision will enable the process of decision-making to be seen and be confirmed as being accurate and appropriate. There are two ways in which an administrative decision can be reviewed. The first is a merits review and the second is a judicial review. A merits review involves a reconsideration of the facts and the law that undergirded an original administrative decision. Unlike a merits review, a judicial review does not consider the merits of the decision. A judicial review considers whether a prior administrative decision was reasonable and fair and was made within the legal limits of the power that the decision-maker held.

The nature of a merits review as a reconsideration of the matter in a way that means the decision may be made anew, makes it potentially *less* vital that the prior decision is predictable (in consequence of its explainability). However, it is very clear that in a judicial review the relative explainability of a decision would be crucial in identifying whether the decision was made within the limits of the powers that the decision-maker held. Earlier in this chapter, I set out the difference between automated decision-making and an AI's decision-making. There, I pointed out that, for an AI, the parameters of the decision-making are not as rigid form as in automated decision-making. This means it becomes crucial to ensure that an AI's decisions are being made in accordance with the appropriate criteria and in accordance with the appropriate laws. If the AI in this hypothetical made a decision regarding a visa application that took into account only spurious correlations that it had identified in the data and not in consequence of the requirements of the relevant law, that would make the decision clearly arbitrary, clearly unpredictable, and clearly liable to a successful judicial review process associated with that administrative decision. In these respects, the relative explainability of the decision is crucial in adhering to ideas associated with the Rule of Law. A very similar conclusion follows when the other element of the Rule of Law – procedural clarity – is considered in terms of an explainable AI's decision. In fact, the connection here could be seen to be even clearer. This element reflects the idea that the *way* in which a decision is been made is crucial. This clearly relates to the need for an AI to be able to explain its decision-making. If it cannot, the element of procedural clarity cannot be satisfied meaning that any decision would be arbitrary and liable to a review.

This does not address the issue of whether the relative explainability of an AI's decision would, of itself, satisfy these two elements of the Rule of Law. And, further, if it would satisfy those two elements, whether there are any other broad-brush Rule of Law objections that may still arise. In addressing the first, there must here be some relative consideration. Whilst it seems inherently to be the case that an AI's decision-making could be arbitrary for any number of reasons even if its decisions are explainable, that would seem to require some form of AI-malice or intent to deceive or make the decisions for the wrong reasons. Yet, the attachment of these sorts of positions to an AI – that is functioning as it should – is not easy. (This caveat is important as instances of AI systems being inadvertently taught, and as a result adopting, traits that are undesirable – for example racist or bigoted ways of making decisions – have been prevalent in the past.[29]) Unlike humans, strict boundaries relating to operating protocols exist for machines that cannot be avoided – or, if they are, and if the system is able to provide an explanation relating to its decisions, it may be more apparent that malice or ill will (and, hence, arbitrariness) is occurring.

What I have illustrated across this sub-section is that considerations of the broad-brush ideas of the Rule of Law – as a general anti-arbitrariness idea or in considering the two elements that can be identified across the Rule's usual suspects' conceptions – illustrate that where an AI is unable to explain its decision-making, its decisions would be rendered contrary to each of these elements of the Rule of Law. In this regard, it becomes difficult to see how the AI's decisions would avoid being seen as arbitrary. This picture does, however, alter somewhat if a future-facing hypothetical is considered in relation to an AI making a decision in circumstances where it *could* explain its decision. Whilst this would not obviate all aspects of conceivable arbitrariness, the potential for an AI to explain its decisions may facilitate predictability and procedural certainty as the two elements of the Rule of Law. (I return to this possibility in the final chapter.) As will be seen, this relative conformity with the function of the Rule of Law only where decisions can be explained remains a feature when a more nuanced approach to the Rule of Law is adopted as well as in the other hypotheticals.

B. Past Rule of Law's Thinkers and Hypothetical One

The first two chapters of this book illustrate the breadth of conceptual (and temporal) space covered by the Rule of Law's usual suspects that make up the Past Rule of Law. Over more than two millennia, their conceptions relating to the need, rationale, and processes associated with the limitation of the application of arbitrary power has differed considerably. When this breadth is considered, any conclusions made in relation to broad-brush ideas of the Rule of Law – or even the elemental approach adopted in the previous sub-section – may be criticised because of their generality. For this reason, this sub-section will highlight some key considerations that would arise when the Past Rule of Law thinkers are considered in terms of this hypothetical.

I do not consider all of the usual suspects in equal detail in this sub-section. Instead, I raise and explore in detail only those that take the consideration of this hypothetical any further. This means most time is spent discussing Dicey, Hayek, and Raz. (By curious coincidence, these are the only three usual suspects that apply and use the term 'the Rule of Law' in their work.) The other usual suspects are of

[29] C Sandvig et al, 'When the Algorithm Itself Is a Racist: Diagnosing Ethical Harm in the Basic Components of Software' (2016) 10 *International Journal of Communication* 4972.

less immediate relevance to this hypothetical. Accordingly, I only briefly touch on them here. (They are, however, not ignored. They are explored in the other hypotheticals in more detail.)

The broad reason that Aristotle, Locke, and Fuller are less relevant to this hypothetical is because their Rule of Law ideas more directly relate to the process of law-*making* in the legislative branch. (For this reason, they are prominently discussed in relation to the third hypothetical.) It is not as easy, for example, to consider Aristotle's Rule of Law ideas associated with the need for slower *legislative* processes in terms of *administrative* decisions.[30] Similarly, Locke was arguing that parliamentary rule should be preferred to royal (or papal) rule. The predictability that he set out as a requirement in the *Two Treatises* is also related to the *law-making* function. Whilst Locke's references to 'absolute arbitrary power', 'established and promulgated laws', 'declared and received laws', 'stated rules' and 'settled standing laws' could be seen to relate to the form of administrative decision-making referred to in this hypothetical, these points are made in the context where 'the legislative, or supream authority, cannot assume to its self a power to rule by extemporary arbitrary decree, but is bound to dispense *justice*, and decide the rights of the subject by *promulgated standing laws, and known authoris'd* judges'.[31] The context of his comments, accordingly, relate more particularly to the legislative processes considered in the next hypotheticals.

Fuller's Rule of Law ideas also are in a similar category. His allegory of King Rex relates fundamentally to the *making* of laws. It is, however, true that Fuller does relate some aspect of his thought to the administration of the laws that have been made. He states '[t]he internal morality of the law demands that there be rules, that they be made known, and that they be observed in practice by those charged with their administration.'[32] Yet, this discussion relates to the idea of legality in a chapter related to the substantive aims of law. These ideas did not form a direct part of the eight ways King Rex failed to make law – which are now taken to reflect Rule of Law ideas – raised two chapters earlier in his book. It is also clear that Fuller was *interested* in the administration of laws themselves – something that is clear in his suggestion that 'a retroactive law is truly a monstrosity. Law has to do with governance of human conduct by rules'.[33] But, the ideas that we take to relate to Fuller's conception of the Rule of Law – encompassed by his eight desiderata: generality; publicity (through promulgation); prospectivity (or, at least, non-retrospectivity); intelligibility; consistency; practicability; stability; and congruence – reflect criteria in the *making* of laws.[34] This is put in terms related to the law-maker that is described by Fuller as a 'craftsman'.[35] It is most starkly

[30] Aristotle, *Rhetoric*, trans W Rhys Roberts (Dover, 2004) 1, Ch 1.
[31] Locke (n 22) II, 137. (Emphasis in the original.).
[32] Fuller (n 22) 157.
[33] ibid 53.
[34] ibid 38–39.
[35] ibid 43.

illustrated in the section title in which the extended allegory of King Rex is introduced 'Eight Ways to Fail to Make Law'.[36] For these reasons, application of Fuller's Rule of Law ideas most keenly fits in the second hypothetical.

Of the Past Rule of Law thinkers, Dicey's conception most immediately relates to this hypothetical and the function of administrative decision-making that it raises. Dicey saw the Rule of Law as being under direct threat from the rise in administrative decision-making that was taking place in nineteenth-century England. His concern related to administrative decision-making that impacted individuals' rights and duties and that this was occurring outside of the court system. This is clear from Dicey's first aspect of the Rule of Law that requires 'that no man is punishable or can be lawfully made to suffer in body or goods except for a distinct breach of law established *in the ordinary legal manner before the ordinary courts of the land*.'[37] Equally relevant is Dicey's second aspect of the Rule of Law that requires 'every man, whatever be his rank or condition, is subject to the ordinary law of the realm and amenable to the jurisdiction of the *ordinary tribunals*.'[38] In the sentence immediately following, Dicey clarifies the meaning of 'tribunals' by stating 'In England the idea of legal equality, or of the universal subjection of all classes to one law administered by the ordinary courts, has been pushed to its utmost limit.'[39] Dicey's third Rule of Law aspect is that 'the general principles of the constitution (as for example the right to personal liberty, or the right of public meeting) are with us the result of judicial decisions determining the rights of private persons in particular cases brought before the courts'.[40]

This makes it clear that Dicey feared these other forms of decision-making where decisions were being made outside of the appropriate (Rule of Law–supporting) venue: the courts.[41] Accordingly, whilst the broad idea of the first two of Dicey's Rule of Law aspects could be seen to relate to making laws, consideration of them in conjunction with the third aspect, and in the context in which they are authored as a solution to a problem regarding the expansion of the administrative state, demonstrates the relevance to this hypothetical that is centred on administrative decision-making.[42] In the widest sense, where Dicey saw an increase in the role played by administrative decisions that impacted individuals' rights as being problematic for the Rule of Law, there seems to be little doubt that the use of AI to expedite administrative decision-making processes (outside of the courts) would also be seen as problematic. The hypothetical considered here relates to an AI system making administrative decisions in circumstances where the AI can

[36] ibid 33.
[37] Dicey (n 2) 188 (emphasis added).
[38] ibid 193 (emphasis added).
[39] ibid.
[40] ibid 195.
[41] BZ Tamanaha, *On the Rule of Law History, Politics, Theory* (Cambridge, Cambridge University Press, 2004) 63–65.
[42] P Burgess, 'Deriving the International Rule of Law: An Unnecessary, Impractical and Unhelpful Exercise' (2019) 10(1) *Transnational Legal Theory* 65, 82.

make the decisions more efficiently than a human. Those decisions relate, directly, to individual rights as, in the example give above, the grant of a visa to enter a state is at stake. Accordingly, when the broad context and nature of Dicey's conception of the Rule of Law is concerned, it seems that the use of AI in this way would see the potential for an erosion of the Rule of Law.

A more nuanced consideration of Dicey's three aspects reveals a similar, but not so stark, conclusion. As noted above, Dicey's first two aspects relate to the need for legal equality among subject and for the absence of arbitrary decisions. Equality in this sense relates to all individuals being subjected to the same rules. There appears to be no fundamental issue in the use of an AI in this aspect. Whilst an initial response may be related to the fact that an individual that is subject to an AI's decision-making may have a decision made in a slightly different or a faster/slower way, this seems unlikely to be different to the relative difference that already exists between human decision-makers; further, the aspect of equality that Dicey reflects does not relate to *outcome* but, instead, one related to the relative rules that apply to individuals. In this regard, as long as the rules that the AI applies are the same as the rules that are applied by human decision-makers, then there is no difference.

This point returns us to the position explored in the previous sub-section; whether the *way* in which an AI has made a decision can be fully known. In other words, is the decision explainable. This point also relates closely to the final aspect of Dicey's Rule of Law: the application of rules should not be arbitrary. As noted in the previous sub-section, in circumstances where the underlying rationale behind a decision cannot be known, there are considerable problems of arbitrariness. This relates to the failure to be able to know what rules have been applied. An AI system that cannot explain its decisions would result in arbitrary decisions that may also be being made in a way that does not satisfy legal equality. This would represent, in Dicey's view, a fundamental threat to the Rule of Law.

What, then, would be the Diceyean position where an AI responsible for making an administrative decision *can* explain its decision-making process? The fundamental objection noted above – that administrative decisions are being made outside of a court – would, of course, subsist. This general objection to administrative decision-making pervades any application of Dicey's idea to an AI making administrative decisions; however, where Dicey remains a usual suspect of the Rule of Law – due to his frequent invocation as a thinker that effectively describes what the Rule of Law *is* – it is clear that Dicey's idea of the Rule of Law remains relevant despite the exponential increase in the number of administrative decisions made in any given state. For this reason, it is useful to push beyond this general objection to consider the Diceyean position regarding an AI making administrative decisions where it can explain its decision-making process.

If a decision can be explained, this alone does not necessarily mean the decision would *not* be arbitrarily made, but at least any instance of arbitrariness could be identified. For example, returning to the visa example, if a visa is denied on the basis of a spurious rationale (that does not involve the proper application of the relevant rules) – and that can be seen in the explanation provided – then a subsequent appeal may be launched, and the relevant decision-making protocol could be changed within the AI system. This process will mean that in the longer term, arbitrary decision-making may be whittled away and, eventually, avoided. At this point, excluding the fundamental objection noted above, the Diceyean conception of the Rule of Law, in relation to arbitrary decisions, would have little objection to this form of decision-making. A similar conclusion, for similar reasons, would result in consideration of the other Diceyean aspect of legal equality; if the decision-making can be seen to follow the same process as human decision-makers, there is no perceivable difference in how individual's rights are treated and, hence, the Diceyean standard would be satisfied.

What can be seen for Dicey, as with the more general consideration of the Rule of Law, is that the fundamental basis on which the ability of the Rule of Law to provide some level of protection from arbitrary decision-making relates to the AI's ability to explain its decisions. As will be seen, similar concerns also exist in relation to the other Past Rule of Law thinkers – Hayek and also Raz – as well as with the other accounts in the other hypotheticals.

As will be apparent from chapter two, FA Hayek's contribution to the concept of the Rule of Law is most easily paraphrased as requiring predictability in the creation of legislation in order that subjects of the law can plan and avoid coercion.[43] Hayek did change certain aspects of his view of the Rule of Law over time, but his view regarding the essentiality and broad importance of predictability remained constant.[44] Hayek suggests succinctly that government:

> … is bound by rules fixed and announced beforehand rules which make it possible to foresee with fair certainty how the authority will use its coercive powers in given circumstances and to plan one's individual affairs on the basis of this knowledge.[45]

This quote has been cemented as the core of Hayek's thesis – not only through the longevity of this aspect of his view (over several decades of writing), but also as it was with an extract of a similar passage that Raz framed his own expression of the concept.[46] If this need to avoid predictability is considered to be representative of Hayek's view, how would Hayek respond to the hypothetical situation where AI is used to assist in a process of administrative decision-making?

As hinted at, there is little to distinguish the broad aims of the Hayekian desire for predictability from the Diceyean desire for predictability. Both thinkers seek to limit the imposition of government control over the subjects of the laws; both require a procedural check relating to the way that laws should be made – or, at

[43] Hayek, *The Road to Serfdom* (n 22) 114; Hayek, *The Constitution of Liberty: The Definitive Edition* (n 22) 210.

[44] FA von Hayek, *Law, Legislation and Liberty: A New Statement of the Liberal Principles of Justice and Political Economy*, 1st edn (London, Routledge, 1982) 115–18.

[45] Hayek, *The Road to Serfdom* (n 22) 112.

[46] Raz (n 22) 210.

least, relating to the nature of the area of effect that the laws may have (in Hayek's desire to prevent unavoidable coercion through laws that cannot be predicted ahead of time). For this reason, all of the conclusions drawn relating to Dicey above also hold in relation to Hayek. In other words, there would be a need for any decisions made to be able to be explained by the AI as this would be the only way that future decisions may be rendered predictable and, in consequence, it is only through being able to understand those decisions that an individual can then plan around them and avoid being coerced.

Joseph Raz does, as noted above, refer to Hayek's view of the Rule of Law in stating his own. Whilst he describes that view as 'one of the clearest and most powerful formulations of the ideal of the rule of law',[47] he merely uses Hayek's idea to springboard into his own conception. This requires, at the most general level for his theory, that a law must be capable of guiding the behaviour of its subjects.[48] Raz, like all other Past Rule of Law theorists, provides a thin view of the Rule of Law; however, in providing some principles that feed into his general idea, and in addition to ideas of prospectivity, openness, clarity, and stability, generality, certainty, and predictability, Raz does include a number of desiderata that do trend toward thicker aspects – for example, there is a stated need for the principles of natural justice to observed.[49] They have already been detailed in chapter two. So, here, only the most pertinent to the hypothetical are explored in any detail.

Raz's need for laws to be prospective, open, clear, and stable, can all be seen to relate to the broad ideas of predictability explored above. Unsurprisingly, similar conclusions follow. These are of particular relevance to the hypothetical; Raz even uses an example not dissimilar to the hypothetical: a licencing authority granting a licence as an example of, what Raz calls, a 'particular legal order'. This form of 'ephemeral' order can be seen to introduce a level of uncertainty and in this way should be contrasted and interpreted in light of general laws that shape the legal order.[50] The ephemerality appears to stem, for Raz, from the application of the particular laws by individuals that includes those issuing a licence. Raz's example readily compares with the issuance of a visa, an administrative decision-making process where there is a level of uncertainty of application in each individual circumstance that is, however, tempered by the broad framework that structures *how* that decision should be made.

In considering the hypothetical with the above aspect of Raz's Rule of Law idea, and the importance of the idea of how a decision is made, means the need for the relative explainability of an AI's decision becomes a particular problem. If it cannot be established that the AI is making the decision in the right way and based on the appropriate general laws (to adopt Raz's term), then there is considerable uncertainty introduced into the process; it would not be possible to see and

[47] ibid.
[48] ibid 214.
[49] ibid 214–18.
[50] ibid 215–16.

understand how the laws are being applied and, as a result, the application of the law would not be able to guide the behaviour of its subjects. This runs contrary to the basic idea of the Razian Rule of Law.

If the AI can explain its decision, Raz's Rule of Law is satisfied. Recall that for Hayek the most fundamental aim is the avoidance of coercion (by rules being announced beforehand) and for Raz the most fundamental aim is that rules must be capable of guiding the behaviour of those subject to those rules.[51] In this sense, the fundamental *knowability* of the rules – and the potential as to what the rules may subsequently be – is crucial. (This aspect reflects the Aristotelean ideas – and those evident in ancient legislative systems – explained above and in chapter two.) The idea of knowability in relation to the Rule of Law has previously been explored by Radin. For her, this included the requirements that rules be public, congruent, non-contradictory, clear and relatively stable.[52] These ideas closely connect to the Razian and Hayekian ideas. It seems, then, that if it is possible to *know* the way that the rules are being interpreted at present, that will provide some element of prospective guidance to those that seek to *know* what the rules may be in the future. On this basis, knowing how an AI is making a decision would, as was the case with the previously considered thinkers, satisfy the criteria seen as fundamental by both Hayek and Raz.

Only one of the Past Rule of Law's usual suspects remains for consideration: Fuller. Fuller's list of eight desiderata – derived from King Rex's failed attempts at leadership – that require there to be rules and that these be publicised, prospective, understandable, non-contradictory, congruent, stable, and actionable can be seen to broadly reflect many of the same areas as those discussed above.[53] The element of a necessary guidance function – reflecting the Razian and Hayekian ideas above – undergirded by the need for publicity and prospectivity in rule setting – reflecting Dicey's anti-arbitrariness ideas and the Lockean ideas – will be, by now, familiar. This similarity makes it unsurprising that the need for explainability is crucial.

In considering the hypothetical in Fullerian terms, the need for rules reflects the existence of a particular law but it is the application of these that can be seen to relate to the way in which a particular decision-maker's decision-making process operates. In this respect, the only way that a decision-making process can be seen to be operating in a way that reflects the Fullerian requirements – and not an arbitrary form of decision-making – is through decisions being explainable. Accordingly, Fuller, like the other thinkers, would require an AI that is making administrative decisions to be able to explain its decision-making.

Unlike the other thinkers, an additional problem that arises for the Fullerian Rule of Law where an AI *could* explain its decision-making. Fuller seems to regard only the need for prospectivity to be an absolute requirement – considering

[51] ibid 214; Hayek, *The Road to Serfdom* (n 22) 112.
[52] MJ Radin, 'Reconsidering the Rule of Law' (1989) 69 *Boston University Law Review* 781, 786.
[53] Fuller (n 22) 39.

retrospective laws to be 'truly a monstrosity'.[54] The other desiderata are able to be satisfied to a greater or lesser degree – with only a 'total failure' to satisfy one of the eight criteria resulting in 'something is not properly called a legal system'.[55] Accordingly, where an AI makes an administrative decision based on the rules and where it *could* explain that this is the case, but that decision or rationale was not (for example) publicised, this would not – for Fuller – be a catastrophic end to the satisfaction of the Rule of Law. It seems that would satisfy the Fullerian criteria – albeit to a lesser degree than may be considered ideal. In other words, as long as there was *some* ability for the AI to be able to explain its rationale – even if that was not made fully available to everyone – that would be sufficient.

This consideration indicates that there may be a degree of latitude that exists within the Fullerian Rule of Law that does not – clearly, at least – exist in the other Past Rule of Law thinkers' conceptions. It is possible to illustrate this through the various accounts' requirement for predictability. As has already been observed, each of the usual suspects' Rule of Law ideas require some element of predictability. Each requires predictability for slightly different reasons, but in broad terms it is to allow the subject of the law to be able to know the way that the law will impact them so as they may avoid the imposition of some form of coercion. Fuller, like all of the other Past Rule of Law thinkers, requires a form of predictability – the ability to achieve a predictable outcome stems from the collective operation of the particular desiderata he lists. But, as noted above, those desiderata do not all have to be absolutely satisfied; which, it seems to follow, would result in the potential for a form of predictability to exist – that would still satisfy Fuller's ideal – that would not be absolute or ideal. The conclusion to draw from this is that whilst Fuller would require a form of predictability, the *level* at which this must exist to satisfy his conception of the Rule of Law may be lower than the other Rule of Law thinkers. In this sense, where the broad idea of predictability is closely related to requirement that an AI (or any other decision-maker) be able to explain the decision that has been made, there may be more latitude in the *level* of explainability that would be required in order to satisfy Fuller's conception. This would not obviate the need for some level of explainability – as noted immediately above; however, it does illustrate a relative point of difference between the difference Past Rule of Law conceptions.

What has been seen in this section is that the ability of an AI to explain its decision-making rationale in making administrative decisions is crucial to the satisfaction of the Rule of Law across all of the Past Rule of Law theorists. Whilst there may be some differences across each of the thinkers, it is clear that there must be some way for an AI to be able to explain the steps that are being taken in order to make a particular decision. The ability of an AI to do so is, at the current stage

[54] ibid 53.
[55] ibid 39.

of technological development, problematic.[56] What this means for the satisfaction of the Rule of Law is returned to in the conclusion to this chapter.

IV. The Present Rule of Law

The Present Rule of Law is constituted by works that were authored, unsurprisingly, after the Past Rule of Law. The last of the Past Rule of Law conceptions was authored in the 1970s; however, this date is not an arbitrarily selected cut off that distinguishes the two forms of the concept. It is a difference in type that distinguishes the two forms. 'Past' and 'Present' are simply an appropriate descriptor. The Past Rule of Law represents solutions to a broadly shared problem regarding the imposition of arbitrary power over individuals by the state. (Although, the precise nature of the problems does allow some differentiation of the solutions they propose.) The precise terms of the Present Rule are not only temporally more contemporary than the conceptions that form the Past Rule of Law, but also are differ in type in two ways.

Each of the two forms of the Present Rule of Law provide a point of difference to the Past Rule of Law. The first provides a form that responds to the exercise of arbitrary power *in general*. This represents a source-based form. The second provides a meaning of the Rule of Law that is an *outcome*-based form that contrasts to the Past Rule of Law's ambivalence toward the outcome of the law-making process. In order to consider what the Present Rule of Law means for the hypothetical, I will first consider the two forms in general (in the next sub-section) before considering the individual thinkers' conceptions. This broadly replicates the approach taken in the previous section – moving from general to specific.

In common with the agnostic approach that I adopt in this book relating to the Past and Present Rules of Law – through not advocating that either one should be considered to be 'correct' – I do not suggest that either form of the Present Rule of Law is more or less correct than the other. This is an important aspect. As was noted in chapters one and two, the theorists' conceptions that have been included as both the Past and Present ideas of the Rule of Law have been identified in virtue of their relative popularity in academic discussions around what the Rule of Law *is*.

A. The Forms of the Present Rule of Law

As noted above, the two forms of the Present Rule of Law reflect two points of difference to the Past Rule of Law. The first contrasts to the *state-based* arbitrary exercise of power on which the Past of the Rule of Law is focused. The second is

[56] For a general overview, see D Minh et al, 'Explainable Artificial Intelligence: A Comprehensive Review' (2022) 55(5) *Artificial Intelligence Review* 3503.

reflected in the Present Rule of Law theorists' interest in outcomes, which contrasts to the Past Rule of Law's view that process is itself important. I expand on these ideas in the next sub-section. Here, the aim is to merely consider the hypothetical based on this broad perspective in the two forms.

In considering the first form, it is the locus of the arbitrary power that is in issue. The Present Rule of Law has no specific locus. Any instance of arbitrary power would be part of the ambit of this Rule of Law. This hypothetical involves a state-based application of power. There is potential for that application to be arbitrary. Accordingly, the first form of the Rule of Law applies to the decision-making process between the AI that is coming to a conclusion or making a decision and the subject of the decision. This would mean that instances of arbitrary decision-making would be clearly combatable by the first form of the Present Rule of Law.

The second form of the Rule of Law introduces the potential need for a particular kind of outcome. This may relate to an outcome considered 'good' for any number of reasons; for example, conformity with human rights or the norms of international law (to borrow some examples that would fit with both of the Present Rule of Law theorists in this form).[57] Other benefits may also be seen as beneficial; for example, the relative speed of decision-making. In the context of the hypothetical, the suggestion is that the AI making visa decisions would be introduced in order to facilitate a more efficient and speedy process. Should this be the case, speed and hopefully accuracy of decision-making may result in a good outcome.

The terms of the hypothetical stated thus far do not specify whether the AI system making the visa decisions is complying with basic human rights or international law. If it does not, there would be a number of other obvious legal recourses that could be made about the system – but the absence of conformity with the law broadly could be seen as a negative outcome with consequences relevant to the outcome-based form of the Present Rule of Law. In other words, the relative illegality of an outcome in circumstances where the system is not adhering to relevant laws would be a Rule of Law concern. Where the AI is programmed in such a way that it does not adhere to the law, this would be a relatively simple conclusion. But the issues of explainability raised in the previous section also become relevant.

The question may be one regarding the nature of the outcome itself – where does the process end and the outcome begin? Given the fact that the Present Rule of Law, as noted above and in chapter two, is contingent on the existence of some form of the Past Rule of Law (at least in terms of the need for core ideas like predictability and certainty), this boundary may not be as crucial as it first appears. This is because in circumstances where there is a failure relating to desiderata like predictability and certainty, the outcome alone cannot make an instance conform with the Rule of Law. If the AI system making the decisions cannot be identified

[57] T Bingham, *The Rule of Law* (London, Allen Lane, 2010); United Nations General Assembly, *Strengthening and Coordinating United Nations Rule of Law Activities – Report of the Secretary-General – Addendum* (No A/68/213/Add.1, United Nations, 11 July 2014).

as achieving a decision in a way that is, to continue the theme, in line with the law, then the outcome itself – even if prima facie a beneficial outcome – would not conform with an outcome-based Rule of Law criteria. This means that, as in the case of the Present Rule of Law, a core requirement would be for the AI to be able to explain that the process that leads up to the beneficial outcome was in line with the Rule of Law. This, in turn, means that for this broad idea of the second form of the Rule of Law, the need for explainability in an AI system remains paramount.

B. Present Rule of Law – Source-Based – And Hypothetical One

As noted above, the first form of the Present Rule of Law contrasts to the *state-based* arbitrary exercise of power on which the Past of the Rule of Law is focused. Each of the Past Rule of Law theorists provide solutions to problems that are caused by the application of power by the state. As was explored in more detail in chapter two, their solutions cannot, without considerable licence being taken with the context of their authorship and/or the words that they use, be seen as solutions to problems that extend beyond the state-based application of power.[58] In brief terms, several of the Past conceptions relate, specifically, to the legislative function: Aristotle seeks a form of legislative due process; Locke argues a parliamentary legislature would be less likely to act tyrannically than a monarch or pope; Hayek seeks predictability in the laws that are made in order that individuals can avoid being coerced by the state; Fuller illustrates through the hapless King Rex eight ways to fail to make law; and Raz provides a formal list of requirement designed to ensure people can be guided by the laws that are made. Dicey is the only Past Rule of Law usual suspect that is not specifically focused on the legislative function; yet his is still focused on the application of *state* power. As expanded above and in chapter two, Dicey's fear was that the Rule of Law is being eroded through the prevalence of administrative decisions that alter individuals' rights when the proper forum for this is the courts.

The Rule of Law solutions that characterise the first form of the Present Rule of Law go beyond this idea of the state-based *source* of exercise of power. The absence of a particular need for the public application of power means this first form of the Present Rule of Law includes accounts that see the Rule of Law as being relevant to relations within in a private setting – that is, individual to individual. As will be seen, this difference represents a substantive potential difference in the way that the hypothetical needs to be considered.

[58] I have previously set out my broad objections to this form of the Rule of Law. However, as I noted in closing that article, those that hold the view that the Rule of Law is solely a matter of the state-based exercise of power are increasingly in the minority. P Burgess, 'Googling the Equivalence of Private Arbitrary Power and State Arbitrary Power: Why The Rule of Law Does Not Relate to Private Relationships' [2021] *International Journal of Law in Context*.

The source-based form of the Present Rule of Law is represented by conceptions authored by two scholars: Martin Krygier and Jeff King. (This is not to say that these are the only two that provide popular conceptions that see the Rule of Law operating in the private sphere. Sanne Taekema, Julian Sempill, and others hold a similar view.[59]) King's *social dimension* of the Rule of Law may in some sense be seen as relevant to the second form of the Present Rule of Law – that relates to substantively good outcomes – as he brings together a substantively 'good' outcome with the suggestion that the Rule of Law should, in its best conception, 'require the provision of a legally structured welfare and regulatory state'.[60] Whilst the provision of welfare is clearly an issue for the state, King's view is that the Rule of Law state has a duty to protect people through law and that this duty extends to creating regulation in both the public and private spheres.[61] In this sense, King's Rule of Law is principally about taming the exercise of arbitrary power wherever it may exist – the relative source of this power is not determinative of the protection that the concept should offer. King's Rule of Law idea creates a duty for the state to prevent various forms of arbitrary power – including those relating to private actors – through positive actions. In other words, for a state to be a Rule of Law state, it must act to prevent the arbitrary application of power from any source – whether in the private or the public spheres.

This has a particular impact in terms of this hypothetical. As this positive duty on the state to act to prevent the application of arbitrary power would mean that there may be a reason why – despite the efficiencies and potential benefits – a state should not implement the sort of system contemplated in the hypothetical unless it can be certain that arbitrariness is not a function of the system. For example, even though the system's parameters seek to ensure decisions are being made in accordance with the relevant laws and are being made in the right way and the system is delivering objectively positive benefits (for example, relating to speed and efficiency), if it is the case that the actual precise decision-making approach is not explainable, there would be a question regarding the potential arbitrariness of the decisions. In considering this aspect of King's conception, there would be a positive duty on the state to prevent this sort of system being used. In other words, where a Rule of Law-positive outcome does not follow,

[59] LM Austin and D Klimchuk (eds), *Private Law and the Rule of Law* (Oxford, Oxford University Press, 2014). JA Sempill, 'The Lions and the Greatest Part: The Rule of Law and the Constitution of Employer Power' (2017) 9(2) *Hague Journal on the Rule of Law* 283. A special issue of *International Journal of Law in Context* introduces this position. K Bhatt, J Lander and S Taekema, 'Introduction: The Rule of Law in Transnational Development Projects – Private Actors and Public Chokeholds' (2021) 17(1) *International Journal of Law in Context* 91. Whilst I was a part of that special issue, I held a contrary view: Burgess (n 58).

[60] J King, 'The Rule of Law' in R Bellamy and J King (eds), *The Cambridge Handbook of Constitutional Theory* (2024) papers.ssrn.com/abstract=4487306; J King, '"Constitutional Boundaries" – The Social Dimension of the Rule of Law', *I·CONnect* (2018) www.iconnectblog.com/2018/04/i-connect-symposium-on-constitutional-boundaries-the-social-dimension-of-the-rule-of-law/.

[61] King cites Sempill's work as a comparable project. JA Sempill, 'Ruler's Sword, Citizen's Shield: The Rule of Law & the Constitution of Power' (2015) 31 *Journal of Law and Politics* 333.

then there would be a duty on the state to either not implement or to discontinue the sort of scheme contemplated in this hypothetical. This goes beyond the Past Rule of Law approach that merely suggests that a lack of explainability would mean the system does not conform with the Rule of Law. King's consideration would require positive action.

The other conception used to illustrate the first form of the Present Rule of Law is illustrated by Martin Krygier. As noted in chapter two, Krygier's work on the Rule of Law has been so impactful that a recent double-special issue in the *Hague Journal on the Rule of Law* that encompasses 35 articles authored by the world's greatest Rule of Law authorities has been published.[62] Krygier's ideas have, unsurprisingly, over the decades of his work, evolved. His more recent works form the basis for the examination in this book. His teleological idea of the Rule of Law seeks to address the question of 'what is the Rule of Law for?' His answer, in brief, is that the Rule of Law is a concept that opposes arbitrary power *in whatever form that arbitrary power takes*.[63] The *telos* of the Rule of Law, Krygier argues, means that the concept is about arbitrary power in whatever form it may take – and the relative source of that power is not determinative as to whether the Rule of Law should operate. This means Krygier's Rule of Law protects against the arbitrary exercise of power in both public and private settings.[64]

Krygier's approach regarding the source of the power – where the hypothetical relates to an administrative decision-making process – makes it clear that, unlike with some of the Present Rule of Law issues relating to whether this is a law-making exercise, the Rule of Law has clear operation in this form of administrative decision. The fact that the decision is made by an administrator is of no consequence when the source of the arbitrarily exercised power is irrelevant. In this regard, if there was arbitrariness – for example, through the absence of explainability noted above – the Rule of Law should clearly respond.

This clear conclusion would also follow even in instances where there is a claim that the decision is not actually made by the AI and is, instead, merely informed by the AI. It will be recalled that this hypothetical relates to a human-in-the-loop scenario; the AI system is conducting enquiries and making some sort of recommendation, but the ultimate decision may be attributable to a minister of state. It could be suggested that in this situation the AI is not exercising state-power but the minister is and, as a result, the conclusions reached by the AI – and the way that those conclusions are reached – are not subject to the Rule of Law. This form of argument could exist and be stronger if the AI system is provided by a

[62] J Waldron, 'Preface' (2019) 11(2) *Hague Journal on the Rule of Law* 251. The Preface to the special issues provides an invaluable starting point and entry into the rest of the pieces.

[63] M Krygier, 'Four Puzzles About the Rule of Law: Why, What, Where? And Who Cares?' in J Flemming (ed), *Getting to the Rule of Law* (New York, New York University Press, 2011) 64; M Krygier, 'Tempering Power' in M Adams, EH Ballin and A Meuwese (eds), *Constitutionalism and the Rule of Law: Bridging Idealism and Realism* (Cambridge, Cambridge University Press, 2017).

[64] Krygier (n 15).

non-governmental private third-party.[65] This form of argument would, however, gain no traction in relation to Krygier's Rule of Law. The source – whether private or public – would be of no consequence. Even if the AI was merely facilitating the decision, but was doing so on arbitrary grounds, then this would run contrary to the Rule of Law.

C. Present Rule of Law – Outcome-Based – And Hypothetical One

The second form of the Present Rule of Law reflects what may be seen, or at least recognised, as the more traditional distinction of thin/thick or formal/substantive conceptions of the Rule of Law.[66] This form represents a difference to the Past Rule of Law in terms of the *outcome* associated with the concept. The Past Rule of Law is constituted by conceptions that are thin/formal. This means they achieve a limitation on the exercise of power through the requirement that there are particular steps or parts of a process that must be followed in order for the Rule of Law to exist. This sort of procedural or formal check means that the nature or kind of the resultant laws is of no consequence to the relative Rule of Law-ness of a legal system; as long as the appropriate formal requirements are satisfied, laws that are morally bankrupt and clearly racist or sexist, for example, can be enacted without impacting the Rule of Law.

This is not to say that theorists that make up the Present Rule of Law seek moral outcomes whilst Past Rule of Law theorists are in favour of morally bankrupt laws. Past Rule of Law theorists may, however, simply hold the view that a procedural approach means the instance of these laws would be obvious and, in a system where accountability is also a feature, would mean both that laws of this kind would be less likely to occur and that there is an impetus to then change laws of this kind. Two examples of this would be Fuller and Raz. Fuller suggests that laws conforming with his desiderata are more likely to reflect what may be deemed good laws; or, at least, that the result will be less likely to reflect bad laws.[67] In this sense, the Fullerian requirements go at least somewhat beyond 'ethically neutral' demands.[68] A similar position can be seen in Raz's most famous Rule of Law analogy – where he analogises the concept to a knife – which is neither good nor bad *of itself*, but can result in good or bad ends illustrates the potential of the concept to be applied in a variety of ways – both good and bad. But, he also stresses that the Rule of Law is not a panacea as it is 'just one important virtue that legal systems

[65] An example of this would be the private development of the COMPAS software that assists judges in predicting recidivism. J Dressel and H Farid, 'The Accuracy, Fairness, and Limits of Predicting Recidivism' (2018) 4(1) *Science Advances* eaao5580.

[66] The classic illustration of this distinction is provided by Paul Craig. Craig (n 16).

[67] Fuller (n 22) 157–59.

[68] Raz (n 22) 225.

should possess'.[69] This acknowledges that there are a range of other concepts that operate in a legal system that may have the prevention of bad laws as their central ideal; the Rule of Law should not be considered in terms of the good or bad laws that follow from a Rule of Law-system.[70] The second form of the Present Rule of Law, unlike these past ideas, is focused on the *outcome* of the legal systems. There is a substantive aim that is attached to the attainment or satisfaction of the Rule of Law. Two proponents of this form of the Present Rule of Law can be seen in the conceptions provided by Tom Bingham and the United Nations (UN).

Bingham sets out an aspirational target relating to what the Rule of Law is – in this sense, he provides normative goals which should be striven for. In setting out his own eight sub-rules associated with the Rule of Law, and as alluded to in the previous sub-section, he acknowledges that the concept is both derived and evolved from conceptions that have come before. As also noted in chapter two, he states his account is an attempt to 'identify what the rule of law really means to us, *here and now*'.[71] It is a reflection of the needs that a contemporary society has placed on the concept itself. In setting out his sub-rules, it is clear that they encompass and include the Past Rule of Law through the requirements that: laws should be accessible, clear and predictable; issues regarding legal rights/liability should be decided through the application of law; and, the law should apply equally to all. There are also similarities to Raz's list in requirements that: public officials should exercise their powers in good faith (and act within those powers); the law must protect fundamental rights. However, he goes beyond the Past ideas by also suggesting the Rule of Law requires: resolution of civil disputes should be provided for (at reasonable costs); adjudicative procedures must be provided and be fair; and, the state must comply with its obligations under international law.[72] Many of his sub-rules are focused on attaining a particular substantive outcome.

The second of the *outcome*-based Present Rule of Law ideas can be seen in the UN's conception of the Rule of Law. Whilst various UN bodies have different conceptions of the Rule of Law, they each have a similar broad focus on outcomes. I will focus on one. The UN, as with other Present Rule of Law conceptions, incorporates the ideas included in the Past Rule of Law and also goes beyond these ideas.[73] It does this by requiring 'fairness in the application of the law, separation of powers, participation in decision-making, legal certainty, avoidance of arbitrariness and procedural and legal transparency'.[74] This happens with a substantive

[69] J Raz, *The Authority of Law: Essays on Law and Morality*, 2nd edn (Oxford, Oxford University Press, 2009) 211.

[70] ibid 225.

[71] Bingham (n 57) 10, 37. (Emphasis added.).

[72] Bingham (n 57). (This is a somewhat simplified version of the list.).

[73] Thick/substantive ideas of the Rule of Law are built on a thin/formal base. Burgess (n 19) 485.

[74] UN Security Council, *The Rule of Law and Transitional Justice in Conflict and Post-Conflict Societies – Report of the Secretary-General* (No UN doc S/2004/616, 23 August 2004) 6: www.un.org/ruleoflaw/files/2004%20report.pdf.

purpose in mind: the achievement of Human Rights.[75] For the UN, the Rule of Law is a vehicle to achieve the substantive aim of rights protection.[76]

Some of the substantive outcomes relevant to Bingham's Rule of Law – that go beyond the formal base examined in the previous section – relate to the need to adhere to human rights and the international law. These were broadly canvased earlier in this section. In this respect, all of the conclusions reached are also apposite here. The common criteria relating to both Bingham and the UN – the enhancement of human rights as being important to the Rule of Law – is relevant to consider in more detail. Whilst these two relations to rights are related, they remain different; Bingham sees human rights as something that a state must have and promote to be a Rule of Law state; the UN sees the Rule of Law as a mechanism for achieving human rights.[77] In this respect, for the UN the Rule of Law is both carrot and stick; whereas, for Bingham, the Rule of Law is merely a carrot. This becomes clear when considered in relation to the present hypothetical.

Bingham's aspirational target that requires adherence to human rights would mean that the use of AI in making administrative decisions would be something that could be implemented by a state – regardless of a failure to adhere to human rights. But this would result in the state not being able to be considered as being a Rule of Law state. Whilst this may seem like a mere analytical/theoretical triviality, it is clear that states do value an association with the Rule of Law – association with the concept seems to hold considerable appeal (even for states that may, traditionally, seem to have very little in common with the concept).[78] This seems to be a fundamental premise on which Bingham's aspirational ideal – as a carrot – of the Rule of Law is premised. Accordingly, the relative normative force that may follow from Bingham's idea when the hypothetical is considered would operate so as to seek positive evidence that human rights are being enhanced through the AI's decision-making process. States would need to be able to show the AI involvement conforms with human rights in order to be able to claim they area a Rule of Law state. In other words, the Rule of Law is the end goal – human rights are achieved by way of attaining this end goal; the rights are a means to a Rule of Law-end.

The assessment – although not the outcome – relating to the UN's Rule of Law differs to Bingham's. The relationship appears to be structured the other way around. For the UN, human rights are an end; the Rule of Law is simply one means to achieve that end. For the UN, the Rule of Law is facilitative. The requirements associated with the UN's Rule of Law simply need to result in an outcome that enhances human rights. There is no particular motivation to achieve the Rule of

[75] ibid.
[76] United Nations General Assembly (n 57).
[77] UN Security Council (n 74).
[78] Krygier (n 63).

Law beyond the achievement of human rights. This relative difference can be illustrated if the two ideas are placed into simplified conditionals:

Bingham:	If we have human rights, we may have the Rule of Law.
UN:	If we have the Rule of Law, we may have human rights.

This undoubted oversimplification serves to illustrate the relative differences in the positions that each hold. Both of these assume that there may be other reasons that the Rule of Law (for Bingham) and human rights (for the UN) may not occur. For Bingham, the Rule of Law cannot be attained if there is not satisfaction of human rights. For the UN, human rights cannot be attained if there is no Rule of Law. There is, however, no substantive difference when either of these approaches is considered in relation to the hypothetical. The hypothetical sees an AI making or assisting in making administrative decisions. This, of itself, would be no reason to suggest that either antecedent could be satisfied.

In opening this section, in considering the broad idea of an outcome-based idea of the Present Rule of Law, I suggested that where an AI is programmed in such a way that it does not adhere to the law, a simple conclusion regarding illegality would follow. The same would be the case regarding human rights. What would also be similar is that even if the program required conformity with human rights, even if the process was prima facie in accordance with human rights, the way in which the decision was *actually* made would also need to be in accordance with human rights. It could not be the case, as was suggested earlier in the chapter that there had been some form of spurious relationship identified by the AI – which was not contrary to any particular human right – on which it was basing its decision. In this respect, and once again, the need for explainability in an AI system remains paramount.

V. Summary and Conclusions

In considering a hypothetical in which an AI is responsible for administrative decision-making – albeit when there remains a human in the loop – conformity with the Rule of Law, regardless of the level of abstraction or specificity that is adopted, can only be satisfied when the actions of the AI are explainable. The way in which this conclusion has been reached takes account of the fundamental contest that relates to the concept of the Rule of Law. Where there is no accepted definition of the concept, a conclusion of this kind could be open to criticism. To avoid criticisms for cherry-picking, in this chapter I considered the hypothetical with the aid of a number of the most popular and influential conceptions of the Rule of Law drawn from the past and the present. By splitting these into categories – of Past and Present Rule of Law ideas – and by examining not only the broad categories, but also the theories that constitute the category.

In considering the hypothetical I was able to identify that the point at which explainability causes a problem for the Rule of Law, and the way in which it causes a problem, does vary when the different levels of abstraction are considered. At the most abstract level, when the Rule of Law is considered to be simply a concept that opposes power, or more specifically, state power, the issue arises that it did not immediately appear to be a necessary outcome that arbitrariness would follow an AI making administrative decisions. (At least, not any more than a human.) When a more specific approach is taken by considering the two broad temporal categories of the Past Rule of Law satisfaction of both Predictability and Procedural Clarity was seen to be problematic where AI's decision-making remains unexplainable. The fundamentality of predictability remained across the specific consideration of several usual suspects of the Past Rule of Law. It also continued in relation to the Present Rule of Law; however, there were some differences. For example, the source-based ideas of the Present Rule of Law were seen to be more capable of providing a solution to the problems caused by the hypothetical as questions relating to the exercise of *state* power were avoided. In relation to the outcome-based forms of the Present Rule of Law, the concerns associated with the Past Rule of Law also applied, but the achievement of the goals sought were not differentially impacted by the use of AI in the administrative process.

In terms of where the relative failure of explainability is so common for this hypothetical, this would raise the question as to what would happen in circumstances where an AI in this form of administrative decision-making role *was* able to explain its decision-making. Brief consideration was given to this point earlier; however, even then, issues remained. The hypothetical in this chapter (and in the next two) could, perhaps, have been extended in a way that stipulated explainability *was* achieved. However, in circumstances where explainable AI remains a core area of interest and research as well as being a beguiling problem in consequence of the ever-increasing complexity of algorithms, simply stipulating that element away seemed like a step that would not assist in identifying some of the key issues raised by the Rule of Law. After considering the issues that arise in two more (increasingly extreme) hypotheticals in each of the next two chapters, the final chapter will see me return to the conclusions drawn here and consider how the conclusions may differ, and what other considerations would arise, if AI was explainable.

5

The Rule of Law and the Use of AI in Creating Secondary Legislation

When the exercise of power by AIs is considered in the context of the Present Rule of Law this chapter echoes the conclusion of the previous chapter: the Rule of Law is not satisfied due to a failure in terms of explainability. However, this chapter reveals different mechanisms for that failure. Issues relating to (the absence of) accountability for AI systems come to the fore when both the Past Rule of Law and Present Rule of Law ideas are considered – but the way in which this manifests is *different*. The conclusions drawn in this chapter, together with the conclusions from chapters four and five, will provide the basis for the final chapter's discussion regarding the broad uses of AI systems in ways relating to the hypotheticals and what this means for the future of the Rule of Law.

The structure and approach of the chapter will not come as a surprise to anyone that is reading this book in a linear way. Similarly, for those same people, many of the ideas and concepts will be familiar. I appreciate, however, that not all people will take this approach in consuming the material in this book. For this reason, I accommodate both kinds of reader by providing minimal explanations that are sufficient to understand the argument being made without, I hope, being too repetitive of the content covered in previous chapters. I do, wherever possible, allude to the more fulsome discussions of the various ideas and concepts that I discuss. Because of the brevity that this affords and because less explanatory material is required, this chapter and the next are somewhat shorter than chapter four.

The chapter structure, as noted above, replicates and will be familiar to readers of chapter four. The chapter has five substantive sections after this brief introduction. The first expands upon the hypothetical that was briefly introduced in chapter three. The additional detail that I provide facilitates a stronger foundation on which to base the discussions in this chapter. The second section then considers the hypothetical through the lens of the most abstract idea of the Rule of Law – what I have called the broad-brush idea. In the two sections that follow, I then narrow the focus from the broad-brush idea and consider the hypothetical in terms of the Past and Present ideas of the Rule of Law – with each occupying its own discreet section. I commence each of these sections with a very brief re-statement of ideas of the Rule of Law that will be considered. (As noted above, the summaries provided here are brief; they are briefer than the detailed explanation provided in chapter two; and, they are briefer than the re-cap provided in chapter four. This may mean the non-linear reader may need to consider those other chapters for additional detail.) The largest part of each of these sections is, however, devoted to considering the various ways in which the hypothetical situation contemplated in this chapter can conform with the various Rule of Law ideas presented. The final substantive section of the chapter provides a brief summary and conclusion.

I. The Use of AI in Creating Secondary Legislation

This hypothetical sees an AI operating in a way that sees it *creating* secondary legislation. In doing so, the AI is charged with making decisions that go beyond merely applying the law and moves into the realm of *creating* rules or regulations that have a normative effect on the world in which they exist. This differs to the first hypothetical in which, it will be recalled, an AI system operated in an *administrative* function. This contemplated the AI system *applying* the existing law to a particular scenario and not creating or changing that law. Where Rule of Law ideas have been seen to come from a context relating to law-*making*, the creative function in the present hypothetical places this chapter more squarely into Rule of Law territory.

Secondary legislation is a form of legislation that is not made directly by the legislature; instead, it is created by an individual or a body to which the legislature has delegated law-making power. This form of norm-creation and power delegation is very common. It is a functional necessity in many modern democracies where the many thousands of regulatory changes that need to be made would not be able to be subject to the normal legislative process – of proposing, debating, and enacting a Bill as a piece of primary legislation. In chapter three, I set out an example of such delegation that can be found in the UK's Misuse of Drugs Act 1971. This Act includes, in section 2(2), the delegation that:

> Her Majesty may by Order in Council make such amendments in Schedule 2 to this Act as may be requisite for the purpose of adding any substance or product to, or removing any substance or product from, any of Parts I to III of that Schedule, ….

This has the effect that the list of Schedule 2 drugs can be amended or augmented by an 'order in council'. Sub-section 2(5) of the Act goes on to provide that an order in council requires, first, a recommendation by an advisory council and, second, that a draft of the order be laid by the Secretary of State before – and approved by way of resolution by – the legislature. This chapter will be based around a similar legislative delegation of power; however, in this hypothetical, and in using the form of delegation in the extract above as an illustrative base, the difference will be that an AI system replaces both the advisory council and the Secretary of State. In other words, there will be a delegation of power to an AI to provide an order in council, by both making a recommendation and laying draft of the order before the legislature.

In construing the hypothetical in this way, it will be the AI's relative (artificial) expertise relating to the potential for drugs to be subject to misuse that will enable it to first form a conclusion (as an advisory council), make a recommendation, and lay the draft before the legislature. As is standard with secondary legislation, at that point, the legislature can – should it wish to – block the passage of the secondary legislation. However, empirical evidence from real legislatures suggests that this is not a course of action that is frequently adopted.[1] In this hypothetical, it is not suggested that the delegation of power to the AI is subject to any different form of scrutiny than the existing (human-based) delegations of power.

It is useful to briefly consider what this would mean in practice. A list of controlled drugs contained within the legislation – in relation to which there are associated criminal offences associated with possession that may carry fines or periods of imprisonment – can be amended by the AI's actions. The relative unease with which this situation may be greeted may be tempered by the suggestion that the fact that this is secondary legislation means that the humans in legislature still retain overall control of the laws that operate within its jurisdiction. However, if the hypothetical scrutiny placed on the AI's delegated legislation is the same as with human-created delegated legislation, this level of scrutiny is generally only of a technical nature and infrequently results in the secondary legislation's content being challenged.[2] The delegation of powers in this way, whilst open to a form of veto, results in the delegation of powers that are exercised with relatively little oversight – resulting in a de facto form of law-making as the resulting rules and regulations are, to many individuals in the public that are subject to the rules and regulations, indistinguishable from laws made as primary legislation by the legislature.

A question may arise at this point as to why, then, the hypothetical is couched in these particular terms. The answer is one related to a desire to avoid the various hypotheticals collapsing into one another. If this hypothetical was conceived in a way so as a high (or higher) level of scrutiny was placed on the AI's secondary legislation making power, this could be seen as largely an administrative decision-aiding tool that does little more than assist law-makers in coming to their own conclusions. In this respect, this would be similar to the hypothetical set out in the previous chapter. In other words, stipulating that the level of scrutiny does not change between the human- and AI-delegated power scenarios, both hypotheticals are able to stand (or fall) alone. This also means that this hypothetical operates as a clear instance of a human-over-the-loop scenario. In contemplating further points of difference in what the AI system is doing in this hypothetical compared with the first hypothetical, it is clear that the relative autonomy of the AI also changes. The AI system is now acting in a function where it can *itself* change legal norms as

[1] JS Caird and E Patterson, *Brexit, Delegated Powers and Delegated Legislation: A Rule of Law Analysis of Parliamentary Scrutiny* (The Bingham Centre for the Rule of Law, 2020).

[2] Eg, the scrutiny system in the UK has been described as being 'broken'. ibid; R Fox and J Blackwell, *The Devil Is in the Detail: Parliament and Delegated Legislation* (London, Hansard Society, 2014).

secondary legislation is created by the AI system in the absence of any intervention by a human actor. There is, as noted above, a human-based check or veto that can exist to prevent this happening. This means that the AI's actions are subject to *some* form of supervision by humans. In this respect, unlike the first hypothetical in which the AI's role was assistive and where there were humans-in-the-loop in making decisions, the hypothetical in this chapter changes the human role to a more supervisory function. In this respect, humans are over-the-loop.

For this hypothetical, as noted above, and in summary, I will adopt a slightly amended equivalent of the *Misuse of Drugs* legislation set out above. The slight change is that an AI will replace the *two* roles that the legislation contemplates. I will also adopt a level of check/veto that is generally applied to delegated legislation in general: which reflects a near-complete state of autonomy for the entity responsible for exercising the power that has been delegated to it. This means that in this hypothetical the AI will, in effect, be charged with making decisions regarding particular substances that should be criminalised/de-criminalised.

II. The (Broad-Brush) Rule of Law

It will be recalled that the broad-brush idea of the Rule of Law reflects the most unobjectionable form of the idea: the Rule of Law is a concept that opposes the arbitrary application of power. It will also be recalled that it is the particular application of *state* power that is of concern for the Past Rule of Law's usual suspects and for many of the Present Rule of Law theorists. This state-based idea represents the broad-brush approach.

Hypothetical two has, prima facie, a closer relationship to the broad-brush idea of the Past Rule of Law than the first hypothetical in chapter four. In that first hypothetical, the nature of an administrative decision-making process was in tension with the broad-brush idea that the Rule of Law relates to the *making* of law – as the Past Rule of Law in its broadest sense relates to the prevention of the arbitrary exercise of power by governments through imposing procedural requirements on the law-making process. (Chapter four also demonstrated that the Present Rule of Law, at least in the forms provided by Krygier and King, are less concerned with this issue as the source of the arbitrary power is not of singular consequence.)

In this second hypothetical, the AI is *making* rules and regulations that have direct and immediate impact on members of the public that are, to many of the individuals that may be within its jurisdiction, indistinguishable from laws (properly so called) passed by the legislature. This distinction could descend into a debate regarding the meaning of 'law' – which is not a question to be answered here. To avoid this, this hypothetical will take a broad view of what law is that includes both primary legislation (passed by the legislature) and secondary legislation (passed by an entity to which power has been delegated by the legislature). This (hopefully) uncontroversial position means that the operation of the Past Rule of Law to this sort of norm creation process will be clear.

The question then becomes one related to whether an AI's exercise of power in this way is necessarily arbitrary *because* it is an AI exercising the power. As with the first hypothetical, the answer seems to be in the negative. There is nothing necessarily arbitrary about an AI being the entity exercising the power. Although, as will be seen below, there will be (now) familiar issues that arise relating to the need for explainability in the AI's creation of secondary legislation.

The question hinted at in the preceding paragraph could also be answered in terms of whether the delegation *to* an AI may, of itself, result in arbitrariness. In other words, is there anything relating to the nature of the delegative act (to an AI) that can render any subsequent act by the AI arbitrary? It certainly seems that there is some scope to answer this aspect of the question in the positive – for example, if the delegation was made on the basis of a known technological inadequacy, or if it were known that the AI was to make its decisions based on spurious data or decision-making methods. These things would certainly call into question the appropriateness of the delegative act itself, which may render the AI's subsequent determinations arbitrary. (Arguably, as this delegation would need to take place via primary legislation, the issue could be considered under the rubric of Hypothetical Three.) Whilst the delegative act itself could be rendered arbitrary in the face of technological inadequacy, in line with the non-dystopian future-facing approach adopted in this book, the remainder of the consideration of the hypothetical delegation will be on the basis that the AI is technologically able to make the determinations in considering the appropriate and relevant data.

After caveating aside these questions regarding whether an AI's exercise of power in this way is necessarily arbitrary *because* it is an AI exercising the power or where the delegation itself would render the exercise of power as arbitrary, it is now possible to consider the potential arbitrariness of the AI's actual exercise of power in contravention of something more nuanced than the broad-brush idea of the Past Rule of Law.

III. The Past Rule of Law

The Past Rule of Law – as set out in detail in chapter two and expanded upon in chapter four – is constituted by the popularly cited Rule of Law conceptions by Aristotle, Locke, Dicey, Hayek, Fuller, and Raz. These represent the usual suspects of the Rule of Law.[3] The conceptions represent solutions to a broadly shared problem regarding the imposition of arbitrary power over individuals by the state. Although, the precise nature of the problems does allow some differentiation of the solutions they propose,[4] there are some similarities. The Past Rule of Law theorists

[3] P Burgess, *The Rule of Lore in the Rule of Law: Putting the Problem of the Rule of Law in Context* 4 June 2019.

[4] ibid.

provide solutions that can be described as thin/formal/procedural solutions that constrain the exercise of power by ensuring that new norms are, amongst other things, predictable.[5]

A. Past Rule of Law Elements

In considering this idea, and as with the first hypothetical, I further expand on the idea of what arbitrariness is with reference to the common elements that exist across the usual suspects accounts that make up the Past Rule of Law: the requirements for predictability and procedural clarity.[6] As noted previously, these reflect the 'need behind the need' inherent in the Rule of Law's usual suspects' conceptions. These are the things they sought to achieve in order to prevent the arbitrary application of power.[7]

The element of predictability can be seen to involve many of the same considerations as the first hypothetical. Actions must be predictable to avoid being arbitrary. And, again, the issue of explainability becomes fundamental. If decisions are made in a black-box and are not able to be explained by the AI, the basis on which rules or regulations are being added to the schedule of proscribed drugs may not be predictable.[8] In this sense, a lack of explainability would result in the absence of predictability. Much of this was explored in the previous chapter; many of the same conclusions follow; for any chance of satisfying the element of predictability, an AI must be able to explain the basis on which a rule or regulation is made. The process of explanation could, in this hypothetical, be more simplistic in some senses. The relative autonomy with which the AI is imbued through the delegation of power means that it may be able to take account of a wider swathe of data in adding any substance to the list; but, understanding the data that is used is crucial. As an example, it could be thought that an AI's decision to add a substance to the schedule was based on 'peer reviewed scientific papers' may not, without more, be sufficient. Without more, it is not clear that the conclusions in those papers are not, for example, 50 years old and have since been refuted by subsequent research. In order to provide an explanation that is truly meaningful, it would need to be more specific. For example, an explanation for a decision may need to state that it was based on 'conclusions made in [*n*] peer reviewed scientific papers – [*papers, p1, p2, p3, … n*] – in top tier journals – [*journals, j1, j2, j3, … n*] – that have not been refuted by

[5] I have previously identified predictability as one of the common themes that exist across all of these accounts. P Burgess, 'The Rule of Law: Beyond Contestedness' (2017) 8(3) *Jurisprudence* 480.

[6] ibid.

[7] ibid.

[8] F Pasquale, *The Black Box Society: The Secret Algorithms That Control Money and Information*, reprint edn (Cambridge, Mass, Harvard University Press, 2016).

subsequent research'. This provides the relative criteria that could be augmented by a list of the particular papers that have been used to arrive at the decision. This augmented explanation would be far more meaningful in explaining a decision. This sort of explanation would assist in providing predictability as the *way* in which a decision has been made would be evident.

This sort of process is, in fact, contemplated in the UK's Misuse of Drugs Act 1971 which requires, as part of section 2(5) that any recommendation must be made on the basis of consultation with an Advisory Council. That Advisory Council produces substantial documents that relate to the addition/removal of items to/from the schedule of controlled drugs that are far more extensive than the example set out above. The published material can include factors that provide a recommendation and broad evidence, but also a detailed consideration of background factors, an explanation of the nature and effect of a drug, the analytical and methodological techniques used to arrive at a conclusion, and extensive appendices.[9] The suggestion here is not that the requirements of explainability associated with predictability in the Rule of Law are satisfied by virtue of the Advisory Council's approach – it is entirely conceivable that the content of any report may *not* be sufficient to achieve predictability. However, the relative baseline that the Advisory Council establishes does indicate that not only is something more than a bare recommendation required, but also that the form of explanation advised above (relating to journal articles) would be considerably briefer than that which already exists. This briefer form may still achieve the end requirement of predictability; yet the level of explainability that is currently seen as being adequate goes far beyond this.

Large language models like ChatGPT can provide an extensive rationale for a position that may appear to satisfy similar criteria to the reports that are currently produced by the Advisory Council. However, whilst the utility and ability of systems like ChatGPT is continually and rapidly evolving, at the time of writing the system is not able to greatly impact either governance or transparency and in medical settings (as well as others) it has been prone to errors and or the fabrication of information.[10] On this basis, at this stage, the potential for a level of explainability at the level of that provided by the Advisory Council, from an AI system that can be relied upon, remains a hypothetical vision.

[9] See, eg, Advisory Council on Advisory Council on the Misuse of Drugs, 'Consumer Cannabidiol (CBD) Products Report', *GOV.UK*: www.gov.uk/government/publications/acmd-advice-on-consumer-cannabidiol-cbd-products/consumer-cannabidiol-cbd-products-report-accessible-version.

[10] RI Sifat, 'ChatGPT and the Future of Health Policy Analysis: Potential and Pitfalls of Using ChatGPT in Policymaking' [2023] *Annals of Biomedical Engineering*: doi.org/10.1007/s10439-023-03204-2; GM Currie, 'Academic Integrity and Artificial Intelligence: Is ChatGPT Hype, Hero or Heresy?' [2023] *Seminars in Nuclear Medicine*: www.sciencedirect.com/science/article/pii/S0001299823000363; M Bhattacharyya et al, 'High Rates of Fabricated and Inaccurate References in ChatGPT-Generated Medical Content' [2023] *Cureus*: www.cureus.com/articles/158289-high-rates-of-fabricated-and-inaccurate-references-in-chatgpt-generated-medical-content.

Accordingly, as with the previous hypothetical, what can be seen is that there is a need for explainability to satisfy the Rule of Law but, the way that this may need to be required in order to match that which exists (in providing an explanation of a decision) cannot yet be achieved by an AI. Once it can, and once the rationale provided can be trusted (unlike with ChatGPT at present, for example), then an AI's function in the role contemplated in this hypothetical could be adequately discharged in a way that facilitates predictability. This would allow this element of the Rule of Law to be satisfied.

The other element of the Rule of Law is procedural clarity. The discussion immediately above, and the explanation relating to the role of the Advisory Council, assists greatly in this regard. The *process* by which any amendment is made in the example above is clear: the Advisory Council considers its recommendation; a draft Order is laid before Parliament; the Schedule is amended; and, the norm that relates to the possession of drugs is changed. In this example, the procedure is clear. In circumstances where the wider hypothetical relates to the delegation of power from a legislature to another body, it seems likely that the terms on which that form of delegated power is delegated may be clear. However, a delegation may also be unclear. For example, there is a broad and unclear delegation of power in Australia's Atomic Energy Act 1965, where in section 65 it is stated:

> The Governor-General may make regulations, not inconsistent with this Act, prescribing matters:
>
> (a) required or permitted by this Act to be prescribed; or
>
> (b) necessary or convenient to be prescribed for carrying out or giving effect to this Act.

An unclear delegative process may also be governed by a general piece of legislation – as, for example, is provided in the Administrative Procedure in Government Agencies Act 1946 (US) – where a broadly-stated delegative process is provided. This broadly stated aspect of procedural clarity would not relate to whether an AI or a human (or other entity) is responsible for actioning the delegation. The key aspect of the delegative function that would need to be clear in terms of AI and the Rule of Law would be the *process* that is adopted by the AI in changing the relevant norm. In this respect, the examination above applies: as long as the AI is following (and can be seen to be following) the required process, then there would be little issue in relation to the broad-brush aspect of the Past Rule of Law. But this would require that the AI that has had power delegated to it would need to be demonstrably following the terms of that grant. As will now be familiar, this means that the AI would need to be able to explain the processes that it has adopted.

B. Past Rule of Law's Thinkers and Hypothetical Two

Do any particular facets of the Past Rule of Law thinkers' conceptions of the Rule of Law suggest a different position to that relating to the broad-brush suggestion above? In considering the terms of the hypothetical – where an AI is creating secondary laws based on its own investigations and conclusions and is doing so in a way that is more efficient and at least as accurate as a human decision-maker – the earliest three usual suspect accounts appear to be the most relevant. Aristotle, Locke, and Dicey provide accounts that, respectively, relate to a form of legislative due process, and the need for accountability in both legislative decision-making and decision-making outside of the courts. These are each explored in more detail below.

This is not to say that the other usual suspects have no relevance. Key ideas relating to predictability associated with Raz, Fuller, and Hayek have already been explored in general terms. Whilst I do not explore them in depth again here, they can equally be attributed to each of the specific thinkers. Hayek's concerns relating to coercion specifically do apply here – as secondary legislation would also be a norm that could facilitate the form of coercion that Hayek seeks to avoid – yet, as noted above, this can be alleviated in circumstances where there is at least some element of explainability to the decision. Where there is no possibility or capability for an explanation, Hayek's concerns – and the general concerns noted in the previous sub-section – remain apposite. The same consideration applies in terms of Raz and Fuller's various desiderata. For example, in terms of the Fullerian dislike of retrospective legislation explored earlier. If it is assumed that the hypothetical AI's creation of secondary laws is not retrospective, then there is no concern; but, if it can make retrospective secondary laws, then the broad-brush principle of predictability would not be satisfied.

Aristotle seeks a form of cool-headedness in the making of laws. He required that such *law-making* decisions be made slowly and with due consideration.[11] I am not suggesting that Aristotle had in his contemplation the creation of *secondary* legislation by an *AI*. After all, Aristotle's comment is made against a classical backdrop that has at its core a very different form of law-making than exists in most contemporary legislatures.[12] Yet, the broad idea that Aristotle suggests does relate to this hypothetical. The notion that laws that are made rapidly by individuals driven by emotions (the passions) will not be 'good' laws,[13] seems relevant to consider when an AI is making laws in a more efficient way then humans – particularly when 'more efficient' here relates to the potential massive increase in the processing speed of a machine over that of a human.

Aristotle's contention raises two relevant worries: first, is the idea that emotions may be problematic in a situation like Hypothetical Two; second, is the suggestion that speed – of itself – is a bad thing as errors will follow. The first would require emotions to exist in the AI that is responsible for creating the secondary laws. It has been suggested that it may be beneficial for some forms of AI to demonstrate

[11] Aristotle, *Rhetoric*, trans W Rhys Roberts (London, Dover, 2004) 1, Ch 1.
[12] This was explored in more detail in ch 2.
[13] Aristotle (n 11) 1, ch 1.

or have emotions.[14] However, replication of human emotions is not without its difficulties and complexities.[15] What is important to consider, however, is that this is not merely an *imitation game*. The Turing Test – where an AI's ability to 'think' and fool a human into believing that an AI with which they are communicating is another human – and the ability for a machine to think more generally may initially appear relevant here especially as one component of that idea relates to the role of emotion.[16] This is not the place to delve deeply into the precise meaning and application of the Turing Test and the role of emotion in machine learning.[17] This is also not the place to consider the actual ability of a machine to emote a real – or even a passable – form of emotion, as what Aristotle seeks is a form of law-making that is *devoid* of emotion. This inability to *have* emotions appears to be something that a machine may have as a default. In this sense, Aristotle's fear about emotion-fuelled decision-making seems to have no purchase. Accordingly, in the absence of a machine being programmed to make decisions emotionally, it seems that the Aristotelean requirement that laws be made in the absence of emotion would be satisfied. This suggests emotions are not problematic in a situation like Hypothetical Two.

The second worry arising from Aristotle's ideas would be that speed – of itself – in making the secondary legislation is a bad thing. The suggestion appears to be either that an increase in speed in human decision-making may result in sub-optimal outcomes either through errors per se or through a lack of fulsome decision-making processes.[18] It is clear that modern AI systems can perform particular calculations many millions of times faster than humans. When this is considered in the context of the fact that computers are, at their core, calculation machines,[19] and they are exceptional at this task, it becomes clear where efficiencies may occur in terms of the deployment of AI systems to perform certain tasks. With this in mind, limitations in relation to processing speed will mean the time taken to make more complicated decisions will increase; however, the

[14] J Martínez-Miranda and A Aldea, 'Emotions in Human and Artificial Intelligence' (2005) 21(2) *Computers in Human Behavior* 323.

[15] L Stark and J Hoey, 'The Ethics of Emotion in Artificial Intelligence Systems' in *Proceedings of the 2021 ACM Conference on Fairness, Accountability, and Transparency* (ACM, 2021) 782: dl.acm.org/doi/10.1145/3442188.3445939; O Oritsegbemi, 'Human Intelligence versus AI: Implications for Emotional Aspects of Human Communication' (2023) 6(2) *Journal of Advanced Research in Social Sciences* 76.

[16] AM Turing, 'I. – Computing Machinery and Intelligence' (1950) LIX(236) *Mind* 433.

[17] One aspect of this debate is explored between these opposing views: M Wheeler, 'Deceptive Appearances: The Turing Test, Response-Dependence, and Intelligence as an Emotional Concept' (2020) 30(4) *Minds and Machines* 513; D Proudfoot, 'Rethinking Turing's Test and the Philosophical Implications' (2020) 30(4) *Minds and Machines* 487.

[18] The increased provision of time to scenario-plan and consider options can lead to the avoidance of failures in decision-making. See, eg, TJ Chermack, 'Improving Decision-Making with Scenario Planning' (2004) 36(3) *Futures* 295. Decision-making under pressure can have an impact on the decision-maker: P Wright, 'The Harassed Decision Maker: Time Pressures, Distractions, and the Use of Evidence' (1974) 59 *Journal of Applied Psychology* 555.

[19] (Pun intended.) See ch 3 for a more detailed consideration of what a computer *is*.

vast numbers of calculations that can be carried out by a machine (compared to a human) and the fact that computer calculations are far less prone to (human) error mean that even decisions based on calculations slowed due to processing limitations are likely to be made far faster and with fewer errors than a human. In this respect, where Hypothetical Two suggests that the AI system is functioning in a way to make the relevant calculations regarding the data available to it, there seems to be no reason why speed, of itself, would be a problem with regard to the Aristotelean worry.

Locke did not have a particular problem with speed in law-making. He sought to argue that a form of rule based in a Parliament – as an entity that was accountable in some way to the people – was superior to a form of royal or papal rule that, he suggested, was more likely to be tyrannical.[20] Dicey also sought accountability. His issue was the relative rise in power of unaccountable administrative decision-makers.[21] These ideas were explored earlier in this chapter. (They were also explored in chapter two and they will be returned to in detail in this chapter when considering the Present Rule of Law). What is notable in this hypothetical is that there does appear to be a relative absence of accountability in terms of the entity making the decision to add or remove a new substance to a list of drugs – as it may be questioned as to whether and to what extent a machine can be accountable; but, as will be seen, there does exist a form of accountability – at least in relation to the state-based decision making apparatus – through the retention of a human-over-the-loop that is contemplated in the process of making secondary legislation that is represented by the legislature's (rarely used) veto-like oversight function.

To consider these ideas, it is useful to recall that Dicey sought to ensure that the entity that was making the rules was also subject to the rules. As noted above, Dicey said: 'every man, whatever be his rank or condition, is subject to the ordinary law of the realm and amenable to the jurisdiction of the ordinary tribunals'.[22] This requirement for legal equality seems to not be possible where an AI system may *not* be subject to the same form of accountability as other legal entities. The present hypothetical relates to the inclusion of a drug on a proscribed drug list, but machines cannot consume these forms of drugs nor could they be punished for their possession. Even beyond this narrow example, machines cannot be held accountable in the same way that humans can in general; they cannot be imprisoned; they cannot be fired; and they cannot lose any reputation.[23] (Although, in relation to the latter two points it is accepted that a machine can be turned off, there is no suggestion that this would operate so as to be an accountability mechanism in

[20] J Locke, *Two Treatises of Government*, Peter Laslett (ed), (Cambridge, Cambridge University Press, 1988) II, 137.

[21] AV Dicey, *Introduction to the Study of the Law of the Constitution*, 10th edn (Basingstoke, Palgrave Macmillan, 1979) 195.

[22] ibid 193.

[23] J Chen and P Burgess, 'The Boundaries of Legal Personhood: How Spontaneous Intelligence Can Problematise Differences between Humans, Artificial Intelligence, Companies and Animals' (2019) 27(1) *Artificial Intelligence and Law* 73.

the absence of it being programmed as being the case.) In these regards, the need for accountability in machines and the inability for accountability to be properly attached to AI systems – especially in public decision-making where there is a need for transparency – represents a substantive limitation.[24]

Locke's need for an accountability mechanism faces a similar hurdle relating to the inability to hold AI systems themselves accountable. His fear, where power was held absolutely in either a monarch or a pope, related precisely to having an entity that was beyond the reach of the laws. Similar to Dicey's suggested need for legal equality, Locke's Rule of Law idea saw a limitation of tyranny by ensuring that the entity that was responsible for law-making was accountable – at least at some level – to the people. When seen in this light, it seems that a fear associated with tyrannical decision-making may remain in some form for Locke where an AI is making secondary legislation. I say 'in some form' as Locke's concern was for primary legislation and laws being made by an absolute sovereign. But, in this hypothetical, the AI system relates to secondary legislation that is, necessarily, made by an entity that is not sovereign and, instead, has had power delegated to it by the legislature. Not only can the powers be revoked, but also the creation of secondary legislation itself is – albeit often only formally – required to be supervised in some way by the legislature. The relative oversight by the legislature, for both Locke and Dicey, provides a relative tempering of the conclusions reached above. The very nature of delegated legislation means that there is some level of a human being over-the-loop. So, whilst Locke and Dicey may have a Rule of Law objection against the exercise of delegated power by an AI, this objection may well be softened because the AI's decisions – much like a conventional delegatee's secondary legislation decisions – are subject to oversight by the legislature.

The relative level of oversight is, however, minimal. The level, at least as it is currently practiced in relation to delegated legislation, is tantamount to nothing more than a potential veto. Furthermore, as noted above, there are still substantive problems associated with what it means to hold an AI accountable that were noted earlier; there is no loss of reputation or any other potential penalty that would likely motivate an AI to operate in a particular way. What this means is that the potential accountability mechanism that could be seen to exist seems incapable of achieving the level of accountability that Dicey and Locke sought in their conceptions. This, severely tempered, conclusion faces further complications when the sphere of accountability is broadened beyond the state-based sphere that the Past Rule of Law idea focuses on. I will return to this issue below in considering the Present Rule of Law.

What can be seen in relation to the consideration of these three Past Rule of Law usual suspects is that the concerns raised by Aristotle, relating to emotion-fuelled and rapid decision-making, may appear to be problematic for an AI

[24] M Busuioc, 'Accountable Artificial Intelligence: Holding Algorithms to Account' (2021) 81(5) *Public Administration Review* 825.

system in this hypothetical, a deeper consideration reveals that this is not the case. Similarly, with Locke and Dicey, the initial problems that arise due to the fact that an AI cannot be held accountable in the sorts of ways that they both wanted law makers to be, there is a form of accountability that still exists through the delegated nature of the law-making powers. This does, of course, indicate that it is the delegated nature of the powers themselves that render the exercise of power by an AI system in the way that is contemplated in this hypothetical potentially acceptable to these Past Rule of Law thinkers. In other words, there is a form of accountability that is maintained through the grant of the delegated power – even though that appears to not be sufficient to provide an effective and fulsome accountability mechanism. This naturally leads to questions related to how each thinker would view the exercise of a primary law-making power. Consideration of these points will take place in the next chapter. Before that, it is first necessary to consider the Present Rule of Law in relation to this hypothetical.

IV. The Present Rule of Law

The precise terms of the Present Rule of Law were set out in detail in chapter two (and expanded upon in chapter four.) The Present Rule of Law is constituted by works authored after those that constitute the Past Rule of Law. The temporal distinction is, however, not an arbitrarily distinguished point. Instead, the distinction between the Past and the Present form can be seen through conceptual differences that take two forms. These are adopted in this book to distinguish two forms of the Present Rule of Law. The first form provides a point of difference to the problem of state-based arbitrary exercise of power in the Past and provides a form that responds to the exercise of arbitrary power *in general*. The second contrasts the formal/procedural nature of the Past Rule of Law solutions that is not concerned with *outcomes* and, instead, provides a substantive meaning of the Rule of Law.

It is important to recall that the Past and Present ideas share fundamental ideas. Both forms of the Present Rule of Law, to some degree, adopt various aspects of the Past Rule of Law. In this sense, the Present ideas are built on a base constructed from the Past Rule of Law.[25] In building on this foundation, the Present Rule of Law goes beyond the requirements of the Past Rule of Law. The ways in which this happens reflect the differences in form. In the first difference, the Present Rule of Law relates to the *source* of the arbitrary application of power – not limiting the source to a state-based exercise of power. In the second, there is a need to achieve substantively good *outcomes* – if laws that are made attain a particular end, the

[25] Thick/substantive ideas of the Rule of Law are built on a thin/formal base. (n 5) 485.

Rule of Law satisfies its function.[26] Whilst the foundational role that the Past Rule of Law plays to the Present blurs the boundary between the two, the difference between conceptions – as a difference in focus between the *outcomes* and in the *source* of arbitrary power – will, I hope, be clear enough lines of distinction even where there is some overlap.

In chapters two and four, I provided further detail relating to the reason why the Past Rule of Law conceptions are limited to the *state-based* arbitrary exercise of power – as they can be seen as solutions to problems that are caused by the application of power by the state. These solutions cannot, without considerable licence being taken with the context of their authorship and/or the words that they use, be seen as solutions to problems that extend beyond the state-based application of power. The first form of the Present Rule of Law goes beyond this idea of the state-based *source* of exercise of power. This means the anti-arbitrariness function of the Rule of Law becomes relevant to relations within in a private setting – that is, individual to individual. Martin Krygier and Jeff King provide the two accounts that I use as illustrative of this form. (Many others also have similar accounts.[27])

The second form of the Present Rule of Law reflects another point of difference to the Past Rule of Law. The second form of the Present Rule of Law has an interest in *outcomes*. The two conceptions I use to exemplify this idea are those provided by Tom Bingham and the United Nations (UN). Past Rule of Law ideas provide procedural or thin solutions to the problems associated with the arbitrary exercise of power – the relative goodness of the laws or decisions that then follow from those processes is of little consequence. (I provided more detail about this in chapter four.) This differs to the Present Rule of Law ideas provided by Bingham and the UN. Each in different ways see *outcomes* as being important in the Rule of Law calculus.

The two forms of the Present Rule of Law – relating to both the *source* of arbitrary power, and the *outcome* of the Rule of Law – are considered below in relation to Hypothetical Two. In order to do this, I first, in the sub-section immediately below, consider the application of the hypothetical in the broad sense of the two forms. Then, in the next two sub-sections, I delve more deeply into the conceptions that make up each of the two forms.

[26] The classic statement of the thin and thick ideas of the Rule of Law is provided by Craig. P Craig, 'Formal and Substantive Conceptions of the Rule of Raw an Analytical Framework' [1997] (Autumn) *Public Law* 467.

[27] LM Austin and D Klimchuk (eds), *Private Law and the Rule of Law* (Oxford, Oxford University Press, 2014). JA Sempill, 'The Lions and the Greatest Part: The Rule of Law and the Constitution of Employer Power' (2017) 9(2) *Hague Journal on the Rule of Law* 283. A special issue of *International Journal of Law in Context* introduces this position. K Bhatt, J Lander and S Taekema, 'Introduction: The Rule of Law in Transnational Development Projects – Private Actors and Public Chokeholds' (2021) 17(1) *International Journal of Law in Context* 91. Whilst I was a part of that special issue, I held a contrary view: P Burgess, 'Googling the Equivalence of Private Arbitrary Power and State Arbitrary Power: Why The Rule of Law Does Not Relate to Private Relationships' [2021] *International Journal of Law in Context.*

A. The Forms of the Present Rule of Law

In the broadest terms, the Present Rule of Law either responds to any form of arbitrary power (source-based form) or that there be substantive aims or benefits associated with the idea (outcome-based form). In considering these ideas in the most abstract sense in terms of the hypothetical in this chapter it becomes apparent that, although issues relating to explainability remain, the Present Rule of Law provides additional protections (in comparison to the Past ideas of the Rule of Law) where power may be exercised by private entities.

In taking a broad source-based approach, as issues of arbitrariness relating to public power have already been addressed in the previous section – and the conclusions drawn remain appropriate here as the Present Rule of Law uses the ideas associated with the Past Rule of Law as a foundation – the consideration is whether this hypothetical raises any *additional* concerns relating to the exercise of arbitrary power. In circumstances where the AI in this hypothetical is creating secondary legislation, that impacts individuals with relatively little oversight – as humans are over-the-loop – the entity that is actually exercising the delegated law-making power may be seen as something other than the AI; it could be seen to be the entity responsible for creating or programming the AI. This entity may not necessarily be a public body. This would represent a problem for ideas of the Rule of Law – like the Past Rule of Law – that have the state as a necessary component.

As has been noted in previous chapters, the creation of technologies that assist in the public execution of laws – like the COMPAS system that has been used to predict recidivism – may be created and developed by private companies for use in the public sector.[28] The creation of the technology and the mechanisms by which it works may be closely held intellectual property that the creators may not wish to share. Even if the basis for the technology is shared, the now-familiar issues associated with the black-box may still occur.[29] In these circumstances, the issue becomes one of identifying the relative sovereign-power in terms of the secondary law-making function; whilst it may appear to be the AI that is making the decisions, the decision-making function may be able to be traced back to the programmers or the entity that created the AI in the first place. (This is explored in further detail in chapter six.)

In circumstances where this may be the case, and where the AI in this hypothetical is largely *creating* rules and regulations that impact the public, a form of the Rule of Law that can apply to private entities has further application that the Past ideas do not. As noted above, the Past Rule of Law would have no direct interest in the private entities – the formulation adopted above would see the Past Rule of Law ideas as being unable to combat any private-arbitrariness. The Present

[28] J Dressel and H Farid, 'The Accuracy, Fairness, and Limits of Predicting Recidivism' (2018) 4(1) *Science Advances* eaao5580.

[29] Pasquale (n 8).

Rule of Law has no such restriction and would directly engage with, and require, that there be no arbitrariness that stems from the private entity responsible for the creation of the AI. This facilitates a deeper layer of Rule of Law protection.

In terms of the abstractly considered outcome-based form of the Present Rule of Law, the question would turn to whether the introduction of the technology has some form of particular or beneficial outcome. In the last chapter, it was noted that the use of AI in many respects is intended to provide benefits that may include the relative, speed and accuracy of decisions. In this respect, in considering the non-dystopian approach of this book, it is assumed that the AI in this hypothetical is functioning as it should in making the decisions – although, issues that have been already addressed relating to the *way* in which decisions are made and the potential for bias to exist in the system remain relevant issues. It is, therefore, assumed that there is some sort of beneficial outcome and that this is desired – as the system would not be introduced if this were not the case. The question as to whether this sort of benefit is of Rule of Law-relevance is addressed in the consideration of the outcome-based accounts of both Bingham and the UN, below.

B. Present Rule of Law – Source-Based – And Hypothetical Two

As suggested in the sub-section immediately above, this hypothetical brings into focus the issue of accountability. This issue will remain a relative constant through the rest of the book as the level of human involvement in the exercise of state power diminishes. The issue is pertinent to both source-based theorists that I focus on – King and Krygier. Their ideas can be seen to provide additional support and solutions in terms of the questions relating to *what* entity is accountable and *how* is the entity responsible.

Krygier's purposive idea of the Rule of Law describes a Rule of Law that has, at its core, the prevention of arbitrary power wherever that power may be located.[30] This means that Krygier, together with many other contemporary Rule of Law theorists, see the Rule of Law as being able to respond to private exercises of arbitrary power.[31] In this hypothetical, the exercise of power by a committee of humans in making recommendations and laying papers, is replaced by an AI. That AI is operating in the same institutional capacity and, in simple terms, replaces the

[30] M Krygier, 'The Rule of Law: Legality, Teleology and Sociology' in G Palombella and N Walker (eds), *Relocating the Rule of Law* (Oxford, Hart Publishing, 2009); M Krygier, 'What's the Point of the Rule of Law?' 67 *Buffalo Law Review* 50; J King, 'Martin Krygier and the Tempering of Power' (2019) 11(2) *Hague Journal on the Rule of Law* 363; L Rodak, 'From Rules of Life to Rules of Law. An Account of M. Krygier Approach to Sociological Jurisprudence' (2019) 11(2) *Hague Journal on the Rule of Law* 283.

[31] For different forms of this approach, see, eg, Bhatt, Lander and Taekema (n 27); Sempill (n 27); Austin and Klimchuk (n 27).

human function. If the exercise of power is seen as institutional, that would designate the power as being of a public body. This means both the Past Rule of Law and the Present Rule of Law would provide solutions. However, if the replacement of the human function with a machine is seen to alter that institutional arrangement, perhaps because – as will be explored in the following sub-section – there is less accountability for the *machine*. In circumstances where accountability represents a fundamental problem for the deployment and use of AI, an alternate mechanism for accountability may be sought.[32] An attempt may be made to pierce the AI veil and hold the entity that created the AI accountable. This would require an alteration of the institutional arrangement; no longer is the entity *making* the decisions being held accountable. I do not suggest this would be the only, or even the best, option available. But it would be one option. Should this happen, the Past Rule of Law would cease to have relevance – as, it is assumed, that the entity that creates the AI would be a private entity. (This is simply based on the fact that public bodies are not in the business of making AI systems.) In this regard, whilst Krygier's purposive approach may not have a particular problem with the hypothetical noted here, his account does provide a more varied and versatile solution than the Past Rule of Law.

King's idea of the social dimension of the Rule of Law would see the operation of a positive duty to take steps to enhance social benefit.[33] Whilst this idea could be seen to apply to the hypothetical more in terms of *how* the arbitrary power is ultimately delegated, the result is similar to that described above; a more versatile solution to the potential arbitrary exercise of power is possible.

If a duty exists that requires actions to be taken that increase social benefit, in broad terms this could operate so as to limit the way in which power could be delegated to the AI – as the power that is exercised is required to be delegated *to* the AI from the legislature. It seems that a corollary of King's social dimension would mean either that the delegation of power itself resulted in benefit or, alternatively, that should the delegation result in detriment, that the delegation should be revoked. In these circumstances, whilst this positive duty aspect would not oppose an AI acting in this delegated role, it must be able to provide a benefit to have the power delegated to it or it must continue to provide a benefit or else it would have the power revoked. These instances would, of course, include the exercise of arbitrary power as a non-benefit. In these senses, the consideration of the social dimension in terms of the hypothetical provides an increased layer of protection when contrasted to the Past Rule of Law.

A further extension of this idea may stretch the hypothetical further. If it can be demonstrated that an AI was able to achieve an objectively *better* result than a

[32] BW Wirtz, JC Weyerer and BJ Sturm, 'The Dark Sides of Artificial Intelligence: An Integrated AI Governance Framework for Public Administration' (2020) 43(9) *International Journal of Public Administration* 818.

[33] J King, 'The Rule of Law' in R Bellamy and J King (eds), *The Cambridge Handbook of Constitutional Theory* (2024) papers.ssrn.com/abstract=4487306.

human-based advisory body, it seems it may be the case that there would then be a *duty* to delegate power to the AI to act in that function. (I merely note this interesting possibility here as this clearly goes beyond the suggestions in this hypothetical that there simply has been an AI invested with power to make decisions.)

C. Present Rule of Law – Outcome-Based – And Hypothetical Two

What becomes apparent when considering this hypothetical in terms of the Present Rule of Law's outcome-based ideas is that the need for accountability in the process is essential. This is the case despite the different ways in which Bingham and the UN see the operation of the Rule of Law. For Bingham, in consequence of the need for accountability, it is difficult for the sort of AI application imagined satisfying his Rule of Law requirements. For the UN, whilst the conclusion is the same, the reasons are different – the need for explainability impacts fairness which, in turn, means the UN's Rule of Law cannot be satisfied.

In order to reach this conclusion, it is useful to consider the sorts of principles that this hypothetical invokes. In general terms, the idea of good governance is an outcome that would be seen as a positive.[34] The idea of good governance is closely related to the positive frameworks that are required in order to realise and protect human rights.[35] For this reason, the idea of good governance can be seen as being relevant to both Bingham's idea – that requires human rights principles to be adhered to in a Rule of Law state – and the UN's idea – that sees the Rule of Law as being a vehicle for the realisation of human rights.

The principle of good governance includes a prominent focus on the need for accountability. This, together with a need for transparency, causes the idea of good governance to be frequently discussed in common with the Rule of Law.[36] In this respect, there is a close interrelationship and a potential overlap. The issues of good governance and, in particular, accountability are key issues here – more so than the hypothetical in the previous chapter – because in this chapter, the AI system is operating more autonomously; the system is one where humans are only over-the-loop in a broadly supervisory function.

States are primarily accountable for respecting and protecting the rights of those within their jurisdiction – the form and nature of this accountability requires

[34] United Nations, Economic and Social Commission for Asia and the, and United Nations Economic and Social Commission for Asia and the Pacific, *What Is Good Governance?*.

[35] United Nations, 'About Good Governance – OHCHR and Good Governance', *OHCHR*: www.ohchr.org/en/good-governance/about-good-governance.

[36] H Addink, 'The Rule of Law and Good Governance' in *Good Governance: Concept and Context* (Oxford, Oxford University Press, 2019) 75; AN Licht, C Goldschmidt and SH Schwartz, 'Culture Rules: The Foundations of the Rule of Law and Other Norms of Governance' (2007) 35(4) *Journal of Comparative Economics* 659.

that there be a body that is responsible and answerable as well as being subject to enforcement mechanisms.[37] The idea of which entity is responsible is seen as being broad. It does not only include the public institution of the state that is responsible – the responsible entity can also extend to any duty bearers that are involved in the adherence or promotion of rights.[38] This means that partners to government should also be accountable – which, in turn, can include both tool-makers and tool-users.[39] The group to which accountability may attach would include individuals and organisations – whether public, private, for profit or not for profit.[40] By conceiving of the sphere of accountability in this way, the use of technology and AI in order to improve public service delivery is encapsulated.[41] This means that good governance, if it is to be realised in the terms of this hypothetical, would require accountability to extend to those responsible for the creation and operation of the AI system that is creating the secondary legislation.

In line with what has been suggested already, the broad ideal of introducing AI for deployment in the public sector would require the advancement of the public good.[42] In addition, and in further overlap with ideas that are common across ideas of the Rule of Law, the introduction of this form of AI would also need to be transparent.[43] Questions related to the nature of accountability when AI is deployed in the public sector have been asked before.[44] In this respect, due in part to the difficulties associated with legal personality, it may not be easy to identify the legal status of the entity in charge.[45] Furthermore, it is not always clear who may be accountable when decisions are made by an AI.[46] All of these complications raise substantial issues that may arise in general when attempting to

[37] United Nations, *Who Will Be Accountable? Human Rights and the Post-2015 Development Agenda* (2013) www.ohchr.org/sites/default/files/Documents/Publications/WhoWillBeAccountable.pdf.

[38] ibid.

[39] DF Kettl, *The Transformation of Governance: Public Administration for the Twenty-First Century* (Baltimore, JHU Press, 2015).

[40] LB Bingham, T Nabatchi and R O'Leary, 'The New Governance: Practices and Processes for Stakeholder and Citizen Participation in the Work of Government' (2005) 65(5) *Public Administration Review* 547, 547.

[41] KP Gupta, 'Artificial Intelligence for Governance in India: Prioritizing the Challenges Using Analytic Hierarchy Process (AHP)' (2019) 8(2) *International Journal of Recent Technology and Engineering* 3756.

[42] C Cath et al, 'Artificial Intelligence and the "Good Society": The US, EU, and UK Approach' (2018) 24(2) *Science and Engineering Ethics* 505.

[43] J Bryson and A Winfield, 'Standardizing Ethical Design for Artificial Intelligence and Autonomous Systems' (2017) 50(5) *Computer* 116; H-Wei Liu, C-Fu Lin and Y-Jie Chen, 'Beyond State v Loomis: Artificial Intelligence, Government Algorithmization and Accountability' (2019) 27(2) *International Journal of Law and Information Technology* 122.

[44] Wirtz, Weyerer and Sturm (n 32).

[45] ibid; Chen and Burgess (n 23).

[46] YK Dwivedi et al, 'Artificial Intelligence (AI): Multidisciplinary Perspectives on Emerging Challenges, Opportunities, and Agenda for Research, Practice and Policy' (2021) 57 *International Journal of Information Management* 101994; S Fatima, KC Desouza and GS Dawson, 'National Strategic Artificial Intelligence Plans: A Multi-Dimensional Analysis' (2020) 67 *Economic Analysis and Policy* 178; JB Bullock, 'Artificial Intelligence, Discretion, and Bureaucracy' (2019) 49(7) *The American Review of Public Administration* 751.

understand the entity that is accountable or responsible for a particular decision. The hypothetical in this chapter encompasses many of these issues; but it also goes beyond these ideas in considering the way that the Rule of Law may be important when they are considered.

These intertwining ideas of good governance, accountability, and transparency are all core components of a functioning system that respects human rights. In this respect, each of the intertwining ideas also relates to the Rule of Law conceptions provided by Bingham and the UN. It will be recalled from the last chapter that one key difference between these two Rule of Law ideas is that the Bingham sees human rights satisfaction as a necessary feature and a way of achieving of a Rule of Law state, whereas the UN sees the Rule of Law as a necessary feature and a way of achieving human rights. As will be seen, these two positions mean the intertwining ideas associated with good governance when considered in terms of the hypothetical result in quite different outcomes.

For Bingham, there is a need for human rights to be satisfied in order to achieve a Rule of Law state.[47] Given the good governance implications above, the satisfaction of human rights will, at least in part, require systems of accountability and transparency. The importance of transparency – at least as it relates to explainable AI – has been explored earlier in the chapter. Whilst those considerations remain relevant to the Rule of Law considerations, it is also necessary to consider them in relation to the human rights elements. When considering these things in terms of an AI system that is creating secondary legislation, the issue of accountability becomes paramount. (This is further explored in the following chapter where it is, arguably, even more important.) For the principle of good governance to be satisfied, a feature that is necessary to provide a human rights-positive system, the use of the AI system will not only need to be transparent, but also there would need to be someone, or something, accountable.

In terms of accountability, I explored in the previous section that humans may have motivators that may assist in making them accountable (financial or reputational for example). In this hypothetical, the humans that provide the recommendations for changes in the schedule of proscribed drugs have been replaced. But, in replacing them with an AI, it is not immediately clear where the accountability – in terms of good governance – may lie. As secondary legislation, it may lie ultimately with the legislature. But this seems to not address the fact that the previous human decision makers were also accountable. The public servants that are responsible for implementing the system may be another avenue of accountability; but, again, this seems to miss holding the actual decision-maker accountable. There exists an accountability gap. In this regard, the AI itself would not be able to hold any substantive form of accountability. Even if it was a legal person, and there is no suggestion in this hypothetical that it is, at least one key element of accountability, that of enforceability, seems to be impotent in the face of attempting to

[47] T Bingham, *The Rule of Law* (London, Allen Lane, 2010) 7.

sanction an algorithm. Accountability could lie with the programmer/s or the entity that created the AI system. There are some legal hurdles in this respect that relate to the locus of accountability/liability; but, even if this is put aside, holding a corporation (or similar) accountable in this way for the purposes of determining – even in part – whether a system is capable of being a Rule of Law system may not be appealing to some. Yet, in circumstances where the broad-based nature of good governance requires a holistic and many-faceted approach to accountability, this conclusion may be more attractive in terms where it is pointed out that the real *absence* of accountability on the part of an entity like this would mean that the system of which it is a part *cannot* be a Rule of Law state. This may seem to be more palatable in much the same way that an absence of transparency – through an unexplainable form of AI, for example – would cause real problems for the Rule of Law.

What this all means is that, for Bingham at least, there would need to be a clear chain of accountability in the creation, operation, and application of the AI system. If there was a lack of accountability in the way that the system is making its decisions, then human rights and, hence, the Rule of Law, would not be satisfied. On the terms of the hypothetical as it has been stated here, it is not clear that this has been satisfied. Given the difficulties that exist in general with the allocation of accountability when private institutions, particularly large technology institutions, provide services to the public sector, the lines of accountability have generally not always been easy to see or make out. In these respects, it is difficult to see how the provision of a form of technology like the one imagined in this chapter would be able to, ultimately, satisfy the requirements for Bingham's Rule of Law.

The requirements, as noted above, for the UN's Rule of Law idea are, however, different. The UN requires the Rule of Law as part of the attainment of human rights. Its version of the Rule of Law does not, logically, require prior satisfaction of the accountability principles (to achieve human rights) to arrive at the Rule of Law. This means that the conclusion reached immediately above for Bingham's Rule of Law does not apply in terms of the UN. It will be recalled from chapter two that the UN's idea of the Rule of Law requires 'fairness in the application of the law, separation of powers, participation in decision-making, legal certainty, avoidance of arbitrariness and procedural and legal transparency'.[48] This compendious idea of what the Rule of Law encompasses incorporates a substantial number of concepts. In circumstances where certain aspects have been addressed in detail earlier in the chapter, two stand out as being important: fairness in the application of the law; and procedural and legal transparency. I will touch on each to illustrate why the UN's Rule of Law results in a different calculus to Bingham's idea, but arrives at a similar conclusion.

[48] UN Security Council, *The Rule of Law and Transitional Justice in Conflict and Post-Conflict Societies – Report of the Secretary-General* (No UN doc S/2004/616, 23 August 2004) 6: www.un.org/ruleoflaw/files/2004%20report.pdf.

The achievement of fairness in the application of the law is a substantive concept that requires a notion of what 'fairness' is. In the context in which it is given – as 'fairness in the application of the law' – there is a clear requirement that would relate to the previous chapter's hypothetical. However, the present hypothetical also requires application of the law in terms of the factors that are stated as being relevant to be considered in identifying a drug that is sufficiently dangerous so as to be added to the schedule. Accordingly, there is an element of application even though there is also the creation of regulations as a result of the AI's decision-making. Fairness in this context could relate to the absence of bias or favour in relation to the application. In order to satisfy this sort of requirement, it would be necessary to identify the *way* that the decision has been made. Which, again, returns us to the importance of explainability. (Which has been explored earlier.)

In considering the other requirement – the need for procedural and legal transparency – we arrive at the same conclusion. It has already been illustrated earlier in the chapter that the AI system in this hypothetical lacks explainability in relation to its processes. This issue, once again, means that the tenets of the Rule of Law cannot be satisfied in the UN's conception.

The hypothetical illustration in this chapter fails to satisfy the outcomes-based form of the Rule of Law, as provided by Bingham and the UN. However, whilst the root-cause of the failure is the same, the mechanisms by which the failures occur are different. For Bingham, at least in one respect, the absence of explainability would contribute to the inability for the AI system to be accountable. This absence of accountability would mean that the requirements associated with human rights could not be satisfied. For Bingham, this means that a system could not then properly be called a Rule of Law system. For the UN, the conclusion is somewhat simpler: the absence of explainability would mean two core ideas associated with its Rule of Law – fairness and procedural/legal transparency – could not be satisfied.

V. Summary and Conclusions

This chapter has explored a hypothetical in which an AI is responsible for the creation of secondary legislation after being delegated power to do so from the legislature. This differs in kind and in substance from the hypothetical in the previous chapter as, here, it is contemplated that the AI acts with additional autonomy. The AI in this chapter is only broadly subject to supervision; there is a human over-the-loop.

Notwithstanding the relative difference in hypothetical construction, the broadly stated conclusion from the previous chapter – that the Rule of Law is not satisfied due to a fundamental failure in terms of explainability – is also found to be the case in this hypothetical. However, the mechanisms by which this occurs are different. In considering this hypothetical in terms of the Past Rule of Law (both in terms of its broad-brush and the elements of predictability and procedural clarity), the absence of explainability represents a fundamental bar to the prevention of the arbitrary exercise of state power. In this scenario, the decisions made by the AI makes it clearer than the first hypothetical that what is happening is an exercise of state power; the regulations that are created – relatively unsupervised by the AI – may result in individuals being fined or sent to prison. Where the way in which the decisions are made is not explainable, the exercise of power would be arbitrary and, as a result, contrary to the Rule of Law.

In considering the most relevant Past Rule of Law usual suspects – Aristotle, Locke, and Dicey – it becomes apparent that prima facie concerns relating to the speed of decision-making and accountability are, at least to some extent, alleviated by the fact that there is some form of accountability through the delegative process. Whilst this does provide a bare and base level of accountability, this is not sufficient to avoid decisions being considered arbitrary.

Consideration of the Present Rule of Law expands upon the consideration of accountability, but it does so in a different sphere. For Bingham, accountability is fundamental because it is necessary as part of the good governance regime associated with human rights; and, again for Bingham, the achievement of the Rule of Law requires a system that is adhering to and enforcing human rights. In circumstances where an AI cannot explain its decision-making process, it is not capable of satisfying the calculus associated with explainability that spans both public and private institutions. (The Past Rule of Law conceptions only relate to the public, state-based, elements of the exercise of power.) In considering the other Present Rule of Law conception, the UN's use of the Rule of Law as a way to attain human rights, the same calculus does not apply; but, the conclusion is broadly the same. In the absence of explainability in the creation of secondary laws, the UN's core Rule of Law ideals of fairness and transparency cannot be satisfied.

What this means is that, as with the hypothetical in the first chapter, the idea of explainability (and its absence) causes a fundamental problem for adherence to the Rule of Law; however, the way in which this occurs *differs* across both the Past and Present ideas of the Rule of Law as well as across the various conceptions that individual thinkers provide. In providing a conclusion to chapter four, I suggested that I could have created a series of hypotheticals in which the AI-made decisions *were* explainable but noted that my doing so would have made many of the conclusions raised in that chapter (and this one) largely irrelevant. However, that course of action seemed to illuminate little in terms of the fundamental *differences* that can be seen across the failures associated with explainability. In the next chapter, when considering the most extreme form of hypothetical of the three, I will illuminate yet more failures of this kind that are also different to the ones before. Then, in the final chapter I will turn to consider the question of what these repeated and constant failures associated with explainability mean for the use of AI by governments (where, it is assumed, conformity with the Rule of Law is required), as well as suggesting what may happen for and to the Rule of Law where AI's decisions *may* become explainable in the future.

6

The Rule of Law and the Use of AI in Creating Primary Legislation (Making Law)

This chapter considers the exercise of power by AIs in making law – as primary legislation – in terms of the Rule of Law. In this chapter, I demonstrate that not only do we see the problems identified in previous chapters – associated with explainability and accountability – but also the identification of new problems that relate to the speed at which the creation of laws may take place when algorithms populate the legislature. The conclusions drawn in this chapter will combine with the conclusions from the first and second hypotheticals in chapters four and five, to provide a basis for an argument that the Rule of Law will need to change in the future if it is to continue to provide protection against the arbitrary application of power.

The structure and approach of this chapter mirrors, precisely, the previous two chapters. Once again, remaining conscious of those that will be consuming this book in a non-linear way, I provide minimal explanations for the basic ideas that are necessary to ground the arguments and observations that I make whilst, hopefully, avoiding being overly repetitious for those that have already read the preceding chapters. In doing this, particularly in setting out the basic ideas, I do provide broad references back to the sections of the book where more fulsome descriptions can be found. The flexibility that this affords means that this chapter, whilst representing a radical hypothetical view that departs quite some way from the current way in which laws are made, is the shortest of the three hypothetical-based chapters.

The chapter structure, as noted above, replicates that of chapters four and five. There are five substantive sections. After first adding further detail to the terms of the hypothetical (as introduced in chapter three), I then consider the hypothetical in terms of the various ideas of the Rule of Law that I have introduced in this book. I do this by, first, considering the most abstract form of the concept – what I have called the broad-brush idea of the concept. Then, in the third and fourth substantive sections of the chapter I narrow the conceptual focus and consider – each in a different section – the Past Rule of Law and the Present Rule of Law. The final section of the chapter provides a brief conclusion and summary.

In-keeping with the brief-recaps noted above, I commence the three sections following the explanation of the hypothetical with a very short conceptual overview of the Rule of Law ideas that will be considered: the broad-brush, the Past, and the Present Rule of Law ideas. Given the stage of the book, these represent little more than summaries of ideas – which may necessitate non-linear readers seeking further detail elsewhere in the book. (In this respect, the most detailed explanations occur in chapter two, with progressively briefer instances occurring in both chapters four and five.) As suggested above, I first I expand upon the precise terms of this hypothetical.

I. The Use of AI to Make Law

This hypothetical concerns the replacement of the institution responsible for making laws – the legislature – with elected AI systems. Each representative in the legislature would be replaced by an individually elected AI system. In effect, this is a one-for-one swap of human legislators for AI legislators. Those AI systems, as elected algorithmic legislators, would then be responsible for proposing, debating, and passing legislation that operates in their jurisdiction in a way that mirrors the role previously occupied by human legislators. In introducing the first hypothetical in chapter four, I suggested that the hypotheticals introduced through the course of the book would become progressively more 'extreme'. This third hypothetical can be seen as the most extreme in two ways: first, it represents the most futuristic consideration of the application of AI – as the technology that would be required to exist in order to satisfy this role (in a way that would likely be acceptable to and accepted by the individuals subject to the law) is a long way from existing; second, because the adoption of this sort of technology would mean that the way that democracy is and has been practiced in many states around the world would require a substantive upheaval.

The hypothetical in this chapter has some differences to those set out earlier in the book: unlike the first hypothetical, the third has no contemporary parallel where AI is already being used in some way;[1] unlike the second hypothetical, the third has no particular example that can be pointed to, to illustrate the way in which the hypothetical may run. The third hypothetical is *purely* hypothetical in this sense. As noted above, the technology and potential acceptance of the technology to do what is being suggested is a long way off. The AI replacement of the human function is systemic and total – humans are removed from the law-making function entirely. The first hypothetical describes a human-in-the-loop scenario; and the second describes a human-over-the-loop scenario. Here, the humans are out-of-the-loop. They play no role in the creation of the laws to which they are subject. (There is an indirect role, however, which I expand upon later in the chapter.)

[1] I have previously explored a similar hypothetical: P Burgess, 'Algorithmic Augmentation of Democracy: Considering Whether Technology Can Enhance the Concepts of Democracy and the Rule of Law Through Four Hypotheticals' [2021] *AI & Society*.

The classical origins of democracy see the legislator's role as one in which individuals hold a civic duty to care for the state and its people. Whilst it could be said that contemporary legislators may sometimes seek election to high office for reasons other-than civic duty and may (in this respect) not live up to the classical ideal, it is not necessarily the case that the various legislative institutions in democratic states around the world have a strong desire or need to replace those legislators with algorithms. In this sense, it is relevant to acknowledge that in the terms of the *purely* hypothetical situation that is imagined, it is not the case that the replacement of human legislators is based in a particular contemporary need in society. The contemporary lack of need may combine with the fact that the implementation of this idea would see the nature of the democratic function being radically altered. This, of itself, seems to confine the idea to a purely hypothetical status. Whilst this illustrates the hypothetical's extreme nature, and whilst the technology is at no stage close to being accepted in this role, this does not mean the consideration of extreme examples is not beneficial. By considering such an extreme hypothetical, especially in conjunction with the consideration of the first two hypotheticals, it becomes possible to identify where certain boundaries, pitfalls, and blind spots may be in relation to the adoption and application of AI technologies in exercising power. (I expand on this in the final chapter.)

The modern idea of a representative government is a common one. In this model, a member, elected by individuals of voting age within a particular constituency or electorate, sits in the legislature to represent the interests of the people of their constituency or electorate. It is the role of those elected members to make laws for the rest of the population. Accountability and responsibility are created due to the fact that the members may be voted out should electors' interests not be acted upon. This hypothetical retains the vast majority of this idea – yet makes one small change that may be seen to have extreme consequences: the individuals that may be put forth for any of the elected seats are not humans – they are individual AI systems. Whilst the idea of democracy being exercised through an elected representative would subsist, the nature of that representative has always been a *human*. This hypothetical changes this relationship from human-to-human to a human-to-machine relationship.

As noted above, the extreme and systemic nature of the hypothetical means that there is no illustrative case-study or instance – like the visa application and addition of a substance to a banned list in the previous hypotheticals. Instead, to frame the hypothetical, a broad caricature of a representative democracy's legislature is adopted. This reflects the broad idea that is common in many democracies of the proposing, debating, and passing a Bill into law. In this respect, I do not seek to ground the hypothetical in a particular jurisdiction. Instead, I seek to ensure that the broadest idea of representative government is encompassed within the discussion. Should any particular jurisdictional applications arise – for example where a jurisdiction may require a certain kind of Bill to only pass one house or may need to go through a sub-committee process – the reader is asked to, in those scenarios, simply replace the elected representatives that perform those functions with the algorithmic representatives that are contemplated here. Where that occurs, I do not think that there would be any substantive differences in the conclusion that are reached below.

In returning to an element of the relative extreme nature of the hypothetical, it is clear that what is imagined is a scenario where we would be required to trust that the laws that govern us are made – on our behalf – by entities that are very *different* to us. This has been seen by some as being problematic in terms of the execution of laws – for example, in the instance of artificial judges determining court cases.[2] Other extreme ramifications may also be considered as being relevant. The very real and significant disparities between the ruling class and the rest of the society in many democratic societies – based on, for example, class, race, or other features – would pale into insignificance should this hypothetical be realised. The laws that govern a particular human society would, for the first time, be created by a completely different kind of non-human entity. (This could, however, be disputed on some levels. Societies that are controlled by religious laws may be said to be controlled by laws created by a non-human entity. This is not the place to debate or discuss the origin of the laws that do control those societies. Accordingly, I will limit the statement made above relating to the creations of laws by non-human entities to secular democracies.)

A further extreme element must be stated and clarified. The hypothetical does not involve a partial delegation of power that can ultimately be revoked. Should this be the case, this would be tantamount to little more than the delegation of rule-making powers that were contemplated in the second hypothetical. The transfer of law-making power that is contemplated here is absolute. The AI legislature would be the *only* way in which primary laws could be made and there would be no way that these laws could be usurped – barring a constitutional revolution in that society. Of course, even if the technology existed and could be trusted in the way that is contemplated in this hypothetical, the various real societies around the world would face particular legal/constitutional challenges of their own in order to affect a transference of power in the way suggested. Whilst this poses an interesting question, I do not offer any suggestions as to how this may take place in any particular society – I simply commence the consideration at a point in the hypothetical future after the transfer has taken place.

Whilst it has been stated earlier in this chapter and earlier in the book, it is important to re-state and acknowledge that the technology to achieve this hypothetical – at least in a way that would satisfy accountability in a representative sense – does not exist. There seems little prospect in even the most technologically trusting society adopting this sort of approach to law-making.[3] However, the

[2] J Boughey et al (eds), 'Public Law Limits on Automated Courts' in *The Automated State: Implications, Challenges and Opportunities for Public Law*, 1st edn (Alexandria, NSW, Federation Press, 2021) federationpress.com.au/product/the-automated-state/.

[3] Opposing views can be stated in relation to the relative trust that does or has existed in relation to AI systems. See, eg, T Araujo et al, 'In AI We Trust? Perceptions About Automated

prospect of it begins to raise the questions for which it is hoped that the discussion in this book may start to provide some semblance of an answer. Those questions relate to the bigger picture of whether the concept of the Rule of Law can provide any form of protection against arbitrary laws passed by this form of non-human legislator. As will be seen in the sections that follow fundamental and basic problems subsist in terms of all ideas associated with the Rule of Law.

II. The (Broad-Brush) Rule of Law

As with the previous sections, I will first consider the broad-brush ideas of the Rule of Law before considering particular thinkers. This means an initial consideration of the function of the Rule of Law as a concept that opposes the arbitrary application of power. In considering the function of the concept of the Rule of Law in the broadest terms in relation to this hypothetical, there does appear to be a considerable potential for the application of arbitrary power where legislative AIs are the *only* entities creating, and are the only entities responsible for creating, legislation. After all, where an entity is granted a power to make laws, and there is no other law-making power that exists above that entity, the absence of any check or counter to that law-making power may, and often has, lead to arbitrary laws being made. In this broadest consideration of the concept, it is useful to consider this potential in order to identify the ways in which power could be arbitrarily exercised.

Constitutional limitations on the extent of law-making powers are common. Constitutional limitations can be included within codified or uncodified constitutions. There are, of course, pros and cons associated with each. Regardless of the form, the function is to delimit the extent of the legislature's power – in this respect, constitutions themselves assist in controlling the potential for the exercise of arbitrary power. Constitutions in this respect can be seen as laws about laws; they are a base template that determines the sorts of laws that can be passed. This may, for example, include a requirement that laws passed by a legislature must be passed in conformity with particular human rights, or it may delimit the kinds of laws that may be made.[4] If it is supposed that a constitutional arrangement exists that provides a similar sort of fetter on law-making power, this may make the creation of arbitrary laws less likely, but it cannot (in this hypothetical or in any

Decision-Making by Artificial Intelligence' (2020) 35(3) *AI & Society* 611; W Frick, 'Here's Why People Trust Human Judgment Over Algorithms' (27 February 2015) *Harvard Business Review*: hbr.org/2015/02/heres-why-people-trust-human-judgment-over-algorithms.

[4] The former can be seen, as an example, Constitution of the Republic of South Africa, 1996 – ch 2, in which it is stated the Bill of Rights contained within the Constitution 'is a cornerstone of democracy in South Africa' and 'applies to all law, and binds the legislature, the executive, the judiciary and all organs of state' ss 7.1 and 8.1 respectively. The latter is prevalent in federated states in order to facilitate a split of law-making powers between states and the federal government – this can be seen in the Australian Constitution and the US Constitution.

other situation) completely prevent arbitrariness. This is clearly the case as, if it was not, there would be no need for the concept of the Rule of Law in states that have a constitution. It is also clearly the case as the nature of arbitrariness, as it has so far been explored, can relate to the *way* in which laws are created and promulgated, which is something very different to the broad nature of the laws that may be limited by a constitution. In these respects, it is the case that legislatures can be arbitrary notwithstanding the existence of a constitution.

The question in terms of the broad-brush idea of the Rule of Law could, then, be considered in two ways: first, whether the application of power by an elected group of AIs would be *necessarily* arbitrary; and second, whether the application may be *more likely* to lead to the arbitrary application of power than a human-filled legislature. In considering the first, there seems to be no reason why the exercise of power by elected AIs would be necessarily arbitrary. If the hypothetical is considered, as with the rest of this book, in non-dystopian terms, it would be the case that the AI legislators would continue to exercise the same sorts of legislative powers as their human legislator predecessors. We are not imagining a system where the AIs will suddenly seek to rise up and seize power for themselves. Nothing has changed other than the locus of law-making-power; or, more particularly, the constituents of the locus of law-making-power. If the elected AIs merely continue doing the same sorts of things as the human legislators, and if it is assumed that the human legislators were able to create laws non-arbitrarily, then whilst there would still be a possibility of arbitrary power being exercised when laws are being created, it also seems to follow that laws may be created without the exercise of arbitrary power. On this basis, where it is merely the law-*maker* that has changed and everything else is held constant, the laws that result from the AI legislature would not necessarily be arbitrary.

The second way to consider the broad-brush of the Rule of Law is in terms of whether the exercise of power by elected AIs will be more likely to lead to the arbitrary application of power than a human-filled legislature. This is not the case, again, if this book's non-dystopian approach is assumed. The change to an AI-filled legislature is imagined as a like-for-like exchange – this means that it is assumed that the AI's function will be as an immediate replacement for the human law-makers and, as noted above, they will perform this task in a way that does not malfunction or have nefarious ends. In this respect, whilst there will be increases in speed and efficiency possible (detailed below), the laws that come out of the legislative process will not be substantially different and the process for making those laws will not be substantially different.

Whilst the laws may be no different, it could nevertheless be suggested that the inability for an AI to explain its actions may increase the arbitrariness of law-making. (This is explored in more detail in considering the elements of the Past Rule of Law, below.) However, in the broad sense it is not always completely clear how humans make decisions – and it is not always clear that human legislators' stated reasons are the actual reasons for a decision. In this respect, the relative opacity that exists in relation to an AI legislator seems to be not dissimilar to a human legislator. In considering the broadest sense of the Rule of Law as being opposed to arbitrary power, the exercise of power by elected AIs will not normally be more likely to lead to the arbitrary application of power.

III. The Past Rule of Law

The Past Rule of Law is made up of the conceptions of the usual suspects of the Rule of Law: Aristotle; Locke; Dicey; Hayek; Fuller; and Raz.[5] These thinkers put forth Rule of Law ideas that provide a solution to the exercise of arbitrary power by the state. Their ideas contrast to the Present Rule of Law explored in the next section in consequence of their focus on the state-based exercise of power and their provision of formal or procedural solutions to the problem. After considering the most abstract and non-controversial idea of the broad-brush idea of the Rule of Law in the previous section, this section increases the relative nuance afforded to the analysis. I do this in two ways. The most nuanced consideration is conducted by drilling into the usual suspects' conceptions. First, however, I provide an assessment that falls between the highly abstract broad-brush approach and the most nuanced individual conceptions by considering the common elements that can be identified within the Past Rule of Law accounts.

A. Past Rule of Law Elements

The conclusions associated with the broad-brush approach can be refined through considering the Past Rule of Law elements: Predictability and Procedural Clarity.[6] This provides a slightly more nuanced perspective. The elements approach was explained in chapter two and expanded upon in chapters four and five. In those previous chapters, I provided a rationale for the identification of these less abstract, but commonly held, ideas across the various usual suspects' accounts. The elements represent points of commonality in the sorts of outcome that the various thinkers are trying to achieve. In considering the hypothetical in terms of the two elements, what becomes clear is that there is no particular Rule of Law problem with the hypothesised form of AI legislature. In coming to this conclusion, it is once again, important to keep the non-dystopian approach of the book in mind. If the potential for malfeasance, or even overt malfunction, is considered in the calculus, the conclusions would necessarily be very different.

In terms of Predictability as a Rule of Law element, it could be the case that the relative predictability of the AIs' actions could *increase* by virtue of the fact

[5] P Burgess, 'The Rule of Lore in the Rule of Law: Putting the Problem of the Rule of Law in Context' (2020) 12 *Hague Journal on the Rule of Law* 333.

[6] P Burgess, 'The Rule of Law: Beyond Contestedness' (2017) 8(3) *Jurisprudence* 480.

that a machine's processes may not be subject to the same passions and emotions as a human. (This is explored in greater detail in the sub-section below in relation to Aristotle.) As was seen in the previous chapter, humans can be motivated by various accountability factors, but may also be motivated by factors or by hate or malice. Crucially, for humans, these factors may be either consciously motivating or sub-consciously motivating – in other words, human action is not necessarily the result of a simple input/output calculation and cannot always be reduced to a simple mechanistic process.[7] (I will return to accountability in considering the Present Rule of Law.) A machine may have some advantages in this respect.

If a machine is conceived in simple linear terms, it would be apparent what sorts of data the machine would consider and how it would process that data to arrive at conclusions. It seems that there is scope for only particular data to be analysed that relates to the actual decision and not extraneous data or biases.[8] (This would describe something like a decision maker.) As explored earlier and earlier in the book in chapter three, this is not to say that AI does not have a problem with biases at this present time – systems have been found to adopt or learn from particular racist or sexist views and manifest the same.[9] Even if these aspects cannot be completely removed from an AI system, this hypothetical imagines a level of AI consciousness that may at least be aware of these biases and can avoid acting on them. (Whilst bias remains a fundamental problem, research in continuing in ways to remove bias from algorithmic decisions.[10]) In these circumstances, the processing of data seems to be able to be conducted in a way that is devoid of *sub-conscious* biases – something that humans may not be able to do if we are not even aware of the existence of those sub-consciously held positions. Accordingly, the level of predictability that may be achieved from a machine in the non-dystopian approach adopted, may be at least equal to, and potentially greater than, that of a human.

A similar conclusion follows when the element of Procedural Clarity is considered. A machine's ability to ensure that it is making the right decision in the right way – as dictated by the programming parameters of the algorithm – is

[7] There does exist a difference between a mechanical view of human behaviour – that is largely input/output dictated – and a less machine-centred approach that is favoured by expectancy-value theorists. In this form, a mental aspect intervenes between the input/output process intervenes and may result in a different output. For a broad overview of the different approaches, see B Weiner, *Human Motivation*, 1st edn (Cham, Springer International Publishing, 1980. 2nd printing edn, 2012).

[8] M Spielkamp, 'Inspecting Algorithms for Bias', MIT Technology Review (12 June 2017) www.technologyreview.com/2017/06/12/105804/inspecting-algorithms-for-bias/; M Mann and T Matzner, 'Challenging Algorithmic Profiling: The Limits of Data Protection and Anti-Discrimination in Responding to Emergent Discrimination' (2019) 6(2) *Big Data & Society* 2053951719895805.

[9] C Sandvig et al, 'When the Algorithm Itself Is a Racist: Diagnosing Ethical Harm in the Basic Components of Software' (2016) 10 *International Journal of Communication* 4972; Spielkamp (n 8).

[10] L Belenguer, 'AI Bias: Exploring Discriminatory Algorithmic Decision-Making Models and the Application of Possible Machine-Centric Solutions Adapted from the Pharmaceutical Industry' (2022) 2(4) *AI and Ethics* 771; B Giovanola and S Tiribelli, 'Weapons of Moral Construction? On the Value of Fairness in Algorithmic Decision-Making' (2022) 24(1) *Ethics and Information Technology* 3.

an important consideration in this. As noted immediately above and in previous sections, there are substantial issues that may be seen in relation to the relative explainability of the process and the decision made by a machine. (I will return to these in a moment.) But, despite not being able to know what may be happening within the black box, it may at least be possible to identify both the data that is going into the box and the parameters that define what the box is doing.[11] There remains a question, however, as to whether this would be enough to satisfy the Rule of Law element of Procedural Clarity.

It is not just the making of laws that is important in this hypothetical. The ability to *see* that the laws have been created in a particular way is also fundamental. Consideration of the *process* that a machine follows in making law is also a crucial factor. The Rule of Law elements that can be seen in the Past Rule of Law relate – most clearly – to the *making* of laws. The uniting feature of the Past Rule of Law is, after all, that it relates to the control of arbitrary power exercised by the state – and the way that a state exercises its power is through its laws. In modern democratic states around the world, there is a performative/public element to the creation of laws. Legislative bodies frequently have galleries that are open to the public. This enables individuals that are subject to the laws to see the processes associated with making the laws. Records of proceedings – like Hansard in the UK Parliament – provide a way for those not present, or those looking back on the proceedings, to 'see' the process of law-making in action.

Procedural Clarity is agnostic in terms of the precise nature of the steps that must be taken, it simply requires that a particular procedure be followed and that it be clearly followed. As with the discussion of Predictability immediately above, and for similar reasons, it is in this respect that machines *may* be able to act in ways that are superior to their human legislator-counterparts. Machines cannot stray from a process – this is the nature of the algorithm that governs their behaviour. Accordingly, in the process of making laws, a machine will carry out that procedure in the way that it has been programmed to do so. In this respect, the 'procedural' aspect of Procedural Clarity is clearly satisfied; however, whilst there may be strict adherence to the procedural aspect, this does not necessarily mean that the 'clarity' aspect is satisfied.

In circumstances where the hypothetical AIs that are being imagined are highly sophisticated, it is clear that the actual and relative processes that take place within the AI systems would be a form of black box; the precise nature of the 'considerations' that are taking place would be opaque. This, of course, has been discussed at length earlier in this book so the basic problem will, by now, be familiar. It does, however, seem that in relation to the performative or public elements of the

[11] F Pasquale, *The Black Box Society: The Secret Algorithms That Control Money and Information*, reprint edn (Cambridge, Mass, Harvard University Press, 2016); T Wischmeyer, 'Artificial Intelligence and Transparency: Opening the Black Box' in T Wischmeyer and T Rademacher (eds), *Regulating Artificial Intelligence* (Cham, Springer International Publishing, 2020) 75: doi.org/10.1007/978-3-030-32361-5_4.

law-making process, this could be achieved through the creation of a dialogue between the various AI legislators. This would replicate Hansard in some respects. This dialogue would include a transcript of the process of proposing, debating, and enacting legislation. (One difference, that will be expanded upon below, and a feature of the ability of machines to process information faster than humans would be that these debates could take place almost instantaneously.)

It does become clear that when humans are out-of-the-loop and where the output from the various AIs' deliberations is the creation of primary legislation that governs human society, a high degree of clarity and explainability is fundamental. The provision of a transcript of the kind advised above would satisfy the procedural element of law-making, but it may not completely satisfy the need for explainability. As with the previous considerations relating to explainability, if this can be satisfied, there is no elemental Rule of Law objection to the making of laws in the way contemplated here. This holds in relation to both Predictability and Procedural Clarity. However, given the nature of the output (laws) and the absence of checks (humans out-of-the-loop), in the absence of a *deep* level of explainability that may reveal particular motivations and rationales inherent in the particular AI's decision-making, an AI parliament may be seen as being problematic for the Rule of Law.

The substantial Rule of Law issues that stem from the need to achieve explainability have been canvased in previous chapters. In those chapters, the need for explainability was frequently responsible for the hypotheticals considered being considered to be contrary to the Rule of Law. In this hypothetical, at least in terms of the Elements of the Rule of Law, the performative elements of the legislative process could enable those that are subject to the laws to see the creation of the laws – enabling a form of explainability to be realised. Whilst the root cause or motivation in the enactment of those laws may remain opaque – as the explainability of an algorithm's decision-making within the black box remains a feature – the publication of debates across multiple AIs relating to the creation of laws may facilitate a form of accountability (regarding the 'view' or 'opinion' of each AI) and procedural clarity. I will return and expand upon the idea of accountability across the rest of this chapter. At this point, in considering the elements of the Rule of Law in this hypothetical, there is (for the first time) a way in which there may be a level of explainability and, hence, Rule of Law compliance. As will be seen in the following sub-section, by considering the various Past Rule of Law thinkers, there is some nuance introduced into this relative black-and-white conclusion; yet the importance of explainability is in no way diminished.

B. Past Rule of Law's Thinkers and Hypothetical Three

At this point in the book, the vast majority of points that need to be made in relation to each of the Past Rule of Law thinkers has already been made. This allows a relatively brief discussion to be had in relation to certain points in this sub-section.

Others, however, will be expanded upon in more detail as the nature of this hypothetical relates more clearly to their particular ideas and aspects of those ideas have not yet been explored. In doing this, I will first briefly touch on the points of overlap before expanding on the most relevant and novel points.

The nature of the broad-brush idea of the Rule of Law and the elements of Predictability and Procedural Clarity mean they can, necessarily, be seen in each of the usual suspects accounts. Accounts that specifically focus on the Rule of Law's anti-arbitrariness function in the law-*making* function include Locke's, Dicey's, and Hayek's. Whilst not mentioned specifically as desiderata for Fuller and Raz, the broad idea of law-making undergirds the function of their ideas. The need for predictability in law-making is, similarly, present in each of the usual suspects' accounts.[12] Finally, the need for procedural clarity is also reflected across all of the accounts – and is especially prominent in Raz's suggestion that the law must be capable of being known, Fuller's ideas of promulgation and prospectivity, and Hayek's idea that coercion can be avoided by law-making being predictable. Each of these ideas has broadly been discussed in relation to the law-making function in the previous sub-section. The arguments made there remain apposite here. In those respects, at least at an abstract level, the conclusion was made above holds: an AI parliament may be seen as problematic for the Rule of Law – but there is some potential for an aspect of explainability that stems from the visibility of the performative aspects of law-making that may arise from various AIs proposing, debating, and passing a piece of legislation. This broad and abstract consideration does not get to the root of each of the individual thinkers' points. As has been suggested earlier, additional meaning can be drawn from considering the context of each of the thinkers – which, in turn, illuminates their Rule of Law ideas. In turn, this adds nuance to the assessment.

As explored in the previous hypothetical, Aristotle sought a form of legislative due process. As has been explored in earlier chapters, the process of law-making should not be one that is subject to emotion and is not one that should be conducted hastily.[13] The context of Aristotle's ideas assists in understanding exactly how the hypothetical may be seen in this chapter. As was also explored in chapter two, the legislature for Aristotle was not involved in the *creation* of law in the same way that contemporary legislatures are. His legislature merely sought to make minimal changes to the laws that already existed. Even with the level of law-making being limited to incremental changes, there was *still* a call for a relative reduction in the speed of the process. Extrapolation from this position may lead to the conclusion that even more care and consideration should be taken in terms of the creation of new laws; but this extrapolation is not adopted in this assessment as this would be anachronistic in terms of Aristotle's point.[14] Yet, there seems to be no

[12] Burgess (n 6).
[13] Aristotle, *Rhetoric*, trans WR Roberts (London, Dover, 2004) 1.
[14] Q Skinner, 'Meaning and Understanding in the History of Ideas' (1969) 8(1) *History and Theory* 3.

problem applying the general idea that there should be some level of due process and consideration in the law-making process.

This hypothetical is centred around the process of law-*making* and has as one of its core ideas and – by virtue of the high speeds at which machines can communicate with one another – the idea of the speed of law-making becomes a crucial factor. The hypothetical contemplates a legislature comprised solely of AI systems. The normal functions of the legislature – including proposing, debating, and passing a Bill – could be conducted in fractions of a second instead of weeks or months. On this basis, a Bill could be passed into law less than a second after the need for the law has been identified. This would not result in a law being retrospective, but it would mean it could be almost instant when compared to the weeks (or months) long process that is currently the case for most pieces of legislation. Legislative enactment at these speeds is far beyond what Aristotle contemplated or feared.

As was contemplated in the previous hypothetical, this should be construed in terms of the element of emotion of which Aristotle also discussed. I previously noted that machines do not experience emotion in the same way as humans and that they (machines) are not prone to mistakes merely because they accomplish a task faster. In considering Aristotle's warnings in these terms, the problems of speed noted immediately above may be tempered by the fact that speed, of itself, does not lead to a decision that would be necessarily worse. In this respect, the AI legislature's speed of law-making is not *internally* problematic to the process. However, this does not mean there is not an *external* problem with speed of law-making due to the fact that the – often relatively lengthy – law-making process itself may serve to both promulgate the potential for the law and provide advanced notice that a law may be coming into effect. This external problem associated with the speed of law making would not be tempered by the publication of the record of debates noted in the previous sub-section; it seems of little benefit in this external element that an extensive and detailed debate that is, for example, constituted of more than 10,000 pages of the virtual Hansard is published when the whole process from proposal to enactment takes less than a second.

Ideas associated with this sort of external idea are prevalent and prominent in the accounts provided by the three most recent usual suspects: Fuller, Raz, and Hayek. Speed of law-making itself was not something that they specifically contemplated. It was not the case, for example, that Fuller's King Rex failed to make laws in the right way because the law-making process that was engaged in was too fast; nor was it the case that Raz specified one of his desiderata to be a slow-moving legislature. The same can be said for Hayek. But, as will become apparent, there is, implicit in the ideas that they do communicate, a strong potential objection to laws that are very rapidly made.

Lon Fuller provides eight desiderata that relate to the making of laws. These are generality; publicity (through promulgation); prospectivity (or, at least, non-retrospectivity); intelligibility; consistency; practicability; stability; and congruence.[15] A failure of the publication of changes in the law may be problematic if the period associated with the debate of the Bill is considered part of the way in which a potential change is communicated. It may be argued this is a tenuous link as there is no specific suggestion that Fuller intended the debating process itself to be part of the promulgatory affect – his notion relates more precisely to the communication of the passage of the law – and the promulgatory aspect of the idea may be satisfied by the publication of the debates relating to the law's passage; but, any promulgatory benefit of this would be rendered nugatory where a debate is provided almost simultaneously with the passage of the new law.

What is more obviously of relevance is Fuller's requirement for stability. Fuller suggests that it is a problem if 'there are such frequent changes in the rules that the subject cannot orient [their] action by them'.[16] Of course, Fuller is concerned with *frequent* changes to legislation not *rapid* changes. I do not think that it is necessary to extend the hypothetical to include the AI legislature's consistent reviews of laws' suitability and their (near) immediate amendment where amendment is required in order to illustrate that Fuller's concern is relevant. In the current terms of the hypothetical, it would be the case that a law could be amended – even if this only occurs once – with near immediate effect. This would be problematic for Fuller's stability (and intelligibility) as, at least in the period immediately after the Bill's passage, this would mean that a subject may find it difficult to orient their actions by them.

Raz's general requirement – that the law should be such that the that people will be able to be guided by it – plus his specific desiderata that laws should be relatively stable would lead to a similar outcome to Fuller's issue of stability.[17] Raz goes on to state that one of the law's key functions, and one of the key functions of stability in the law, is that knowledge of what the law *is* can facilitate both short-term and long-term planning. (I return to a similar point in considering Hayek immediately below.) Long-term planning may not be impacted by the near instant changes in the law that are contemplated here – as the time difference between the moments it may take for an AI legislature to pass a Bill and the several months it may take a human legislature may be inconsequential when planning a decade into the future. However, short-term planning may clearly be impacted. Raz uses the example of how much alcohol is allowed to be purchased duty-free as one instance of short-term planning.[18] With a near instant change in the law, it is conceivable that the duty-free limit may change between the time a customer enters a shop and their purchase two minutes later. In this respect, the shopper would be unable to be guided by the law in consequence of its near instant change. Thus, near instant law changes would represent a problem for Raz's Rule of Law.

[15] LL Fuller, *The Morality of Law* (New Haven, Yale University Press, 1964) 38–39.
[16] ibid 39.
[17] J Raz, 'The Rule of Law and Its Virtue' in *The Authority of Law: Essays on Law and Morality*, 2nd edn (Oxford, Oxford University Press, 2009) 210, 213–14.
[18] ibid 215.

As has been previously noted, Hayek's Rule of Law idea is fundamentally based around the need for predictability in law-making so that individuals can plan around the creation of laws in order to avoid being coerced.[19] Hayek, like Fuller and Raz, also required knowledge of the law in its subjects. He stated that '[w]ithin the rules of the game, the individual is free to pursue [their] personal ends and desires, certain that the powers of government will not be used to frustrate [their] efforts.'[20] The issue here relates to what happens when the rules of the game – as laws – change rapidly. This represents a similar consideration to Fuller. In the Hayekian sense, it seems that this could result in governmental actions frustrating the efforts of individuals that thought they were acting within the rules. Accordingly, as was the case with both Raz and Fuller, there is at least some uncertainty associated with the conformity of near-instant passages of legislation with the aims inherent in Hayek's Rule of Law.

The relatively obvious answer in relation to the above criticisms would be for the AI legislature to introduce a mandatory constitutional 'cooling off' period, or to ensure that any laws that are passed – regardless of whether the debate and passage of the Bill was almost instantaneous – do not take effect for a period of time that would be appropriate in the circumstances of the particular law. If the constitutional element was such that the legislature does not have absolute legal sovereignty and cannot, therefore, change this requirement by a piece of legislation, this would address many of the concerns that are raised above in relation to the speed at which the particular laws are passed. It would, however, introduce a further complication relating to the application, extent, and operation of such a delay. There would be considerable questions associated with how long a delay should be and why. (It would also raise questions regarding what would need to happen in circumstances where 'emergency' legislation is required.) Whilst not insurmountable, this may of itself introduce considerable uncertainty into the law-making process – which would raise further issues for each of these thinkers. The potential *way* in which the decision regarding the delay to be implemented would also introduce a relatively new form of arbitrariness into the process – this could occur through the requirement to make a decision regarding the period of the cooling off, as to whether this should be a fixed period (a week, a month, a year, for example) or whether this should be variable (based, for example, on the nature of the law). This would need, at some level, to be arbitrarily decided. As arbitrariness is an element of law-making that the Rule of Law is fundamentally seeking to avoid, the introduction of further arbitrariness in an attempt to satisfy a Rule of Law desiderata would be contradictory.

Both Locke and Hayek seek to avoid the application of power becoming tyrannical. The context and focus of their works relate to concerns relating to tyranny

[19] FA von Hayek, *The Road to Serfdom*, B Caldwell (ed), (Chicago, University of Chicago Press, 2007) 112.

[20] ibid 112–13.

seen as a result of, respectively, the Glorious Revolution and World War II. The potential harm of power being exercised in a way that was unconstrained and unchecked was provided either explicitly or implicitly in their works.[21] Dicey was also concerned regarding the application of state power in the hands of unaccountable administrative decision-makers.[22] These points were canvased briefly in the second hypothetical. Many of the Past Rule of Law worries were tempered in consequence of the accountability mechanism that exists in relation to the creation of secondary legislation – in that hypothetical, the creation of secondary laws was still subject to some sort of oversight and that oversight was provided by a legislature populated by humans that were accountable. (There were some additional accountability worries that were raised in terms of the Present Rule of Law in chapter five. Consideration of those in relation to the present hypothetical will be deferred until the next section.) In the hypothetical in this chapter, that accountability mechanism has been removed; here, the humans are out-of-the-loop. Accordingly, that tempering effect cannot occur.

The law-making ability of the AI legislature in this hypothetical is fundamentally problematic when considered in terms of the removal of this accountability mechanism. The potential for tyranny that may result from unconstrained power is a key concern of, amongst others, Locke, Dicey, and Hayek. In this hypothetical, there is the potential for laws to be created by the AI legislature with no human oversight and, as was also discussed above, the relative impact of accountability mechanisms on machines means that the power wielded by an AI legislature may be expressed in a way that is not subject to clear constraints. In other words, the fact that machines cannot be held to account in the same way as humans – through a mechanism facilitating responsible actions that relate to enforceable steps against entities that are answerable – represents a problem.[23] This lack of accountability problem precisely reflects some of the fears that Locke, Dicey, and Hayek identified and sought to solve with their Rule of Law ideas. By hypothesising a law-making body that cannot be held accountable for its actions in the same way that a legislature that was once populated by individuals could be, and in the absence of any indication that algorithms can be made accountable in the same way, there appears little prospect of Locke, Dicey, and Hayek seeing the AI legislators as being in conformity with their ideas of the Rule of Law.

What this means is that the exercise of the power by an AI legislature faces a substantive series of Rule of Law objections when the individual Rule of Law usual suspects' accounts are considered. Whist the performative elements associated with

[21] Throughout the Rule of Law chapter in Road to Serfdom, Hayek reflects back on the Nazi regime. He also was concerned regarding the broad nationalisation of state assets following the war. ibid 112. Locke's *Two Treatises* was an argument in favour of parliamentary control in preference for the absolute power that was evident in royal or papal rule.

[22] AV Dicey, *Introduction to the Study of the Law of the Constitution*, 10th edn (Basingstoke, Palgrave Macmillan, 1979) 195.

[23] See the discussion of the United Nations in ch 5.

law-making provide a level of explainability and predictability the relative lack of accountability of the AI law-makers means that the scenario contemplated in this chapter is highly problematic in terms of the Past Rule of Law usual suspects.

IV. The Present Rule of Law

The key differentiating features between the Past and Present Rule of Law are conceptual (not temporal). The Present Rule of Law is made up of two forms each reflecting a distinct point of differentiation from the Past Rule of Law. The first, reflected in the conceptions of Martin Krygier and Jeff King, differs in terms of the *source* of arbitrary power. In this form, the source of arbitrary power is not limited to the exercise of power by the state. The second, reflected in conceptions provided by Tom Bingham and the UN, differs in terms of the outcome-based nature of the accounts. In this section, I first consider the chapter's hypothetical in terms of these broadly stated conceptual differences, before considering the way in which the source-based and then the outcome-based thinkers' conceptions may respond to the creation of primary laws by an AI-populated legislature. I will demonstrate that whilst familiar issues arise in terms of explainability, significant problems arise in relation to a focus on achieving particular outcomes; yet, at least one of the Present Rule of Law conceptions provides a solution to the problem of an AI legislature being *more* arbitrary than human-populated legislatures.

A. The Forms of the Present Rule of Law

In considering the Present Rule of Law in broad terms it is possible to consider the hypothetical in terms of *any* form of arbitrary power (source-based form) or in terms of any substantive aims or benefits associated with the idea (outcome-based form). In thinking broadly about the source-based aspect of the Present Rule of Law, this hypothetical's focus on the legislature reveals a less stark contrast to the previous hypotheticals. The source-based idea that the Rule of Law may also apply to private exercises of power is relatively inconsequential where it is a clear expression of public power that is contemplated. However, as will be seen below, the idea that *any* exercise of power becomes relevant if the exercise of power by *humans* is considered to be a particular aspect of the Rule of Law has not previously been conceived. This means that a source-based idea that combats arbitrary power wherever it arises – unlike the Past Rule of Law – may operate in circumstances where an AI exercises power and not a human. (This is explored below in more detail in relation to Krygier's conception.)

The broadly construed outcome-based idea of the Rule of Law involves some form of thick or outcome-based idea of what the Rule of Law is or does. There are difficulties, however, in ensuring that the aim or desired outcome does not result in unintended consequences. The attempts to dictate a particular goal may operate so as to dictate the *nature* of the laws that could be passed by an AI legislature. This is different to the *scope* of the laws that may be passed as this would be, per this hypothetical, set out in a constitutional document that cannot be amended simply by a simple piece of legislation. But the way in which the scope of laws is programmed or communicated to an AI would be fundamental to achieving a particular outcome. For example, if it is programmed into each of the elected/electable AIs that they cannot pass laws that contravene human rights, that may – from the bottom up – curtail the nature of the laws that can be passed: here, for example, human rights contradicting laws may not be passed. This would operate as a form of constitutional bar, but at the programmer level. This may be seen as a problem as, on occasion, laws may need to be passed by a legislature that do curtail human rights. This is an obvious example and it would not be difficult to imagine – especially in the context of this already extreme hypothetical – that the AI could be programmed to operate in a very similar way to current human legislators in terms of human rights. But, even under this broad consideration, the example does illustrate the potential for literality and (potentially) unexpected consequences in machines that adhere to a strict algorithm and may not be in a position to identify or implement solutions that go beyond this. The relative difference between the unconstrained (cognitive) autonomy of a human, and the need for programmed/predetermined 'autonomy' to act as an AI represents a key differentiating factor. This will be explored further later in the chapter.

B. Present Rule of Law – Source-Based – And Hypothetical Three

The broad-based considerations outlined immediately above lay some foundations for a more nuanced consideration of the source-based idea of the Present Rule of Law. What can be seen by considering King's conception, is that there is also a level of overlap with the issue regarding how the AIs may act in a given circumstance. In considering Krygier's, we can see that the potentially wider application of the Rule of Law to non-humans provides a potential solution to a human-centred interpretation of Rule of Law ideas.

Krygier's Present Rule of Law idea identifies a teleological approach to the concept. He suggests the very purpose of the Rule of Law is to combat the arbitrary application of power and it is of no great distinction as to where that power originates.[24] This contrasts to the Past Rule of Law idea that sees the *source* of

[24] M Krygier, 'Four Puzzles About the Rule of Law: Why, What, Where? And Who Cares?' in J Flemming (ed), *Getting to the Rule of Law* (New York, New York University Press, 2011) 64; M Krygier, 'What's the Point of the Rule of Law?' 67 *Buffalow Law Review* 50; M Krygier, 'The Rule of Law: Legality, Teleology and Sociology' in G Palombella and N Walker (eds), *Relocating the Rule of Law* (Oxford, Hart Publishing, 2009) ('Legality, Teleology and Sociology').

power being confined to the state. Of course, the suggestion in this hypothetical is that it is the state that is exercising law-making power. This suggests that the Past Rule of Law would be of particular reference. However, certain aspects of the Past Rule of Law relate to particular human-specific elements. As was outlined earlier in the chapter and in chapter two, Aristotle's Rule of Law ideas, for example, were focused on the idea that *humans* were prone to acting rashly and based on emotion.[25] Furthermore, as was also suggested earlier in this chapter, the structure of accountability mechanisms is relatively human-centric – for example, those seen in Past Rule of Law thinkers like Locke and Dicey – meaning that machines may not be subject to these things.[26] In these circumstances, it is possible to conceive of the Present Rule of Law being particularly confined to the traditional way of making laws: via a *human* populated legislature. Accordingly, Krygier's wider view of the potential for the Rule of Law to respond to arbitrariness *wherever this may arise*, may enable a non-human form of arbitrary power to be combatted where the Past Rule of Law may not.

The conclusion raised immediately above may also provide *additional* protection – even within the rubric of the Present Rule of Law – if the creation of laws by an AI legislature is seen to be, in some way, *more* arbitrary (than a human legislature). As has been noted in several chapters thus far, there is an ongoing inability for AI systems to provide an explanation of their decision-making processes. This, it has been suggested, may cause decisions to be considered arbitrary – in contravention of the broad ideas associated with the Rule of Law (in chapters four, five, and above). This would mean that the Past Rule of Law ideas that are taken as being foundational to and shared with the Present Rule of Law would not be satisfied. In the final chapter, I will conduct a deeper discussion of how the conclusions I draw across chapters four, five, and six would apply if the decisions are explainable. However, it is relevant to note at this point that the extension of Krygier's idea may provide *more* scope for identifying alternate forms of arbitrariness that are not related to just humans. In other words, Krygier's purposive approach does more than merely change the source from solely public applications of power; it expands the very nature of what sorts of arbitrariness may be included within the idea of the Rule of Law. This would mean limitations that may be seen to exist relating to conceptions that are anchored in a human-populated source institution are no longer relevant, resulting in an extension of the concept's protective function.

A core facet of Jeff King's *social dimension* of the Rule of Law relates to legislators' positive duty to act in a way that provides forms of benefit to society.[27] This positive duty would, in the terms of this hypothetical, need to be applied to the

[25] Aristotle, T Sinclair and TJ Saunders, *The Politics* (London, Penguin UK, 1981) 1287a23.

[26] R Kennedy, 'The Rule of Law and Algorithmic Governance' in W Barfield (ed), *The Cambridge Handbook of the Law of Algorithms* (Cambridge, Cambridge University Press, 2020) 209.

[27] J King, 'The Rule of Law' in R Bellamy and J King (eds), *The Cambridge Handbook of Constitutional Theory* (2024) papers.ssrn.com/abstract=4487306; J King, '"Constitutional Boundaries" – The Social Dimension of the Rule of Law', *I·CONnect* (2018) www.iconnectblog.com/2018/04/i-connect-symposium-on-constitutional-boundaries-the-social-dimension-of-the-rule-of-law/.

AI-populated legislature. The application of this sort of duty may, at a superficial level, be questioned in terms of a machine's inability of being the subject of rights and duties – especially in the face of issues around legal personhood for AI systems.[28] However, that seems to be a disingenuous way to view the idea. The duty is on the institution itself – as a law-making institution – and not on the individual entities that constitute the institution. On this basis, the relative personhood status of those entities seems to not represent a problem.

Notwithstanding the conclusion immediately above, the requirement that an *institution* act in a particular way may still be seen to represent a conundrum for the entities within it. Whist there may be a duty on the institution, there would still be some autonomy for the individuals within that institution. This may represent a dilemma in terms of how an algorithm should conduct itself as a legislator. Issues relating to the difficulties of programming an algorithm – in terms of achieving specific objectives – were hinted at above. This is not a book about coding or programming, so I will not consider those aspects in any detail. I will merely say that the programming aspects of defining what the AI is and does, and how it should conduct itself as a legislator, will be highly impactful on the potential nature of the laws that may follow. Again, as hinted at above, the programming within a legislative AI algorithm would dictate the way that it would operate. This means that, once it is elected, the programming itself could operate as a quasi-constitutional bar regarding on what the machine may or may not do or how it can or cannot conduct itself. This could be contrasted to the ways in which a human may be able to choose between ways they should or should not conduct themselves. The relative importance of core programming in achieving an end would raise fundamental questions about where the seat of power may ultimately lie. With the ability of another entity – the programmer – being able to limit the scope of conduct of the lawmaker, it becomes difficult to determine which entity is responsible for a decision and, accordingly, which entity is ultimately exercising their power. In this sense, this potentially generates a completely new form of arbitrarily made decision; one that is pre-determined in consequence of the underlying programming directing what can and cannot be acted upon.

Consideration of these two source-based ideas of the Present Rule of Law expose very different facets of the hypothetical. One exposes the potential for new forms of arbitrary decision-making, and the other suggests a broader way that the Rule of Law may respond to arbitrariness. The next sub-section illustrates a concern with both of these issues as well as highlighting new ones.

[28] RD Brown, 'Property Ownership and the Legal Personhood of Artificial Intelligence' (2021) 30(2) *Information & Communications Technology Law* 208; J Chen and P Burgess, 'The Boundaries of Legal Personhood: How Spontaneous Intelligence Can Problematise Differences between Humans, Artificial Intelligence, Companies and Animals' (2019) 27(1) *Artificial Intelligence and Law* 73; VAJ Kurki and T Pietrzykowski (eds), *Legal Personhood: Animals, Artificial Intelligence and the Unborn*, 1st edn (Cham Springer International Publishing, 2017).

C. Present Rule of Law – Outcome-Based – And Hypothetical Three

In addition to echoing some of the concerns noted in the sub-section above, the outcome-based ideas of the Rule of Law, exemplified by Bingham and the UN, also illustrate Rule of Law non-compliance can arise due to the non-explainability and accountability issues. These were touched on in the previous chapter in relation to outcome-based ideas but they will be expanded in relation to this hypothetical.

The requirement for accountability relates to this hypothetical most clearly as here the AI systems are operating autonomously with humans out-of-the-loop. What is more, they are doing this in circumstances where they – the algorithms – are making primary laws. The idea of a democratically elected legislature is premised on the idea of law-makers being accountable for their actions. Legislators making laws that are not in the interests of the wider population can be, in a well-functioning democracy, removed from power at the next election. This form of accountability seeks to ensure that those that are acting in the representative function within the legislature continue to act in the interests of their constituents. As was highlighted in chapters four and five, there are substantive difficulties in holding an AI to account in the same way as a human. If a machine has no ego, no interest in power (per se), or no particular drive to achieve a particular desirable state of affairs, it may not be possible to motivate it with the potential of being voted out at the next election (without building in some inherent motivation to hold onto power – which, itself, seems an undesirable trait in an AI). Whilst accountability was an issue in previous hypotheticals, the necessary level of accountability in relation to the body responsible for creating laws where the body is acting autonomously is more substantive. This level of accountability plays a fundamental role in relation to *both* outcome-based ideas of the Present Rule of Law.

For Bingham, adherence to the idea of the Rule of Law requires adherence to both human rights and international law. I have canvased issues in the previous sub-section in relation to legislative processes and programming. Similar issues arise in relation to adherence to principles of human rights and international law. It is sometimes the case that legislative bodies may not always adhere to these ideals. It may also be the case that these ideas are not always principal drivers of the legislative agenda. This is one reason why Bingham's Rule of Law is an aspirational form of the concept. There may be many reasons for such non-adherence. But, as was explored previously, the ability or otherwise to make this distinction may lie with the programmer and not with the AI itself. In this respect, and where the ultimate source of the decision-making authority lies with the programmer, there is no level of accountability. The AI as a law-maker may be unable to do certain things in consequence of the programming; and the person or entity that is responsible for the programming (and, therefore, for the decision) is not democratically accountable. This relative constraint, as noted above, may also mean that the decision itself may be arbitrary – as it is not based on the actual criteria that may exist and is, instead, based on pre-determined criteria at the programming level. This broad conceptual issue is further compounded by the issues of explainability that have already been explored in the chapter – as the inability to see and understand how the AI is making decisions will mean that the relative influence of the underlying programming may never be apparent. The nature of what it is to be an algorithm therefore, in relation to the idea in this hypothetical, represents real problems for the realisation of Bingham's Rule of Law.

It will be recalled that the UN's approach to the Rule of Law is that it is not determined by the realisation of human rights (and other things) as is the case for Bingham but, instead, is a vehicle used for the achievement of human rights.[29] The same considerations relating to the programmers' influence also exist here in relation to the relative focus of the AI legislature on achieving human rights in their society. The issues noted above relating to accountability, transparency, and explainability would also exist when the UN's idea of the Rule of Law is considered.

V. Summary and Conclusions

This chapter has explored a hypothetical in which an AI is responsible for the creation of primary legislation: laws. The hypothetical represents an extreme in terms of the sort of technology that would be required to achieve this. It is also extreme in terms of the changes in the societal conscience that would need to accept it. On a different measure it would also be considered extreme given the kind of revolutionary constitutional and institutional changes that would be necessary to move from a law-making body that is, as it always has been, staffed by humans, to one that is composed of a number of elected algorithms that fulfil the precise same role as the prior human legislators. By constituting the hypothetical in these extreme terms, it becomes possible to extend the relative level of the AI's autonomy by having no check over the AI's operation. In other words, in this imagined scenario, humans are out-of-the-loop in creating legislation.

In considering what this means for the Past and Present ideas of the Rule of Law – at varying levels of abstraction – problems that have already been identified in previous chapters re-emerged and new problems were identified. But, surprisingly, given the relative extreme nature of the hypothetical, there were also some areas in which there may be distinct benefits from the use of AI legislators. In considering the Past Rule of Law, in the broad-brush ideas as well as the elements of Predictability and Procedural Clarity, there appear to be situations in which machines may be able to provide an enhanced form of legislative process;

[29] United Nations General Assembly, *Strengthening and Coordinating United Nations Rule of Law Activities – Report of the Secretary-General – Addendum* (No A/68/213/Add.1, United Nations, 11 July 2014).

however, even here, the familiar issues associated with explainability can be seen. A more nuanced consideration of Past Rule of Law thinkers revealed that speed of legislative enactments may not, of itself, be a problem internally within the law-making process as computers do not make more mistakes simply because they process data faster; but an external manifestation of the speed – being near instant laws – appeared to be a Rule of Law problem for many of the usual suspects. Other familiar considerations also arose that included problems associated with accountability and explainability. These were seen across both the Past Rule of Law thinkers and in the Present Rule of Law.

Considering the Rule of Law and AIs making law also demonstrated some commonality across several Present Rule of Law accounts. The purposive form of the Rule of Law was noted to be of wider potential application – than other forms – in consequence of its clear applicability beyond *human* legislators. In this sense, it may be more suited to provide a response to machine exercised arbitrary power than the institutionally anchored Past Rule of Law ideas. More nuanced consideration of King and Bingham's ideas in terms of this hypothetical also revealed the possibility for a bottom-up quasi-constitutional limitation on an algorithm's decision-making power. This, itself, may also result in a different form of arbitrariness in an AI-populated legislature.

As it seems clear that AI use in some form may have *some* benefits – even in circumstances where the form adopted is not the extreme idea adopted in this chapter – it seems likely that the use of AI by governments will continue to grow. (These benefits may be as simple as increased efficiency in terms of time or costs.) It also seems to be the case that many states seek to conform with – or at least appear to conform with – the tenets of the Rule of Law. In these circumstances, in the next and final chapter, I will consider the question of what the repeated and constant failures associated with explainability and accountability may mean for the use of AI by governments. I will also consider how some of the conclusions raised in the chapters so far may be different should AIs' decisions become explainable in the future and, in consequence, what this may mean for the Future Rule of Law.

7

The Future Rule of Law and AI: The Necessary Evolution of a Concept

This chapter provides an assessment and consideration of the conclusions that have already been reached together with an extension of those ideas in order to identify what this means for the Future Rule of Law. The chapter provides an answer to the question posed in the book's first paragraph: how will the concept of the Rule of Law need to evolve in order to account for artificial intelligence being used to exercise public power in the future? To answer this question, I detail the nature of the shortcomings and indicate the ways in which the Rule of Law must evolve – in terms of both the Past and Present ideas – in a future where the use of AI seems only likely to increase and where the relative contribution, input, or supervision by humans seems likely to decrease.

To answer the question initially posed in chapter one, the analyses included in the previous six chapters are used to frame the structure of this chapter. These are, themselves, posed as questions that need to be answered in order to arrive at the ultimate answer. After a brief section that reflects on the conclusions revealed in the previous chapters (which also presents the conclusions in a different way), the questions that frame the following sections are: what do the hypotheticals mean for the Rule of Law (and what can states use AI for); how will explainable AI alter these Rule of Law conclusions; is AI a new form of power; and, what will the future Rule of Law be? (Further questions are raised and answered within each of these sections.) In the final section, after answering all of these questions, I come to a briefly stated conclusion: our Future idea of the Rule of Law must be conceived on a blank canvas (without recourse to prior Rule of Law ideas) in order to solve the problems that the exercise of power by AI will generate.

This conclusion – and these questions – are important. The Rule of Law is a concept that, despite the level of contest that surrounds its meaning, is seen as a vitally important concept to many different states around the world. There seems to be no immediate prospect of this changing. But, if the use of AI is to increase, the way in which the Rule of Law operates needs to change. This, as will be apparent from the adoption of the Past and Present paradigms in this book that illustrate there has been a change over time, is not unprecedented. After all, the meaning of the concept of the Rule of Law, contested as it is,[1] is based at the most fundamental

[1] J Waldron, 'Is the Rule of Law an Essentially Contested Concept (in Florida)?' (2002) 21(2) *Law and Philosophy* 137; P Burgess, 'The Rule of Law: Beyond Contestedness' (2017) 8(3) *Jurisprudence* 480.

level on our acceptance of what the concept *is*. Our understanding of the content of the Rule of Law is varied. However, there are limits; we would all likely agree that the meaning of 'the Rule of Law' is not, for example, the same as the meaning of 'a chair'. The meanings associated with the concept of these two things is just *too* different to be said to be the same thing. The popularly accepted Past and the Present Rule of Law ideas are not as different as this example. But they are still different. What is more, the temporal difference in their authorship indicates significant changes do occur in what we may accept the concept to be over time.

The change over time can be illustrated by pointing to just two of the accounts that have both featured heavily in this book: Dicey and Bingham. Both were English jurists writing, primarily about what the concept means in their jurisdiction at their time of writing.[2] Yet, as will likely be apparent to anyone reading the book linearly, there are considerable differences between the two accounts. It does not seem to be too much of a stretch to suggest that Bingham's early twenty-first century Rule of Law would, a little over a century earlier, have been *too* different for Dicey to have recognised it as being the same concept as his Rule of Law.[3] Whilst there is clearly some overlap (noted in chapter two) there are fundamental differences in kind that relate to both the thin/thick natures of their conceptions as well as the way in which they operate. There are also differences in the way that they talk about the concept. Dicey provides an account that is largely *observational* – he suggests that the account exists in England (but is under threat).[4] Bingham provides an aspirational idea of the Rule of Law – he puts forth the concept as something that states should strive toward.[5] Yet, these are not random and fringe accounts. They are both accounts that are widely accepted as being ideas that provide an indication of what the Rule of Law *is*.[6]

It may be that Bingham's account would have been as widely accepted in the late-nineteenth century as it is now. We have no way of knowing; but what we can see across the dichotomy of the Past and the Present ideas of the Rule of Law is that there seems to have been a substantive turn in relation to the acceptance of what the Rule of Law *may* mean. I do not mean to suggest that there have not been any substantive accounts that pre-date any of the Past Rule of Law authors. What I do mean is that there has not been popular acceptance of more substantive accounts of the Rule of Law until more recent decades. Given this substantial change in relation to the relative acceptance of more substantive ideas – to the extent that some of the Present ideas of the Rule of Law would be unrecognisable to the authors of

[2] AV Dicey, *Introduction to the Study of the Law of the Constitution*, 10th edn (Basingstoke, Palgrave Macmillan, 1979); T Bingham, *The Rule of Law* (London, Allen Lane, 2010).

[3] Bingham (n 2); Dicey (n 2).

[4] Dicey (n 2) II.

[5] Bingham (n 2).

[6] The two texts used in institutions where I have taught Public Law both refer to these (and others). M Elliott and R Thomas, *Public Law*, 4th edn (Oxford, Oxford University Press, 2020); LB Crawford et al, *Public Law and Statutory Interpretation: Principles and Practice*, 2nd edn (Alexandria, NSW, Federation Press, 2021).

the Past Rule of Law – there is no reason not to think that changes in what we are willing to accept as an idea of what the Rule of Law *is* will not continue to evolve into the future. Given the extreme kinds of differences noted above, there is no reason to think that any future change may also not be extreme. In other words, if the relative sources or way in which arbitrary power may be exercised may change, and if we want the Rule of Law to prevent or limit the arbitrary exercise of power in the future, our understanding of what 'the Rule of Law' *is* must evolve in order to account for those changes. The question remains, however, as to what that form of evolution will look like. Through the course of this chapter, I will seek to provide an answer.

I. Rule of Law Reflections and Ramifications of AI's Use

This section provides a brief restatement as well as a different view of the conclusions reached across chapters four, five, and six. In the sub-section that follows, I present the conclusions reached in those chapters not in the context of each hypothetical – as they were considered in the chapter – but in the context of the Past and Present conceptions of the Rule of Law. In adopting this different perspective, different trends, similarities, and differences can be observed. This different perspective enables broader conclusions to be drawn as to what the hypotheticals mean in terms of the interrelationship between the use of AI and the Rule of Law. In addition, it enables conclusions to be drawn regarding what states can – if they are adhering to the Rule of Law – use AI for. I deal with each of these in a distinct sub-section.

Before providing the *different* perspective, it is useful to very briefly summarise the conclusions reached in each of the chapters that explored the different hypotheticals. In chapter four, the first hypothetical related to the use of AI to make administrative decisions – the running example was using an AI to process visa applications. As an administrative decision-making process, any decisions were subject to review – so this was considered to be a human-in-the-loop scenario. This hypothetical represents the least extreme of the three hypotheticals – as the technology that is required to do this largely already exists and has been deployed in some form in some states. (These were explored in chapter three.) In considering the range of Rule of Law ideas, from the broadest anti-arbitrariness idea, through to individual popular Rule of Law conceptions, it became clear that a need for any decision-making steps that the AI takes must be explainable. This fundamental need pervaded all hypotheticals and all levels of abstraction.

The second hypothetical – presented in chapter five – imagined an AI taking the place of an advisory body that was responsible for adding or removing particular substances to a list of proscribed drugs. These actions resulted in the creation of secondary legislation – as a form of regulation – in consequence of power being delegated to the AI from the legislature. Whilst the legislature did still hold a form of veto over the exercise of the delegated power, the hypothetical assumed that this would be rarely exercised (as this is the case in current real situations where such powers are delegated).[7] This resulted in a human-over-the-loop scenario where the AI exercised a considerable level of autonomy.

As with the first hypothetical, it was clear in the second hypothetical that explainability remained fundamental – its absence resulted in a system that could not satisfy the requirements the Rule of Law at any level of abstraction. Several other novel issues relating to Rule of Law compliance also became apparent. The most prominent of these was that the increased autonomy exercised by the AI meant that a problem also arose in relation to accountability of an algorithm. This became a problem at different points for different kinds of thinkers. For example, Past Rule of Law thinkers like Locke and Dicey expressed concerns regarding the need for accountability in general; Bingham, as a Present Rule of Law thinker, required accountability in order to satisfy elements of good governance that would be required for his conception of the Rule of Law. Another problem that was first explored in this hypothetical included issues associated with the relative speed of decision-making and the interrelationship of speed and emotion. These problems were, to some degree, tempered by the legislature providing some level of human-over-the-loop supervision – which provided a minimal level of accountability. What was also seen for the first time in Hypothetical Two was that some Rule of Law accounts provided the potential for increased levels of protection. The Present Rule of Law accounts, in particular King and Krygier's *source*-based accounts, illustrated ways in which requirements like a positive duty to delegate and the ability to hold non-public bodies accountable under the Rule of Law would provide more protections than exist under the Past Rule of Law accounts.

Chapter six presented the third and most extreme hypothetical. In this hypothetical, elected algorithms replace all of the elected humans in the legislature. The elected algorithms are then, constituted in the legislature, solely responsible for the proposing, debating, and passing of new laws. This describes a humans-out-of-the-loop scenario. This hypothetical illustrated similar patterns but also a different way in which the problems manifested. Problems that had been identified in previous chapters, notably the need for explainability and accountability were also present in Hypothetical Three. In addition, the speed of decision-making was also identified as a problem; but the nature of this problem differed to the previous hypothetical. Here, it related to an *external* manifestation of the speed-problem. This increased speed did not lead to a problem in terms of increased errors. Instead, it resulted in problems relating to certainly, predictability, and knowability – fundamental desiderata for several theorists across the Past and Present Rules of Law.

[7] JS Caird and E Patterson, *Brexit, Delegated Powers and Delegated Legislation: A Rule of Law Analysis of Parliamentary Scrutiny* (London, The Bingham Centre for the Rule of Law, 2020); R Fox and J Blackwell, *The Devil Is in the Detail: Parliament and Delegated Legislation* (London, Hansard Society, 2014).

Hypothetical Three did also reveal a number of relative benefits. In considering issues related to accountability, speed, and explainability, certain benefits offered by an AI-populated legislature manifested. This included the ability to clearly satisfy the performative elements of law making. Relative benefits that had also been identified in relation to the second hypothetical – like the ability in the Present Rule of Law to hold non-public bodies accountable under the Rule of Law – were also see in the third hypothetical. In these respects, there seemed to be some considerable benefits offered by the Present Rule of Law over the Past Rule of Law; however, one problem that did become apparent when considering the Present Rule of Law was the potential difficulties that may follow from attempting to ensure an algorithm adhered to a paradigm that facilitated particular specified outcomes. This related to the difficulty associated with being able to program an algorithm in a way that provides direct autonomy. This arises as an AI may only act or have power to act within a pre-determined set of parameters. (In contrast to an autonomous human that can act in *any* circumstance.) These could include ensuring social benefit or adhering to principles of human rights. In this circumstance, it becomes clear that the relative autonomy of the algorithm must be limited – and this limitation of the law-making function at the level of the law-maker's code operates as a quasi-constitutional limitation that is created and applied by an entity (the programmer) that is not directly accountable.

II. What do the Hypotheticals Mean for AI and the Rule of Law?

The very brief summary provided in the preceding section – whilst an efficient way to outline the preceding chapters – does not identify what these findings mean for the Rule of Law. The overall conceptual organisation of this book was, however, designed to facilitate this answer. The division of the accounts into Past and Present ideas of the Rule of Law, whilst somewhat reflective of the frequently seen thin/thick divide,[8] was adopted in order to more clearly identify the potential direction of any future evolution of the concept. With this in mind, in the paragraphs immediately below, I provide a conceptual perspective that differs to that adopted in the previous chapter. I do this to assist in bringing out the similarities and differences across the two forms of idea. I then use this in order to better illuminate what this means for the Rule of Law. Then, in the next section, I reflect on what states can use AI for under the existing – Past and Present – ideas of the Rule of Law.

What is immediately clear from the hypotheticals across both Past and Present ideas and at all levels of abstraction – from broad-brush strokes to individual conceptions – is that the need for explainability is fundamental. The inability of

[8] For the classic statement of this, see P Craig, 'Formal and Substantive Conceptions of the Rule of Raw an Analytical Framework' [1997] (Autumn) *Public Law* 467.

AI to be able to provide explanations of its decision-making (in each of the hypotheticals) represents a fundamental Rule of Law problem. In almost all instances, this will mean that if a state wishes to adhere to any idea of the Rule of Law (Past or Present), the AI that it uses in ways that reflect the hypotheticals must be explainable. On the basis of present technology, where explainable AI represents a fundamental and ongoing problem, this means that the use of AI in the ways hypothesised remains contrary to the Rule of Law whatever the view adopted. (Given the fundamentality of this issue, later in this chapter I consider what would happen if AI *was* explainable.) If explainability is put to one side, it is possible to consider the other issues that arise. Several were noted in the summary provided earlier. Here I will focus on issues relating to accountability and speed of action as well as considering the new problems and solutions that arise.

Accountability is a Past and Present Rule of Law problem that arises as soon as the level of autonomy provided to the AI extends into the human-over-the-loop and human-out-of-the-loop scenarios contemplated in Hypotheticals Two and Three. In Past conceptions, it was shown to be a problem for particular thinkers like Locke and Dicey. In Present Rule of Law accounts, accountability overlaps with explainability and transparency. For the UN and, for Bingham, it was seen to be a necessary feature in good governance that is essential if a state is to be considered a Rule of Law state. The problem that arises in each instance is that an AI cannot be held accountable in the same way as a human and, furthermore, the accountability mechanisms that we presently have are largely human-centric.

Whilst a problem in both the Past and the Present, the need for accountability revealed some differences between the two ideas. Past ideas revealed a form of tempering of the problem through the performative aspects of law-making. There could, at least, be some way that elected AIs could be held to account as their actions in proposing, debating, and passing legislation could be scrutinised. But, this may not be sufficient to obviate the problem completely in circumstances where AIs may not be motivated to remain in power in the same way as humans. This tempering effect could also alleviate some of the concerns associated with explainability – at least by providing an outward facing manifestation of the AI's decision-making process. (Whilst this would not be truly reflective of how decisions are being made this may be on par with how human legislators communicate.) This tempering effect did not arise, however, in consideration of the Present Rule of Law. Although, as many of the Present accounts also require the satisfaction of many of the same desiderata as the Past Rule of Law conceptions, this is not to say it would not occur at all.

At least one of the Present Rule of Law ideas does provide an *increased* level of accountability protection when contrasted to the Past. Krygier's purposive account seeks to tackle arbitrariness wherever it may arise.[9] In this sense, a form

[9] M Krygier, 'The Rule of Law: Legality, Teleology and Sociology' in G Palombella and N Walker (eds), *Relocating the Rule of Law* (Oxford, Hart Publishing, 2009) ('Legality, Teleology and Sociology');

of accountability could be seen to apply *beyond* merely applying to the wielder of public power (as contemplated by the Past Rule of Law). In this respect, Krygier's account would provide an additional form of protection if the application of the concept of the Rule of Law was read very narrowly so as to apply only to humans – taking literally the suggestion that the Rule of Law means that it is the law that rules and not people.[10]

It is not only the extension of Rule of Law protection in terms of a narrow reading of the human operation of the Rule of Law that can be seen as a difference. The Present form of the Rule of Law provides other increased or extended protections over those offered by Past ideas. The source-based Rule of Law accounts – by Krygier and King – have the effect that responses to applications of power may be possible *beyond* the public-sphere.[11] Where accountability is a key issue in the sorts of scenarios raised in chapters five and six, the ability to hold private entities (programmers or corporations that create the algorithms) could be seen as a significant advantage over Past ideas that cannot be extended in this way.

A further area in which there are differences between the Past and Present ideas relates to the issue of speed (of decision-making). When AIs are used to make decisions, speed was not seen to represent a problem in *internal* terms – in the actual making of decisions. This was because the speed of machine-based decision making is not more prone to error simply because it is faster than humans' speed. The relative speed did, however, represent an *external* problem in circumstances where the ability of those subject to laws to keep up with, and properly comprehend, the decisions that could be made in a fraction of a second became a particular problem for Past Rule of Law ideas. This external manifestation of speed increases uncertainty and unpredictability – as two key Rule of Law desiderata. However, there was also found to be a potential benefit of the performative elements of AI operation – particularly prevalent in the third hypothetical – that may temper, at some level, the relative negative impact of the speed of decision making. These would assist with the Procedural Clarity and promulgatory requirements that exist at different levels of the Past Rule of Law. These speed-related issues were not as prevalent in the extended notions of the Present Rule of Law. (Whilst, again, noting that many of the Present Rule of Law ideas are built on a formal base, which means the issues would also be seen in terms of the shared foundation of common Rule of Law ideas across Past and Present.)

The extension of Past Rule of Law ideas into the Present Rule of Law ideas was also seen to create new duties and, as a corollary, new problems. The new duties arise particularly in consideration of King's Rule of Law conception that requires

M Krygier, 'Four Puzzles About the Rule of Law: Why, What, Where? And Who Cares?' in J Flemming (ed), *Getting to the Rule of Law* (New York, New York University Press, 2011) 64; M Krygier, 'What's the Point of the Rule of Law?' 67 *Buffalo Law Review* 50.

[10] Aristotle, T Sinclair and T J Saunders, *The Politics* (London, Penguin UK, 1981) 1287a23.

[11] J King, 'The Rule of Law' in R Bellamy and J King (eds), *The Cambridge Handbook of Constitutional Theory* (2024) papers.ssrn.com/abstract=4487306; Krygier, 'What's the Point of the Rule of Law?' (n 9).

positive action to promote social benefit.[12] This idea is already a departure from the Past ideas of the Rule of Law that are not generative of the same duties. This difference becomes starker when the hypotheticals are considered. If it is the case that the AI systems contemplated may produce a *greater* social benefit than the human-based practices, there would be a duty to enhance this benefit by delegating the power to the AI systems in preference to humans. This represents a radical difference to the Past Rule of Law ideas that do not see any such additional duty arising.

The duty to delegate to the AI systems that forms at least a part of the Present Rule of Law may, however, be part of a process that creates novel problems that do not arise under the Past Rule of Law. These problems have been seen to be the potential creation of a new form of arbitrary power through the outcome-based ideas of the Rule of Law. This results from the need to code algorithms to be targeted at achieving a particular outcome for Bingham and the UN and through King's source-based ideas that see the Rule of Law as creating a positive duty to enhance social benefit. The novel problems that are illuminated through consideration of the hypothetical are, it is suggested below, not only reflective of some of the different views associated with thin/thick ideas of the Rule of Law but are also sufficiently problematic so as to obviate the potential benefits that may be seen from the Present Rule of Law ideas.

The problems would arise even if the outcomes that are targeted are accepted as being universally good or desirable – for example, the enhancement of social benefit or the promotion of human rights. By stipulating a *particular* objective for an algorithm to seek to achieve, whatever that objective may be, this imposes a relative constraint on its autonomy and decision-making process that is imposed by non-elected, non-accountable, programming entities (made up of, for example, a software company or a programmer). This constraint, particularly in circumstances where the relative autonomy of the AI is at a high level – in the second two hypotheticals, most obviously – results in the relative power-base related to the creation or application of laws either moving to a programming entity or being partially shared between the algorithm and the entity. It creates a bottom-up quasi-constitutional constraint on the way in which laws are made or applied and could be seen as the creation of a *new* form of arbitrary power. This sharing – whether explicitly or implicitly apparent – could be seen to represent serious challenges for several other big-picture public law principles beyond the Rule of Law – for example, democracy and the separation of powers. What this, and the other broadly stated conclusions relating to the Past and Present ideas of the Rule of Law, means for the future of the Rule of Law is explored across the following two sections.

[12] King (n 11); J King, '"Constitutional Boundaries" – The Social Dimension of the Rule of Law', *I·CONnect* (2018) www.iconnectblog.com/2018/04/i-connect-symposium-on-constitutional-boundaries-the-social-dimension-of-the-rule-of-law/.

III. What can States Use AI for?

The question framing this section is broadly stated. However, it represents a crucial step in both the analysis provided across this book and in the potential practical application of the ideas that have been presented. The broadly stated answer is that the relative in-explainability of complex algorithmic processes that underlie each of the hypotheticals explored in this book renders each incompatible with the Rule of Law regardless of the form or level of abstractness that is preferred. This means that, if a state values the Rule of Law and if the AI processes are not explainable, then states cannot use AI in the ways contemplated in this book. This must, however, also be considered in terms of the next section that moves beyond this relatively bleak contemporary conclusion and seeks to explore what states may be able to use AI for in circumstances where this problem may be remedied.

What will be clear by this point in the book is that across both the Past and Present Rule of Law ideas – regardless of the level of abstraction that those ideas are viewed at – the issue of explainability is fundamental to the satisfaction of the Rule of Law. This has been shown to be the case in each of the three hypotheticals that have been considered in chapters four, five, and six and summarised above. Despite the non-dystopian and future-facing approach that is adopted in this book, the construction and framing of the hypotheticals did not seek to explain or wish-away the relative and current inability of AI technology to be explainable; the opaqueness of the algorithmic black-box was maintained.[13] The reason for the retention of this problem despite the hypothetical situations being considered is due to the relative intractability of the problem.[14] (I do, however, briefly consider the possibility of this problem being solved in the next section.)

Past ideas of the Rule of Law – across levels and across all of the hypotheticals – require explainability. This can be seen in the common desiderata related to predictability and certainty, as well as in both of the Rule of Law elements relating to Predictability and Procedural Clarity. These ideas, and many other commonly stated ideas related to stability and certainty, for example, reflect the idea of explainability. Where decisions are not explainable – whether at the level of administrative decision-making or in secondary or primary law-making – the exercise of power would be rendered arbitrary and, thus, contrary to even the broadest idea of the Rule of Law. Even if the potential for some explainability were to be facilitated – for example in the performative aspects of primary law-making explored in chapter six – this would not be sufficient to provide a level of explainability that would satisfy the requirements of the Rule of Law. This has the effect that any of the uses contemplated across the hypotheticals would be rendered contrary to the

[13] F Pasquale, *The Black Box Society: The Secret Algorithms That Control Money and Information*, reprint edn (Cambridge, Mass, Harvard University Press, 2016).

[14] D Minh et al, 'Explainable Artificial Intelligence: A Comprehensive Review' (2022) 55(5) *Artificial Intelligence Review* 3503.

Past Rule of Law and, as a result, states (that consider themselves to be Rule of Law states) would not be able to deploy AI systems in the ways contemplated here.

As noted above, and noted in chapter two, the Present Rule of Law, and the conceptions that have been considered within that idea, are each based on a foundation of Past Rule of Law basic desiderata. As suggested in the previous paragraph, these foundational desiderata include ideas like certainty, predictability, and stability. The non-compliance with the Past Rule of Law due to a failure of explainability noted immediately above would have the effect of also rendering each of the hypothetical applications contrary to the Present Rule of Law. In other words, as was the case immediately above, any of hypothesised applications would be rendered contrary to the Present Rule of Law. This would mean that Rule of Law states would not be able to deploy these kinds of AI systems (if they wish to remain Rule of Law states).

These conclusions, whilst based around theoretical exploration and hypothetical scenarios have profound real-world implications. AI systems are increasingly being used and deployed by various states around the world. Some of the ways in which AI is already being used relate closely to some of the hypothetical scenarios. For example, the processing of visa applications has already, in some states, been partially delegated to AI systems.[15] The conclusions described above mean that if those uses of AI are not able to be fully explained, they would be being used contrary to the Rule of Law – no matter which popular form of the Rule of Law is preferred. As the Rule of Law is a political concept, this does not mean those decisions are necessarily *legally* challengeable – but it does mean that the continued use of AI systems in this way can be criticised from a Rule of Law adherence perspective. This, of itself, may be sufficient to generate substantial normative force where states continually appear to strive to be seen as Rule of Law adherent.

The conclusions also mean that Rule of Law states' future policy directions related to the implementation of AI systems across broad-ranging public functions like administrative decision-making and the creation of (primary and secondary) laws must depend on the ability of those systems to be explainable. The effect of this is that whilst these may be very real cost and time efficient benefits relating to the deployment of AI systems, the realisation of these benefits must, in Rule of Law states, await the development of AI technologies that are explainable.

The fundamental bar that the Rule of Law creates in relation to the deployment of AI systems in the ways contemplated in this book is not only clear, but also exists across the various ideas and levels of abstraction considered in the book. The future-facing approach of the book would not, however, be complete without considering what may happen in a future where explainability *can* be achieved.

[15] Treasury Board of Canada Secretariat, *Digital Operations Strategic Plan: 2018–2022* (13 May 2021) www.canada.ca/en/government/system/digital-government/government-canada-digital-operations-strategic-plans/digital-operations-strategic-plan-2018-2022.html; UK Cabinet Office, *Government Transformation Strategy 2017 to 2020*: www.gov.uk/government/publications/government-transformation-strategy-2017-to-2020.

In other words, what would happen if the explainability of algorithmic decision-making was no longer a fundamental Rule of Law bar to the use of AI in the ways conceived in this book.

IV. How will Explainable AI Alter Rule of Law Conclusions?

In this section I consider a very brief extension to the hypotheticals already considered. The focus of this 'what if?' relates to the most prevalent and problematic element for the use of AI by governments across both the Past and Present Rule of Law ideas: explainability. Whilst this book has taken a future-facing and non-dystopian view of the potential for AI's use, it did not simply assume that one of the most difficult and beguiling features of AI use – that of explainable AI – could be solved. As noted earlier, current research suggests the issue is increasingly prevalent as algorithms become more complex and these more complex algorithms do not appear to be any more explainable. For this reason, dealing with the potential that this may not be solved in the previous chapters seemed sensible. Yet, it does also seem useful to consider how the conclusions that have already reached may differ where the explainability problem could be solved.

When this happens, the conclusions drawn thus far may be seen to suggest that the Present Rule of Law ideas – in virtue of the increased protections that they offer – may mean that not only would those ideas be better suited than Past Rule of Law ideas to addressing many of the problems that arise in relation to the hypotheticals, but also that the protections may be sufficient to alter the relative bar expressed above. This simply put position is not, however, fully reflective of the relative differences across the Past and Present ideas and does not take account of the relative problems that the Present Rule of Law may generate. What this means is that even where an AI's decisions may be explainable, several Rule of Law problems suggest AI cannot be used by states in the ways contemplated in this book.

In earlier sections I have outlined the conclusions that follow from the earlier analysis in this book. The potential efficiency, accuracy, and speed benefits – as the sorts of benefits that AI deployment often provides – that may occur in the hypothetical situations raised in this book must be considered in terms of the Rule of Law problems that may arise. When going beyond the explainability problem, these include the externalised problems associated with the increased speed of decision-making that may impact the clarity and predictability of decision-making for those subject to those decisions. In previous sections and chapters, it was noted that this problem may be tempered by – at least in the law-making function in the third hypothetical – the publication and promulgation of the outward-facing aspects of decision-making. One form of this was taken to be Hansard-type records of debates in the legislature. This tempering effect was considered too insufficient to offset the external speed problem when considered in conjunction with the explainability problem. Yet, if the explainability problem is removed, the potential for an AI system to be able to provide a rationale for and explanation of its decision-making process would need to be considered together with the tempering effect. In this respect, the performative element would provide an *additional* level of scrutiny. In these circumstances, the relative speed benefit that AI can bring would be able to be realised in a way that satisfies the Past Rule of Law (as well as aspects of the Present Rule of Law that share requirements for predictability, stability, and certainty as foundational ideas).

Accountability was also identified above and in previous chapters as being a problem across both the Past and Present ideas of the Rule of Law. The Past Rule of Law identified accountability issues that stemmed from the accounts of thinkers like Dicey and Locke. The Present Rule of Law identified more complex issues relating to accountability's role in good governance and in concert with issues like explainability and transparency. The issues associated with accountability had two aspects. The first was related to explainability – as it was difficult to hold an entity to account if it was not clear what the entity was doing. The second was related to the ability to hold an entity to account for its actual actions. If the explainability problem is solved, this leaves only the second issue. There were two hypotheticals where accountability was raised as a fundamental issue: Hypotheticals Two and Three. In this regard, the Past Rule of Law problems regarding the fears Dicey and Locke held – relating to the implementation of decisions in circumstances where there was no way to hold the decision-maker accountable – could, then, be partially remedied. This is only partial as the explainable nature of the decisions only results in the *mode* of decision-making being able to be identified. The ability to explain a decision does not address the second of the issues that relates to the ability for the decision-making entity to be truly held accountable. It may be possible to see which AI made a decision and, crucially, *why* it made a decision. This means accountability can be attributed to the process of decision-making. However, this does not cause an AI to be able to be held accountable in the same way as a human – as it remains the case that AI systems cannot be held to account in the same way as humans.

The Present Rule of Law identified *additional* considerations relating to accountability. In particular, this related to the outcome-based Present Rule of Law ideas of Bingham and the UN in which the idea of accountability forms part of a chain of good governance that was either required to satisfy the Rule of Law or that overlapped with the Rule of Law. In these instances, similarly to the explanation immediately above, it remained the case that AI could not be held accountable in the same way as humans. Krygier – as another Present Rule of Law theorist – does, however, contemplate that the Rule of Law protections should not only extend to public bodies (for example, legislative institutions) but also to private entities. In this respect, there would be some accountability-related benefit as it would be possible to consider the creators of the AI systems that were being held to account as, in turn, also accountable. At some level, this addresses the inability of holding an AI to account by sheeting home a form of responsibility to another – human or corporate – entity. In this sense, there is a form of additional accountability mechanism that may operate in excess of the Present Rule of Law forms of accountability. (This aspect feeds into the discussions below regarding the relative problems that stem from the application of new duties and increased protections.)

It is also apparent that there are other forms of *increased* protection that exist in relation to the Present Rule of Law idea when compared to the Past. Some of these were touched on immediately above in terms of Krygier's view. They include the ability to hold non-public bodies to account from the idea that the Rule of Law should respond to and oppose arbitrary applications of power regardless of the source.

The creation of explainable AI is not, however, all problem-solving. I also pointed out that there are novel problems that arise in relation to either the potential creation of a positive duty to act – in King's source-based Rule of Law conception – or in the desire to achieve particular outcomes either in order to satisfy the Rule of Law or in using the Rule of Law to achieve other substantive outcomes – as in the outcome-based conceptions of Bingham and the UN, respectively. As noted above, where this would require the achievement of a particular focus on a particular kind of action to be included in the algorithm's code, this would remove autonomy from the algorithm and would result in the source of the relevant power being moved, at least in some degree, from the decision-making algorithm to the programmer.

In the hypotheticals, the AI systems are exercising public power. It is in this sense that the issue of accountability raised earlier is a key consideration in terms of the Rule of Law. The relative shift in power to the programming entity would be invisible. It would form a new opaque element in the decision-making process. Further, as outlined earlier in the chapter, the coding of the algorithm would operate so as to create a quasi-constitutional constraint on the laws or decisions that may be made. The exercise of a constraint on the AI that is either making decisions or laws would mean that the difficulties associated with holding the AI accountable would be complicated further by a level of accountability lying with the programming entity. In considering the teleological Present Rule of Law conception provided by Krygier, it would be the case that the Rule of Law anti-arbitrariness function would be able to be applied to the programming entity – even if this was a non-public body. But this does not address the fundamental issues that arise that contravene principles like representative democracy and the separation of powers – public law ideas that often are seen to operate hand-in-hand with the Rule of Law.

What this means is that the requirements that relate to three of the Present Rule of Law ideas – requiring the achievement or targeting of certain goals or aims – are constitutive of substantial problems that not only cause substantial issues associated with the Rule of Law, but also with other fundamental public law ideas that exist together with the Rule of Law. The scope and nature of these problems is sufficient to suggest that, even where AI is explainable, the implementation of AI in the ways hypothesised in this book would be profoundly problematic for the Present

Rule of Law. When taken with the earlier conclusion in this section – that the hypotheticals are problematic for the Past Rule of Law (even where it is assumed that explainability can be addressed) due to the problems associated with holding AIs to account – it becomes clear that there are substantial Rule of Law problems associated with the use of AI in the ways hypothesised. It appears that, for different reasons, there are ultimate problems associated with the use of AI across all levels of abstraction in both the Past and Present conceptions of the Rule of Law. In other words, even if explainable AI can be achieved, there are still several Rule of Law reasons why AI cannot be used by states in the ways contemplated in this book.

V. What will the Future Rule of Law Be?

In this final substantive section of the book, given the pessimistic conclusion arrived at above, I consider what the various conclusions arrived at thus far may mean for the Future Rule of Law. This section is focused on providing an overall answer to the question that has informed the book more broadly: how will the concept of the Rule of Law need to evolve in order to account for artificial intelligence being used to exercise public power in the future? My rationale for seeking to provide this answer, notwithstanding the conclusions thus far, stems from the fact that there is no reason to suspect that the Rule of Law will cease to be a concept that is considered to be important to states around the world. What is more, there is also no reason to think that states will not seek to exploit the potential benefits of deploying AI systems in ways that may be akin to some of hypotheticals raised here. If these assumptions are correct, but if Past or Present ideas of the Rule of Law cannot be satisfied where AI is used to exercise public power, our understanding of the concept must change.

Putting this another way, if there are Rule of Law problems with these sorts of uses of technology but a state adopts them anyway, it could not be considered to be a Rule of Law state. This of course would only hold if the commonly accepted views of the Rule of Law explored in this book – that were considered in terms of the Past and Present of the Rule of Law – were seen as being reflective of the Rule of Law in the eyes of the state that was deploying the AI. And, as was noted earlier in the chapter and as is apparent in the Past and Present dichotomy, the meaning of the Rule of Law is able to change or be reinterpreted. Where it is the case that the Past and Present of the Rule of Law explored here *are* the most widely adopted ideas associated with the Rule of Law, it seems that the state would need to hold a *different* view of the Rule of Law than these conceptions. This section considers, albeit very briefly, how that form of the Rule of Law – the Future Rule of Law – would need to differ from the Past and Present ideas already explored.

In order to do this, and in order to consider how our understanding of – and acceptance of – the concept will need to evolve, I will need to address a point that has been touched upon previously: whether AI being used in the way contemplated in this book is a *new* form of power or simply a new *way* of exercising power. I do this first before considering the necessary form of the concept's evolution. Once I have done this, I then consider what the Future Rule of Law may need to be in order to provide protection against uses of AI similar to those considered in this book.

A. Is AI a New Form of Power or Simply a New Way of Exercising Power?

The above question represents a fundamental foundational consideration in identifying the Future Rule of Law. In earlier chapters, I alluded to suggestions that the protection from the arbitrary exercise of power contained within the Rule of Law relates to power that is exercised by *humans* – as the rule of law is preferable to the law of people.[16] I do not seek to claim this alone should be taken as evidence of the inherent humanness of the Rule of Law. But what is clear is that the problems that all of the Rule of Law conceptions seek to solve stem from decisions made by *humans*. It is correct to say that many of the exercises of arbitrary power are institutional – that is, by a legislature – but legislative bodies are constituted by and their institutional mind is informed by humans. In this sense, it seems relevant to consider whether the exercise of power by an AI constitutes a *new* form of power and, as a result, would be beyond the remit of the Rule of Law. Whilst this may seem to be an overly technical distinction it is a relevant one. After all, some conceptions of the Rule of Law – particularly thin conceptions like those of Raz – seek to confine the concept's operation to a conceptually narrow sphere of operation.[17] Whilst the consideration is brief, I conclude that the exercise of power by an AI is not a new form of power and, instead, is a new way of exercising power.

Part of the consideration of this question is, of course, intertwined with an issue that has already been identified as being fundamentally problematic for the operation of both the Past and the Present ideas of the Rule of Law; the idea of accountability. The issues relating to the relative inability to hold an algorithm to account in the same way as a human exist even where an AI may be granted legal personhood.[18] Should it be the case that it is a new form of power *and* be unable to be held accountable, and given the importance of accountability to the Rule of Law that has been explored in previous chapters, this would mean that there would likely be no scenario where giving the AI power would be able to conform

[16] Aristotle, Sinclair and Saunders (n 10) 1287a23.

[17] J Raz, 'The Rule of Law and Its Virtue' in *The Authority of Law: Essays on Law and Morality*, 2nd edn (Oxford, Oxford University Press, 2009) 210.

[18] J Chen and P Burgess, 'The Boundaries of Legal Personhood: How Spontaneous Intelligence Can Problematise Differences between Humans, Artificial Intelligence, Companies and Animals' (2019) 27(1) *Artificial Intelligence and Law* 73.

with the Rule of Law. If the exerciser of the power *cannot* be held accountable, this alone does not determine the answer to the question as to whether the exercise of power by an AI represents a *new* form of power. It seems that it may be a new form of power yet, for the reasons already explored, we may not be able to hold it to account in the same way as humans (or at all).

The potential status of AI as a legal person may, however, offer some way to answer the question of whether AI may constitute a new form of power. If, for the moment, we assume that the trend of extending the categories of personhood moves more toward contemporary theories of personhood there is scope for an AI of the kind contemplated to be a legal person; yet, this may not solve the accountability problem. As one example, Kukri's *Bundle Theory*, claims that there should be nothing intrinsic behind an entity to be considered as a legal person.[19] That idea holds that it is not about right-holding or duty-bearing in general and, instead, it is about the holding of particular types of legal entitlements and burdens.[20] In this sense, it is for the law to decide if such an entity is or is not treated as a legal person. Where the grant of personhood has been made to inanimate objects or parts of the natural environment,[21] it seems that there would be scope to grant personhood status to an AI.[22] (At least to the sort of sophisticated AI that is being contemplated here.) In this situation, the entity that is exercising decision-making or law-making power would be a legal person. This would reflect only a very minor difference to the current human-based situation in which personhood is not involved. The mere fact that an AI becomes a legal person would do little to get beyond the relative lack of motivational effect that potential sanctions may have on the AI (in comparison to a human). In this scenario, it is difficult to see why the exercise of power by the (legal person) AI should be seen in fundamentally different terms – the accountability problem subsists.

Even if the personhood status is removed, the difference – at least to the individual *subject* of the law or decision-making process – could *still* be seen as similar: an entity, often removed from the subject, makes a decision by coming to a conclusion based on the facts available to it, according to a procedure that it has been required to follow. This process, that reflects a decision-making process that may, for example, take place in making an administrative decision like that contemplated in Hypothetical One. This is very similar to a broad definition of a computer introduced in the first chapter that I first learned in school: 'a computer is a machine that under the control of a stored program automatically accepts and processes

[19] VAJ Kurki, *A Theory of Legal Personhood* (Oxford, Oxford University Press, 2019) II.

[20] VAJ Kurki and T Pietrzykowski (eds), *Legal Personhood: Animals, Artificial Intelligence and the Unborn*, 1st edn (Cam, Springer International Publishing, 2017) 84.

[21] SM Solaiman, 'Legal Personality of Robots, Corporations, Idols and Chimpanzees: A Quest for Legitimacy' (2017) 25(2) *Artificial Intelligence and Law* 155; RL Jr Cupp, 'Moving beyond Animal Rights: A Legal/Contractualist Critique' (2009) 46 *San Diego Law Review* 27; G Teubner, 'Rights of Non-humans? Electronic Agents and Animals as New Actors in Politics and Law' (2006) 33(4) *Journal of Law and Society* 497.

[22] Chen and Burgess (n 18).

data and supplies the results of that processing'.[23] For this reason, whilst this very brief consideration cannot do this much deeper question sufficient justice,[24] I will not consider the exercise of power by an AI to not be a new form of power. Instead, I consider it to be a *new way* of exercising power.

This conclusion means that the concept of the Rule of Law remains relevant in the control of the exercise of power. Yet, as stated above, the way in which the Rule of Law has been conceived in the Past or Present cannot provide a solution to the problems that arise when AI is used to exercise public power. Accordingly, if the Rule of Law is to continue to protect against the arbitrary application of power, our understanding of what the concept is (or does) must change.

VI. How Must the Rule of Law Evolve to Prevent the Future Arbitrary Exercise of Power?

The suggestion in the titular question above that the Rule of Law must evolve could be seen as a misnomer. It could be suggested that the Rule of Law does not and cannot evolve as the concept is both essentially contested – so the actual meaning and content of the concept is never agreed – or that itself is not capable of evolving as it is simply a reflection of what we accept it to be at any particular time. This second alternative is the paradigmatic basis on which this book has been framed – different instantiations of ideas that we now associate with the concept in both the past and the present were aggregated together in an effort to gain an understanding of whether the use of AI in exercising public power may contravene the Rule of Law across a variety of ideas and levels of abstraction. The briefly stated answer reached earlier in this chapter was that as there are fundamental problems in terms of both the Past and Present Rule of Law ideas – relating to, most obviously, explainability, accountability, and speed – the use of AI in the ways hypothesised should not be used in the exercise of power in states that profess to adhere to the Rule of Law.

It was also noted that the use of AI is increasing and that the efficiency benefits mean that AI will likely be increasingly used in the exercise of power. In these circumstances, if there is to still be some anti-arbitrariness function played by the Rule of Law, the question becomes one of what the Future Rule of Law must look like in order to continue to play its traditional anti-arbitrariness function. The answer to this can most simply be provided by addressing the problems in Rule of Law compliance noted earlier – that there must be a way to ensure that AIs are

[23] Whilst I learned this definition in the 1980s, it is still used. See, eg, O Bevan, TJ Dixon and S Hargitay, *Microcomputers in Property: A Surveyor's Guide to Lotus 1-2-3 and DBASE IV* (London, Taylor & Francis, 2014) 1.

[24] The nature of this question is such that a fulsome answer would require at least a complete article and, potentially, a book-length answer.

(in some way) accountable for the decisions that they make and that the ideas of the Rule of Law that result in directing AIs to achieve certain goals are either removed or are implemented in such a way that the AIs retain a level of autonomy. I briefly address these before concluding with an alternative, and more radical, suggestion.

Simply addressing the problems themselves is not, however, the aim; doing this would not be a way to imagine a Future Rule of Law. In circumstances where we remedy the problems, all we would be doing is changing the way that power is exercised in order that either the Past or the Present ideas of the Rule of Law could be achieved. For example, in addressing the accountability issue, it could be suggested that algorithms are developed that have ambition, fear of public humiliation, or a desire to stay in power in order that they can assist in creating a more successful society. If that was the case, where it is imagined that an algorithm may be motivated by some of the same motivations and desires that drive humans, this may mean that they could be considered to be accountable in the same way as humans. (This may, however, create other problems for the Rule of Law that were disposed of because machines are devoid of emotion in their decision making.) It could also be the case that it is imagined that the hard-coding issue that takes away an AI's autonomy and shifts power to the programming entity – introducing Rule of Law, separation of powers, and representative government issues – was also solved. Doing these things would be a way of making the exercise of power compliant with current ideas of the Rule of Law. This, of course, would not be a bad thing if it could be achieved. If it could be achieved, there would be no need to consider what the Future Rule of Law must look like. Accordingly, in what follows, I consider what the Future Rule of Law must look like in circumstances where the problems already identified subsist.

VII. A Reimagined Future of the Rule of Law

The Rule of Law is a solution concept.[25] The Past and the Present of the Rule of Law represent solutions to problems that existed at the time that the conceptions were authored.[26] If the Future of the Rule of Law is conceived in a similar way, and assuming the concept will not be overly radically reimagined (akin to the 'chair' example described earlier), the future form would need to provide a solution to the problems associated with the arbitrary exercise of power that have been identified throughout this book. This provides a positive way in which to frame the Future Rule of Law. There is also a negative way to frame the Future Rule of Law as a way

[25] Waldron (n 1) 158; M Krygier, 'Democracy and the Rule of Law' in J Meierhenrich and M Loughlin (eds), *Cambridge Companion to the Rule of Law* (Cambridge, Cambridge University press, 2021).

[26] P Burgess, *The Rule of Lore in the Rule of Law: Putting the Problem of the Rule of Law in Context* 4 June 2019.

to suggest what the Future concept does *not* need to be. In the few paragraphs that follow, and in suggesting one way in which the Future Rule of Law could be conceived, I consider both.

In conceiving a positive Future for the Rule of Law, the problems most pertinent to solve relate to explainability, speed, and accountability. These problems are fundamental reasons why the anti-arbitrariness function of the Rule of Law (conceived in the Past and Present) cannot be achieved when AI is used in the ways contemplated across this book. Of course, the challenge in conceiving a Future Rule of Law conception stems from retaining the anti-arbitrariness function reflected in the problems whilst also accounting for the use/application of AI. The broadly thin or formal ideas that inform the entirety of the Past Rule of Law and form a foundational part of the Present Rule of Law conceptions, may give one way to think about constraining AI's power. In this sense, with some of the problems identified in this book in mind, a Future Rule of Law may seek to temper the exercise of power both in a way that must be made *slowly enough* to be externally comprehended and in a way that ensures the exercise of power can be *communicated* in a way that can be comprehended by those that are subject to the power. Whilst these ideas relate to the problems associated with speed and explainability, the process-based suggestions do not simply remove the problem. They are solutions as they could be implemented where, for example, explainable AI is never realised.

The negative aspects of the Future Rule of Law relate to things that the concept would not do or need to be in order to respond to the arbitrary exercise of power by AI. In one respect, this could be seen as avoiding situations that generate some of the problems set out above. For example, the problems that arise when seeking to have an AI achieve particular outcomes or in seeking to discharge a particular duty – as was seen in the conceptions by Bingham, the UN, and King. In this respect, thin/ner ideas of the Rule of Law appear to be less problem generative – which accords in the broadest sense with the process-based positive approach above.

Another respect in which the negative aspect of the Future Rule of Law that could be considered involves a specific non-reliance on prior authorities of (the Past or Present) Rule of Law. As noted at the start of this section, the solution-based nature of the Rule of Law in prior authorities is highly contextualised – each of the authors is providing a solution to a problem that they have in *their* societies. It is difficult to conceive of even the Present Rule of Law accounts as being intended to solve the problems relating to the exercise of power by an AI. In this respect, the Future Rule of Law does not include process-based ideas *because* Locke, Dicey, Bingham, or anyone else considered them to be Rule of Law desiderata; it includes these things because their inclusion may achieve the broad purpose of the Rule of Law – as a concept that opposes the arbitrary application of power – in a world in which AI exercises power. This idea of 'creating' a Rule of Law from a blank canvas that responds to a particular contextual problem is not unprecedented. In popularising the phrase 'the Rule of Law', Dicey described a concept without recourse to any preceding accounts of (what we now consider) the Rule of Law.[27] His account identified a problem that existed in his society and identified the facets of the Rule of Law that existed in his society that could combat that problem. In the same way, and where the context and problems of all prior ideas of the Rule of Law are fundamentally different to those raised when AI exercises power, the Future Rule of Law should not be premised on or reliant on the content of prior accounts – even highly popular accounts – of the Rule of Law.

The fundamental problem of accountability is not encompassed in the positive or negative solutions stated above. The motivators that have traditionally been used to hold power-wielding entities accountable have been human-centred. These may include removal from power, sanctions, fines, imprisonment, or reputational damage. There seems to be no immediate way to make a machine accountable in this way. (Barring the intuitively unpalatable suggestion that we build power-hungry machines.) On this basis, the Future Rule of Law would require the inclusion of a human-in-the-loop to *be* accountable. This is not necessary for fear of ineffective technology or malfunction, but to ensure that the exercise of power has a human actor that is always accountable.[28] (In this sense, compliance with the Future Rule of Law may bar, completely, the situation considered in the third hypothetical where AIs are solely responsible for law-making.)

If there must always be a human-in-the-loop, this suggests that the actual exerciser of the power may not be the one that is ultimately held accountable – it may be, for example, an AI that makes a decision, but a government minister may be the human-in-the-loop. It is conceivable that the exercise of power could be a public exercise, but the accountable human-in-the-loop may be a private entity. In this scenario, whilst it could be said that the Rule of Law may operate in relation to the public exercise of power, the relative normative force may extend to the private sphere. The idea of the Rule of Law has traditionally been about the exercise of public power, more contemporary views have moved away from this view. Of those considered in this book, King and Krygier see the Rule of Law operating beyond only the public sphere. I have argued against this wider view in circumstances where there is continued reliance on prior Rule of Law ideas to support the private exercise.[29] However, this argument does not hold where there is no reliance on prior accounts in accordance with the negative aspect of the Future Rule of Law and where the Future Rule of Law is painted on a blank canvas. On this basis, the Future Rule of Law may need to have a role in the public or private sphere, or a hybrid form. Where multiple areas need to be covered, Krygier's suggestion that

[27] Dicey (n 2) 183.

[28] This approach is broadly in line with the dissenting view that the idea of what constitutes a decision (in an administrative law context) needs to evolve in order to reflect decision-making in an age where decisions may be made by machines. *Pintarich v Deputy Commissioner of Taxation* [2018] Cth Federal Court of Australia – Full Court 79.

[29] P Burgess, 'Googling the Equivalence of Private Arbitrary Power and State Arbitrary Power: Why The Rule of Law Does Not Relate to Private Relationships' [2021] *International Journal of Law in Context*.

the Rule of Law should respond to *all* exercises of arbitrary power would be of greatest effect within the Future Rule of Law.

It is with a simple conclusion that I will end the book. In identifying the Future Rule of Law, we need to consider the specific problems that AI's exercise of power raises and that we should do this from a position that does not rely on the previous canon of the Rule of Law. This may seem like a radical proposition. But I do not think that it is. I have suggested earlier that the very nature of the Rule of Law ideas – across the Past and Present – differ considerably to one another; the conceptions provided by theorists like Locke or Dicey (and their focus on procedural constraints on state power) sit uncomfortably with, for example, Krygier and King's ideas that see a much wider application of the concept and the creation of positive duties on the state. In these respects, there have already been radical shifts in popularly cited ideas of the Rule of Law. A shift of the kind I am suggesting, of itself, is not in this sense unprecedented.

The Future Rule of Law that I do suggest is also not a radical departure. It retains the core anti-arbitrariness function that is common across ideas of the Rule of Law – which I take to be a necessary feature in any concept that could be conceived of as being a Rule of Law concept. (This stems from the positive idea of what the Future concept may look like.) What may be considered as being radical is the suggestion that the content of the Future Rule of Law should, beyond the broad anti-arbitrariness function, not be premised on the ideas that have come before it. Even if this is considered radical, it is a necessary approach to avoid the anachronistic application of problems to authors' prior conceptions that were unable to take account of the situations that this book raises. (I have made similar arguments relating to the abandonment of a reliance on past ideas in relation to the international Rule of Law and in seeking to justify contemporary ideas through recourse to past ideas that are too contextually different.[30])

The Rule of Law-related problems that the Past and Present accounts sought to solve are so fundamentally different to those that will arise when AI is being used in the ways contemplated in this book that our Future idea of the Rule of Law must be conceived in a way that solves *those* problems and does not seek to adapt or change the accounts that have come before. Whilst the suggestion that I set out above is not the only way to do this, it provides one option that we can use to begin to evolve our idea of the Future Rule of Law.

[30] P Burgess, 'Deriving the International Rule of Law: An Unnecessary, Impractical and Unhelpful Exercise' (2019) 10(1) *Transnational Legal Theory* 65; Burgess (n 29); P Burgess, 'Why We Need to Abandon "The Rule of Law"', IACL-IADC Blog (21 September 2021) blog-iacl-aidc.org/2021-posts/2021/9/21/why-we-need-to-abandon-the-rule-of-law.

INDEX

www.ingramcontent.com/pod-product-compliance
Lightning Source LLC
LaVergne TN
LVHW010324200225
804096LV00003B/69